Celebrating Poetry

East – Fall 2007

Creative Communication, Inc.

Celebrating Poetry East – Fall 2007

An anthology compiled by Creative Communication, Inc.

Published by:
CREATIVE COMMUNICATION, INC.
1488 NORTH 200 WEST
LOGAN, UT 84341

Printed in the United States of America

ISBN: 978-1-60050-156-2

Foreword

The poets between these pages are not famous...yet. They are still learning how language creates images and how to reflect their thoughts through words. However, through their acceptance into this publication, these young poets have taken a giant leap that reflects their desire to write.

We are proud of this anthology and what it represents. Most poets who entered the contest were not accepted to be published. The poets who are included in this book represent the best poems from our youth. These young poets took a chance and were rewarded by being featured in this anthology. Without this book, these poems would have been lost in a locker or a backpack.

We will have a feeling of success if upon reading this anthology of poetry each reader finds a poem that evokes emotion. It may be a giggle or a smile. It may be a thoughtful reflection. You might find a poem that takes you back to an earlier day when a snowfall contains magic or when a pile of leaves was an irresistible temptation. If these poems can make you feel alive and have hope in our youth, then it will be time well spent.

As we thank the poets for sharing their work, we also thank you, the reader, for allowing us to be part of your life.

Thomas Worthen, Ph.D.
Editor
Creative Communication

Enter Our Next Poetry Contest!

Why should I enter?
Win prizes and get published! Each year thousands of dollars in prizes are awarded in each region and tens of thousands of dollars in prizes are awarded throughout North America. The top writers in each division receive a monetary award and a free book that includes their published work. Poems of merit are also selected to be published in our anthology.

Who may enter?
There are four poetry contest divisions. Poets in grades K-3, 4-6, 7-9, and 10-12 may enter the contest.

What is needed to enter the contest?
You can enter any original poem 21 lines or less. Each entry must include the poet's name, address, city, state and zip code. Entries need to include the poet's grade, school name and school address. Students who include their teacher's name may help the teacher qualify for a free copy of the anthology.

How do I enter?

Enter online at:
www.poeticpower.com

Or, *Mail your entry to:*
Poetry Contest
1488 North 200 West
Logan, UT 84341

When is the deadline?
The contest deadlines are August 14th, December 4th, and April 8th. Poets may enter one poem in each contest.

Are there benefits for my school?
Yes. We award $15,000 each year in grants to help with Language Arts programs. Schools qualify to apply for a grant by having a large number of entries of which over fifty percent are accepted for publication. This typically tends to be about 15 accepted entries.

Are there benefits for my teacher?
Yes. Teachers with five or more students accepted to be published receive a free anthology that includes their students' poems.

For more information please go to our website at
***www.poeticpower.com**,*
email us at editor@poeticpower.com or call 435-713-4411.

Table of Contents

States included in this edition:

Alabama
Arkansas
Connecticut
Delaware
Florida
Georgia
Kentucky
Louisiana
Maine
Maryland
Massachusetts
Mississippi
Missouri
New Hampshire
New Jersey
New York
North Carolina
Oklahoma
Pennsylvania
Rhode Island
South Carolina
Tennessee
Vermont
Virginia
Washington D.C.
West Virginia

Fall 2007 Poetic Achievement Honor Schools

** Teachers who had fifteen or more poets accepted to be published*

The following schools are recognized as receiving a "Poetic Achievement Award." This award is given to schools who have a large number of entries of which over fifty percent are accepted for publication. With hundreds of schools entering our contest, only a small percent of these schools are honored with this award. The purpose of this award is to recognize schools with excellent Language Arts programs. This award qualifies these schools to receive a complimentary copy of this anthology. In addition, these schools are eligible to apply for a Creative Communication Language Arts Grant. Grants of two hundred and fifty dollars each are awarded to further develop writing in our schools.

A L Burruss Elementary School
Marietta, GA
Lisa Brown
Katie Gaudette
Iris Rice

Alpena Elementary School
Alpena, AR
Sherry Choate
Ginny Hulsey
Dawn Keys
Mr. Nichols
Mrs. Phillips
Ruthie Weidenfeller

Alvaton Elementary School
Alvaton, KY
Carolyn Gifford*

Alvaton Elementary School
Alvaton, KY (cont.)
Jane Kirby
Mary-Anne Powers*

Anne Frank School
Philadelphia, PA
Christine M. Schuler*

Bailey Elementary School
Bailey, NC
Frances Anderson*

Belfast-Elk Garden Elementary School
Rosedale, VA
Christy Bowman
Janette Miller

Bensley Elementary School
Richmond, VA
Carolyn Booth
Donna French
Ms. Griffin
S. Perry

Berkeley Lake Elementary School
Berkeley Lake, GA
Ana-Lisa Johnson*

Blakeney Elementary School
Waynesboro, GA
Missey Greene
Lorteea Johnson
Mrs. Richardson
Mrs. Walker
Mrs. Williams

Bradford Township Elementary School
Clearfield, PA
Pamela L. Gabel
Mary Jo Seprish*

Briarwood Christian School
Birmingham, AL
Martha Bickford
Joie Black
Jenny Burdick*
Mrs. Chastain
Kari Cuenin*
Mrs. Cuneo
Mary Beth Fields
Kristin Fincher
Jennie Gillon
Mrs. Griffin*
Susan Johnson*
Miss Jones
Ms. Kirkpatrick*
Mrs. Leonard*
Mrs. Pardue
Ms. Peters
Joanne Peterson

Briarwood Christian School
Birmingham, AL (cont.)
Mrs. Petty*
Mary Ann Pickell
Paige Robinson*
Mrs. C. Smith
Mrs. L. Smith
Cheryl Vincent
Miss Wagner

Broadway Elementary School
Broadway, NC
Susan Brown*

Byrns L Darden Elementary School
Clarksville, TN
Mrs. Downing
Mrs. Elkins
Mrs. McDonnough
Ms. McKeethen
Ms. Murray
Sandi O'Bryan*
Mrs. Purcell
Mrs. Rivers
Mr. Rogers
Mrs. Siegle
Ms. Thomas
Mrs. Wooten

Catherine A Dwyer Elementary School
Wharton, NJ
Sue Fuchs
Ms. Greenwald
Nancy Reeves
Sandra Struble*
Elyse Termatto
Dan Warnock

Central Park Elementary School
Plantation, FL
Norma Callinan
Roni Graham
Lori Lucci*

Central Park Elementary School
Plantation, FL (cont.)
Kristen Marsolek
Virginia Mihajlovski*
Melissa Schultze
Mark Siegel
Maria Tzounakos

Chelsea Heights Elementary School
Atlantic City, NJ
Mayra Cruz-Connerton*

Chestnut Street Elementary School
Kane, PA
Robynn Boyer*

Clover Street School
Windsor, CT
Pauline Reale
Lisa Thomas*

Collingwood Park SDA School
Neptune, NJ
Oretha Bennett
Dr. R. Iola Brown

Concord Elementary School
Pittsburgh, PA
Marcy Grollman*

Consolidated School
New Fairfield, CT
Amy Johnson*

Contentnea Elementary School
Kinston, NC
Birta Battle*

Cool Spring Elementary School
Cleveland, NC
Aimee Adkins*
Tonya Cassidy
Mrs. Duncan
Stephanie Flammang

Cool Spring Elementary School
Cleveland, NC (cont.)
Kenneth Lindstrom
Sandra Milholland

Coral Cove Elementary School
Miramar, FL
Mrs. Burnside
Mrs. Curtis
Ms. Novell
Dr. Peralta
Mrs. Salcedo
Mrs. S. Williams

Dr Martin Luther King Jr School Complex
Atlantic City, NJ
Mayra Cruz-Connerton*

Evangelical Christian School
Germantown, TN
Nadia Alm
Shireen Brandt
Lisa Chandler
Lindy Murley
Cathy Short
Tammy Umlauf
Annette Wright
Barbara Yelverton

Fishing Creek Elementary School
Lewisberry, PA
Miss Hessler
Clair E. Richcrick*

Forest Street Elementary School
Orange, NJ
Deine Garner*

Guardian Angels Catholic School
Clearwater, FL
Debbie Mahle
Mrs. O'Brien
Patricia Powers

Hilton Head Christian Academy
Hilton Head Island, SC
Mrs. Hilton
Nadine Peters

Holland Township School
Milford, NJ
Stephanie Bacskai*
Jill Conti
Deb Croasdale
JoAnn Gitto
Laurie Hughes
Dayle Johnson
Rosemary Martin*
Cathy O'Rourke
Donna Widmer
Joanne Winn

Hunter GT Magnet Elementary School
Raleigh, NC
Lisa Kaszycki*
Angie Parham*

Infant Jesus School
Nashua, NH
Elaine Hebert*

John Hus Moravian School
Brooklyn, NY
Leila Baird
Hortense Morgan

John T Waugh Elementary School
Angola, NY
Kathy Dole*

John Ward Elementary School
Newton Centre, MA
Brad Hammer
Naomi E. Singer

Lee A Tolbert Community Academy
Kansas City, MO
Elizabeth Deardorff
Zanova Gasaway
Valerie Guy
Pamela King
Rayma Moburg
Cindy Salomone
Dana Tiller
Janice Yocum*

Lincoln Elementary School
Pittsburgh, PA
Cynthia Biery*

Long Meadow Elementary School
Middlebury, CT
Joan Kelly
Susan Shaw
Noel Siebern*

Madison Station Elementary School
Madison, MS
Betty Mahaffey*

Marie Curie Institute
Amsterdam, NY
Jerilynn Einarsson*
Theresa Featherstone
Shannon Loveland*
Linda Sawicki

Marie Durand Elementary School
Vineland, NJ
Joan Bergamo*

McKinley Elementary School
Elkins Park, PA
Mr. Beam*
Ms. Garry
Miss Guglielmelli
Mrs. Hartzell
Mrs. Heil
Miss Livingood

McKinley Elementary School
Elkins Park, PA (cont.)
Carol Louis*
Mrs. McGettigan*
Natalie Pawell*

Melwood Elementary School
Upper Marlboro, MD
Mr. Collins
Karen Daniels
Erica Daniels
Mrs. G. Gutrich
Mr. Hartling
Pia Jones
Mrs. C. Richmond
Ms. Tucker
Mrs. C. Walker

Memorial School
Bedford, NH
Courtney Hannah
Tara Shortt
Miss Wroblewski

Miami Country Day School
Miami, FL
Barbara Brown
Judy Finny*
Jo Ann Labaton
Marion McKinnon*
Barbara Mink
Julie Ruben

Mother Seton Inter Parochial School
Union City, NJ
Lorraine DePinto
Sr. Patricia Gatti
Mrs. Giron
Darling Magner
Alexander Pino
Marisol Rodriguez*
Hector Sanchez
Patricia Sanchez

Nativity Catholic School
Brandon, FL
Mrs. Daigle
Mrs. Denison
Mrs. Hamel*
Mary Anne Musella*
Toni Tarsi

Noonan Academy of Fort Myers
Fort Myers, FL
Mrs. West*

North Star Elementary School
Hockessin, DE
Mrs. Becker
Margo Miller*

Northeast Baptist School
West Monroe, LA
Carol Medlin
Lisa Navarro
Diane Tidwell*

Northeast Elementary School
Brentwood, NY
Ms. Betzold
Mrs. Bloom
Ms. Chu
Mrs. Correa
Mrs. Dale
Mrs. Ferro*
Ms. Giancaspro*
Mrs. Hanlon
Marge Leonard
Alison Maggio
Mrs. Martin*
Robert Melo
Lisa Patrick
Ms. Smith
Ms. Tapen
Mrs. Tejada

Oak Ridge Elementary School
Harleysville, PA
Ross Pollack*

Our Lady of Hope School
Middle Village, NY
Martha Madri*

Paine Primary School
Trussville, AL
Gina Gamble*

Perrywood Elementary School
Largo, MD
Amy Louden
Ms. Schiery

Pike Liberal Arts School
Troy, AL
Tisha Norman
Linda Scott

Public School 148 Ruby Allen
East Elmhurst, NY
Lois Ricupero*

Public School 152 School of Science & Technology
Brooklyn, NY
Mrs. Aris
Ms. P. Dong
Ms. Lutjen
Mrs. McGuire
Anna Randisi*
Christina Romeo

Public School 205 Alexander Graham Bell
Bayside, NY
Fran Bosi
Meri Naveh

Reidville Elementary School
Reidville, SC
Lindsey Edens*
Mrs. Fowler
Mrs. Hanke
Mrs. Maxwell

Ross Elementary School
Pittsburgh, PA
Mrs. Brunner
Karen Jones*
Mrs. Lewis

St Alexis School
Wexford, PA
Mrs. Phillips
Sandra Ross*

St Anselm School
Philadelphia, PA
Mrs. Erwin
Mrs. Milligan
Freda M. Terrell-Tait*
Mrs. Whartenby

St Charles Homeschool Learning Center
St Peters, MO
Heather Nuehring*

St Joseph Catholic Grammar School
Jersey City, NJ
Jessica Orellana
Robert David Stenzel*

St Mary of the Assumption Catholic School
Butler, PA
Adrienne J. Ofcharsky*

St Mary's School
Pompton Lakes, NJ
Mrs. Andrews*
Lily Bendezu

St Mary's School
Pompton Lakes, NJ (cont.)
Sr. Mary Byrnes
Edie Kimak*
Carol Porada*

St Stephen's School
Grand Island, NY
Kristy Pasko*

Stone Academy
Greenville, SC
Christen Josey
Cathy Kennedy
Mrs. Merrill
Debbie Roper

Sundance School
North Plainfield, NJ
Carina Bellmann
Claudia Canchola*
Shellie A. Hess
Archana Sankar
Betsy Schneekloth*
Donna Turlik

The American Academy
Philadelphia, PA
Dr. Sharon Traver*

Tuxedo Park School
Tuxedo Park, NY
Natalie Easter*

United Hebrew Institute
Kingston, PA
Lesley Baltimore
Amy Baylor*
Timothy Showalter
Barbara Welch*

Virginia A Boone Highland Oaks Elementary School
North Miami Beach, FL
Terri Cohen*
Stephanie Sheir*
Morgan Taylor

Wanamassa Elementary School
Wanamassa, NJ
Mrs. Francisco
Peggy Keane
Deborah Kiss
Kathleen Marmora

Wapping Elementary School
South Windsor, CT
Karrie Noble
Daria Plummer

Watsontown Elementary School
Watsontown, PA
Mike Butler
Mrs. Danowsky
Ann Duncan
Becky Geiger
Holly Howrilla*
Alison Newman
Dana Pick
Marcia Saam

Wellington School
Seminole, FL
Mrs. Antequera
Kathy Carley
Donna Perkins

Westlake Christian School
Palm Harbor, FL
Mary Barbaccia*
Kimberly Fleming*

Wolcott School
West Hartford, CT
Matthew Dicks*

Woodland Elementary School
Radcliff, KY
Mrs. Hall*

Worthington Hooker School – K-2 Campus
New Haven, CT
Christina Amato
Kathy Lembo*

Yeshiva Ketana of Long Island
North Woodmere, NY
Mrs. Shoshana
Mrs. Sussman
Mrs. Weitzman

Zervas Elementary School
Waban, MA
Rebecca Deeks
Kathleen Eakin
Michael Stern

Language Arts Grant Recipients 2006-2007

After receiving a "Poetic Achievement Award" schools are encouraged to apply for a Creative Communication Language Arts Grant. The following is a list of schools who received a two hundred and fifty dollar grant for the 2007-2008 school year.

Acadamie DaVinci, Dunedin, FL
Altamont Elementary School, Altamont, KS
Belle Valley South School, Belleville, IL
Bose Elementary School, Kenosha, WI
Brittany Hill Middle School, Blue Springs, MO
Carver Jr High School, Spartanburg, SC
Cave City Elementary School, Cave City, AR
Central Elementary School, Iron Mountain, MI
Challenger K8 School of Science and Mathematics, Spring Hill, FL
Columbus Middle School, Columbus, MT
Cypress Christian School, Houston, TX
Deer River High School, Deer River, MN
Deweyville Middle School, Deweyville, TX
Four Peaks Elementary School, Fountain Hills, AZ
Fox Chase School, Philadelphia, PA
Fox Creek High School, North Augusta, SC
Grandview Alternative School, Grandview, MO
Hillcrest Elementary School, Lawrence, KS
Holbrook School, Holden, ME
Houston Middle School, Germantown, TN
Independence High School, Elko, NV
International College Preparatory Academy, Cincinnati, OH
John Bowne High School, Flushing, NY

Language Arts Grant Winners cont.

Lorain County Joint Vocational School, Oberlin, OH
Merritt Secondary School, Merritt, BC
Midway Covenant Christian School, Powder Springs, GA
Muir Middle School, Milford, MI
Northlake Christian School, Covington, LA
Northwood Elementary School, Hilton, NY
Place Middle School, Denver, CO
Public School 124, South Ozone Park, NY
Public School 219 Kennedy King, Brooklyn, NY
Rolling Hills Elementary School, San Diego, CA
St Anthony's School, Streator, IL
St Joan Of Arc School, Library, PA
St Joseph Catholic School, York, NE
St Joseph School-Fullerton, Baltimore, MD
St Monica Elementary School, Mishawaka, IN
St Peter Celestine Catholic School, Cherry Hill, NJ
Strasburg High School, Strasburg, VA
Stratton Elementary School, Stratton, ME
Tom Thomson Public School, Burlington, ON
Tremont Elementary School, Tremont, IL
Warren Elementary School, Warren, OR
Webster Elementary School, Hazel Park, MI
West Woods Elementary School, Arvada, CO
West Woods Upper Elementary School, Farmington, CT
White Pine Middle School, Richmond, UT
Winona Elementary School, Winona, TX
Wissahickon Charter School, Philadelphia, PA
Wood County Christian School, Williamstown, WV
Wray High School, Wray, CO

Young Poets Grades K-1-2-3

Note: The Top Ten poems were finalized through an online voting system. Creative Communication's judges first picked out the top poems. These poems were then posted online. The final step involved thousands of students and teachers who registered as online judges and voted for the Top Ten poems. We hope you enjoy these selections.

Top Poem Grades K-3

Wind

Blowing around the tree,
Listen very carefully.
When you're hot,
It helps a lot.
Sometimes it's just a light breeze,
Other times it'll make you freeze.
It is clear,
And it's something you hear.
It tickles my face,
Like a bunch of white lace.

Caroline Fredericks, Grade 3
Ellicott Road Elementary School, NY

Top Poem Grades K-3

The Beach

Relaxing.
Quietly.
I am feeling so nice.
Quietly.
Quietly.
Quietly.
The wind is pushing me.
The water is falling on me.
It is still quiet.
People playing.
The sun is so hot, hot, hot.
Quietly, I fall asleep on the beach.
ZZZZZ, I am sleeping under the clouds.
ZZZZZ.
Now I leave the beach.

Max Grossman, Kindergarten
Public School 290, NY

Top Poem Grades K-3

A Horse Named Pete

A horse was walking down the street.
I took him home and called him Pete.
I still have him this very day,
And Pete and I still love to play.

I wish those lines were really true,
Except Pete could end up in a zoo.
If he started saying "moo,"
What in the world then would I do?

Maggie Harnish, Grade 1
The American Academy, PA

Top Poem Grades K-3

Math Test!

What? A surprise test!
Starting now, first one's easy
now on to number two.
Number three's tricky
oh, what should I do?
Now I remember just how to divide,
and finished three with pride.
I am very good at this
and number four is simple.
Now number five. Multiplication!
Division! I just can't do this!
My brain is going to explode!
This is number eight and now number nine.
Bubble answers? I don't know them!
I have to think and think and think
and finally get the answer, four thousand one!
Now number ten. Great!
This is the last one.
Now think, think
think, write,
DONE!

Katie Hicks, Grade 3
Lucille Hunter GT Magnet Elementary School, NC

Top Poem Grades K-3

The Knock

God knocked on my heart
I said "Come in."
Our Lord then smiled down on me,
And I felt Him from within.

I became a Christian in that moment,
And in my actions all can tell
How much I love the Lord
In me forever He will dwell.

There are times when I am scared,
Then I remember that He is there.
He makes me feel warm and safe,
Our Savior tells me He will always care.

I love to praise the Lord at church and school
I hope that all my friends will see
The changes that have affected my heart
That God now lives within me.

Cole Jackson, Grade 3
Evangelical Christian School, TN

Top Poem Grades K-3

Prejudice

Everyone is different,
But we're really all the same,
Because we all have feelings,
Getting hurt is not a game.

Some may be short,
Others might be tall,
A person may be large,
And humans might be small.

Personalities might take different tracks,
Our skin colors could make a rainbow,
Religions come in different brands,
A wheelchair might be the way to go.

So if you think that you are cooler,
Stop, think, and slow down your pace,
Remember that you are unique too,
And we are all in the human race.

Katharine Kurz, Grade 3
Hunter GT Magnet Elementary School, NC

Top Poem Grades K-3

Sewing with My Mom

I love to dance the Highland fling
More than the "Sword Dance," the "Lilt" — anything.
My mom and I are making a dress for me —
A red, plaid kilt for the audience to see.
My mom has a sewing room where we sew my dress.
My dad (who does the vacuuming) yells, "Don't make a mess."
The outfit is national; it's called Stewart tartan
I wore my first one, aged six, kindergarten.
Excited that the dress was going to be mine,
I had to cut the fabric right on the line.
I learned to iron edges, make a crease and a fold,
To thread bobbins and pedal hard, as I was told.
Sometimes the pins would fall on the floor,
And Dad would complain to us, "Please, no more."
Dancing in a dress my mom and I made,
In a competition, I will never be afraid.
Three shedding right foot, step, close, and a bow.
Once the "Flora MacDonald Fancy," it's the "Irish Jig" now.

Sarah Null, Grade 3
The American Academy, PA

Top Poem Grades K-3

Dreaming

Blooming flowers, purple berries
Eating apples, picking cherries
Falling leaves and bumblebees
Blue skies and a soft, calm breeze
Hot sand and tall, strong trees
Dewdrops fall through hot, misty air
Tigers roar in their dark, gloomy lair
Water pours from the dark gray clouds
Walk down the stone path to where I am now

Emma Roush, Grade 3
Brimmer and May School, MA

Top Poem Grades K-3

The Wind

The wind began to blow.
The wind is a friend to know!
It gave my jacket a tug,
It felt like a great big hug!
The wind is a friend to know!

Jude Sumner, Grade 1
St Vincent De Paul Elementary School, MO

Top Poem Grades K-3

Magical Land

Magical Land, magical fruit
A magical train that goes "Toot, toot!"
A lot of rainbows, a bright bright sun
We can tell this land is very fun!
Yummy candy we can taste
Creative things at school we cut and paste.
I love the store's famous dress
The best part in Magical Land is no stress!
So many friends, so many smiles
The happy car can drive 20 miles.
Beautiful flowers blooming in spring
The shining river is my favorite thing!
A pretty pond and all of that
The band plays a rat, tat, tat!
And these are the things that I like
Decorations at Christmas and my dog named Spike!
In Magical Land there is so much to do
Maybe we should go together, just me and you!

Sydney Wedin, Grade 2
Stone Academy, SC

The Zoo

zoo
fun, hot
showing lots of animals
selling souvenirs
zoo

Jacob Martin, Grade 2
Bensley Elementary School, VA

Cold Rainy Day

Icebergs a plenty
Snow day, so cold
Rain sprinkling
Cold, wet, puddly.

Just want to go home.

Sad faces
Shining in the cold
Wet, soft snow
Sprinkles everywhere.

Oh home sweet home.

Clara Runfola, Grade 2
Annsville Elementary School, NY

Landforms

Landforms form shapes on land
Some lay plainly as can be
And so we call them plains
Some are high, broad and flat
And see we call them plat-eau
Oh don't you know?
Some we call hills
And they are like babies
Who wish to grow up
To be tall mountains
Pointing upward to the sky
And if you want to dip down low
Then to the valley you must go
Landforms give the Earth its shape
And that's the thing that makes
My planet great!

Nadja McKenzie, Grade 3
Public School 235 Lenox, NY

My Shark

shark
big, dangerous
swimming in the blue ocean
eating other fish
shark

Ben Iracheta, Grade 2
Bensley Elementary School, VA

Lizard

A lizard has a lot of colors
Like black, blue, brown,
Green, orange, purple,
Red and white.
A lizard has a long tongue.

Emerson Wells, Grade 3
McKinley Elementary School, PA

Autumn

A utumn is fun
U nder the leaves is more leaves
T rees make the leaves fall
U sing a rake
M y brother loves sunflowers
N ow you know

Dovid Schwartz, Grade 2
United Hebrew Institute, PA

My Mom

She buys me things
school things
She's as beautiful
as a red flower
She's kind to
all children
and people
My mom
is a beautiful
woman
She's as beautiful
as a red flower
a
rose.

Yoseline Rodriguez, Grade 3
Public School 148 Ruby Allen, NY

Veteran's Day

V ery special day
E ach person in the Civil War was fighting for our world
T imes they have fought for our world
E very person has to have a lot of energy
R ed, white and blue represent our flag
A lot of veteran's care about this special day
N ot a lot of people are alive from the Civil War
S o many people fighting in the war

D angerous
A merica is a good place to live
Y ou can get hurt badly

Amber Cina, Grade 3
Susquehanna Community Elementary School, PA

My Dad

I LOVE MY FAMILY.
It's just me and my DAD.
We have fun and we play lots of games.
He makes me laugh and laugh. He tells funny jokes.
He buys LOTS of things.
We go on trips and see fun things to do.
I LOVE MY DAD.
We watch movies and go to the MALL.
He's the BEST.

Chinell Vaughn, Grade 3
New Orleans Free School, LA

Ode to My Tiger

Oh, my wonderful tiger.
I got you on my fifth birthday.
You were the best present of all.
You have been with me for two years.
You are special because my dad's friend gave you to me.
You are made out of love.
When I hug you I hear you purring in my ear.
You are as soft as a cloud.
You look like a cute bear,
With your nose that is as pink as a peach.
You sneak out of my blankets when I am sleeping.
I am going to keep you forever because you are so special.
I will never have to miss your tickle whiskers because you will always be mine.

Sara Thakur, Grade 2
Worthington Hooker School – K-2 Campus, CT

My Family

My family is special —
They are one of a kind.
They love me so much,
When I make mistakes
They don't even mind!

Sydney Smith, Grade 2
Briarwood Christian School, AL

My Brother

Happy, playful, helpful
Running, throwing, sleeping, watching
Friend, cleaner, listener
Peyton

Parris Johnson, Grade 2
St Mary's School, NJ

Spider

Spider
black, small
spinning, catching, finding
happy, mad, sad, furious
sleeping, helping, getting
hairy, ugly
Bug

Aubrey Mallard, Grade 3
Blakeney Elementary School, GA

Books

Books are fun
Books are cool
Books are plentiful
in school.

Books are amazing
Books are magical
They hold lots and
lots of funny tricks.

Books hold secrets
So many secrets
I love to read the
secrets they hide.

Fareed Safo, Grade 3
John Hus Moravian School, NY

Snow

S now is cold
N ice snow comes from clouds
O ver onto the trees
W hen will snow come again?

Jeffrey Mann, Grade 1
Annie Belle Clark Primary School, GA

Vixen-Ku

Vicious, cute, soft, fox
Hunts in the woods for food yum
Red, fluffy, mean, gross

Olivia DePew, Grade 2
Paine Primary School, AL

Hurricanes

H orrible
U nexpected
R uin land
R am into trees
I nappropriate
C an cause damage
A ctive
N ot nice
E xtremely bad
S imilar to tornados

Rachael DeBenedictus, Grade 2
Marlboro Elementary School, NY

Winter Is Coming

Winter is coming
just wait and see.
Snow will fall
on you and me!

Jocelyn Dytko, Grade 3
Concord Elementary School, PA

Pop!

Pop 'em in my mouth.
Pop, pop
POP ROCKS oh my gosh!
Pop, pop, crackle, crackle,
POP, POP!

Sierra Hermann, Grade 2
Trinity East Elementary School, PA

Natural Resources

The water is fresh so we can drink it.
The trees give us oxygen from their leaves.
The soil is full of minerals to grow flowers.
The gold is for us to wear.
The oil is for us to put in our cars and get going.
And the air that we breathe

Brianna Evering, Grade 3
Public School 235 Lenox, NY

Soccer

Soccer is my sport,
Everybody scream.
Soccer is the best,
Better than all the rest.
Soccer is hard,
I think I need a guard.
Soccer is so cool,
The school has the tool.

Libby Szlaifer, Grade 3
Virginia A Boone Highland Oaks Elementary School, FL

The Little Penguin

A little penguin called Peter
Who sat on ice.
He is not black, he is blue and red.
His dad was eaten by a whale.
Now it was just him and his mom.
He was seven years old
And he liked Santa Claus
And loved to decorate for him.
He can eat 100 mice.
One night his mother made fish.
He did not like them very much.
He only liked mice.
He played with dice and spy gear.
Peter had a brother which always got him in trouble.
Although his brother got him in trouble so much,
He still liked to play with him.
He loves for Santa Claus to bring him gifts.
Although he liked to decorate, eat mice, play with dice
And spy gear, he loved his family more than anything in the world.

Hunter Steed, Grade 3
Pike Liberal Arts School, AL

Weightlifting

Life is like weightlifting

I thought it was
Exciting
Impossible to do
Sweaty.

As I lifted
those extremely
heavy weights

I looked
up and saw
that I had done it.

Brad Apgar, Grade 3
Holland Township School, NJ

The Cloud

The fat white cloud
in the blue sunny sky
galloped like a horse
in the deep forest

Myah Luper, Grade 3
Wellington School, FL

Proudness

It takes
proudness
to score goals.
I have excitement
when I do stunts.
I wear slippers
in dance class.

Natalie Martin, Grade 3
Holland Township School, NJ

What Is Yellow?

The daisies in the field,
Sour like lemon juice,
Sweet like a banana candle,
Soft like a baby duck,
Music in my ears.

Asjiá Harris, Grade 3
Scott Elementary School, MO

About Me

I'm fun to play with!
Athletic, flexible girl,
Clever, talented.

Rachel Engel, Grade 3
Thelma L Sandmeier Elementary School, NJ

Ice

Fire!
Hot, dangerous,
Flaming, burning,
Cold, calm
Ice.

Shawn Valiani, Grade 3
Springfield Park Elementary School, VA

Fall Is When…

the air is as cold as ice.
the trees are as colorful as a rainbow.
the leaves are as yellow as gold.
the birds sound like music.
the animal's coat is as warm as a blanket.
the cider smells like apples.

Jada Fraser, Grade 3
Coral Cove Elementary School, FL

My Scary Hair Day

I quiver when my mommy combs my hair.
She has to coax me but I run everywhere.
I scream in terror like a mad bear.
But in the end I have elegant hair!

Faith Layer, Grade 3
Forest Street Elementary School, NJ

Dance Class

When I'm at dance class
I'm sorry it doesn't last
We do ballet and tap
And never take a nap
It's hard work and fun
All rolled into one
Everyone is welcome, big and small
So if you are thinking, come on come all!

Saudia Bowers, Grade 2
Forest Street Elementary School, NJ

My Noisy Animals

My noisy animals are so loud!
The jumping jaguar jumped on me.
Splish…splash! I fell into the fish's bath.
The white tiger roared.
It scared the horse…"Neigh"
"Shh, calm down," I cried.
Then, the fish got water on my cow. It went, "MOOO."
In all this commotion the bird wouldn't stop chirping.
The horse crashed into the bath.
Now I had quite enough.
Then the slithering snake bit the unsuspecting white tiger.
"SSSSS" he was so suspicious.
Crish crash, the jumping jaguar jumped again.
It was a noisy day!

Jenna Rose White, Grade 3
Briarwood Christian School, AL

My Skateboard

I have the best skateboard in the world.
I ride it during the day and night.
When I ride it at night people yell "MOVE OVER"
with a terrible fright!!

Elijah Aguirre, Grade 2
Mother Seton Inter Parochial School, NJ

Briner Sealey

Jumpy like a rabbit, chatty like a monkey, but sometimes as quiet as a swan,
working like a beaver, quick as a jaguar, imaginative like a cat,
playful as a puppy, as mad as an eagle, but there's much

more…

As hard as a rock, but sometimes as soft as a marshmallow,
as helpful as a chipmunk, understanding as an owl, as balanced as a flamingo,
but sometimes as *un*balanced as a bear, but wait there's

more…

At night as tired as a sloth, and sometimes as cold as a polar bear,
but other times as warm and cozy as a bird. I'm like a lot of things,

but, at different times.

Briner Sealey, Grade 3
Hunter GT Magnet Elementary School, NC

My Dreidel

My dreidel whirls, it twirls around,
I do not want it to fall to the ground.
My dreidel, dreidel, spin, spin, spin.
If I get gimmel, I'll win, win, win!
With all the other people who play,
I hope I win, please just today.
Here comes my turn. I have to go,
Did I get nun? No! No! No!
Yay, I got gimmel! Way to go!

Emily Moss, Grade 3
John Ward Elementary School, MA

Summer Days

I like summer days
My birthday is in July
I like swimming pools

Avi Hoch, Grade 3
Yeshiva Ketana of Long Island, NY

Ben

My cousin Ben
he is ten
he fell off a stool
into a pool

Damien Kinsman, Grade 3
The Parke House Academy, FL

Bruno

Nice
Helps
Loyal
Wishes to stop war
Dreams of a clean Earth
Wants to make a
Better Earth
Who fears snakes
Who likes to be a builder
Who believes in God
Who loves dogs and cats
Who loves mom and dad.
Who loves friends
Who plans to help.

Brunoslav Kunstek, Grade 3
Central Park Elementary School, FL

Heroes

United States Marines are heroes,
Let me tell you why.
They fight for the freedom
Of our country.
They make our world
A safer place.
I know that is so true,
My uncle is a Marine.

Arisley Rodriguez, Grade 1
James H Bright Elementary School, FL

Bunny

The bunny hops fast
And has two long ears

They're very soft and friendly
And get very scared

When they eat yummy carrots
And see someone near

They run very fast
Because of their fear

I once had a bunny
Mocha was her name

I loved her very much
I always watched her play

Alexandria Veneziano, Grade 3
St Alexis School, PA

Halloween

Scary ghosts
Creep spiders
Crawling around,
Jack-o-lanterns
Lit outside.
Bats flying
All around.
Kids dressed up
With scary masks.

Aubrey Schmitt, Grade 2
Annsville Elementary School, NY

Songs

I hear songs everywhere,
Songs are very good to listen to,
Songs are for sing alongs,
Songs are very good to exercise with,
Songs to make you feel happy, sad, and excited,
Songs to cry with.

Alyssa M. Orengo, Grade 2
Marie Curie Institute, NY

Summer Time

It's summer time! Let's have fun! We can play in the hot sun.
Let's build castles in the sand, while we get a nice suntan.
Here we go into the ocean, wearing our suntan lotion.
We will swim with the clown fish. Swim right, swim left, with the fish.
I'm hungry, let's have a snack. We packed grapes in our backpack.
Come on, come on, to the pool! Swim! Jump! Dive! Splash! It is cool!
I got water up my nose! Something tickled my toes!
Who, who, who tickled my toes! My dad or brother? Who knows!
We will walk on the boardwalk, while we talk and talk and talk.
Let's play at the park tonight. It will be a pretty sight.
Let's eat a bowl of ice cream. If I drop it, I will scream.
It's summer time! We had fun! We played all day in the sun!

Kensie Verratti, Grade 3
St Alexis School, PA

A Nice Cool Swim for the Day

On a day of my soccer game, it was really hot. All I could think of is what can I do to cool down? Swim in my pool sure has a good sound. From back and forth and up and down, splashing all around. And playing with my friends before the sun goes down.

Oh how refreshing we all feel now after having cool drink and laying by my pool. Ah! Just what we needed was a nice cool swim on this hot sunny day.

Austin Burns, Grade 3
Noonan Elementary Academy of Fort Myers, FL

My Horse

My horse goes down the path click clock clack,
Click clock clack.
She stops and hears a noise.
Giddy up, giddy up go I say! Go, go, go!
It's a pity she won't giddy up and go.

Marlee Tomlinson, Grade 3
Briarwood Christian School, AL

Falling Leaves

Leaves are falling down
They are dropping to the ground
All sorts of colors

Matthew Benedict, Grade 3
Tuxedo Park School, NY

Puppies

Puppies sleep a lot.
Puppies love to play with you.
Puppies might bite you.

Elizabeth Sevier, Grade 2
St Peter the Apostle School, GA

My Favorite Color

I like blue.
The sky is blue.
My house is blue.
A blueberry is blue.
I like blue.

Abraham Bustamante, Grade 1
Northeast Elementary School, NY

Dog

Dog
Fun, playful
Swims, chases, fights
Follows my dad places
Tucker

Andy Pogue, Grade 3
Clinton Christian Academy, MO

Winter

in winter it's cold
in winter we throw snowballs
in winter it snows

Avi Kafka, Grade 3
Yeshiva Ketana of Long Island, NY

My Cat

My cat likes to climb up on the couch.
He comes and climbs on my lap,
He falls asleep.

Noah Hawkins, Grade 1
Cool Spring Elementary School, NC

Horse

Horse
Smooth, playful
Runs, jumps, gallops
I love wild horses.
Colt

Megan Walrath, Grade 3
Clinton Christian Academy, MO

Will

Will
Small, fast
football, basketball, baseball
always helpful to others
lightning

Jordan Harmon, Grade 3
Briarwood Christian School, AL

My Dog Snowflake

My dog Snowflake
he loves me so much
he is as white as a ghost
he loves to jump just
like me
We have a lot in common
We like to make noise
like
woof, woof, woof
his tail wags so fast like windshield
wipers he feels like the soft
snow falling from the sky
Snowflake,
Snowflake,
you're my
dog.

Kiona Gédéon, Grade 3
Public School 148 Ruby Allen, NY

Lions

Big, scary, furry
Scratching, eating, chasing, roaring
Claws, mane, paws
Lions

Jessica Leonard, Grade 2
St Mary's School, NJ

Candy

Candy is sour,
Candy is sweet,
I can't live without it,
It can't be beat.

Liel Balaila, Grade 3
Virginia A Boone Highland Oaks Elementary School, FL

Thanksgiving

Every Thanksgiving there is always something you should do.
Spend time with family and friends letting them know I love you.
It's not about football or the sale at the mall,
but about giving thanks for the greatest gift of all.
Life, family, friends, shelter, clothing,
and who can forget turkey, turkey, turkey!

Kaila Cuvilly, Grade 3
Springfield Park Elementary School, VA

Bedtime with Sisters

On Tuesday evening, getting ready for bed,
Something hit me, smack, right in the head!
I turned around, and — wouldn't you know —
There was my sister, saying, "Oh, Oh!"

"I'm sorry — really I didn't mean it!"
Cried Maggie, looking like *she'd* been hit.
Then Susanna came running into the room.
And she said, "Why did I hear that boom?"

Maggie, standing by our bed,
Said, calmly, "I hit Molly in the head."
Susanna screamed and ran to tell Mom
But, of course, Mom's busy on www.kingofprussia.com!

"Mom, Maggie hit Molly in the head!"
Behind Susanna is Maggie, dragging our bed.
She's terrified and wouldn't you be?
"Mom, will you really drop water balloons on me?"

Mom is really fighting mad,
And Maggie is so very sad.
But you, of course, must sympathize with Mom;
After all, she *was* on *www.kingofprussia.com!*

Molly Harnish, Grade 3
The American Academy, PA

Cats

Purr. Meow.
Tummy growls. Licking,
Sleeping all day long.
Scratch!
Jaime Alphonso, Grade 2
Clover Street School, CT

Dogs

Dogs go to school
Dogs are really cool

Dogs hate cats
They hate sleeping on mats
Angelina Kelly, Grade 2
Anne Frank School, PA

School

I like school
and coloring too.
It is so cool
school is fun.
Laila Wilson, Kindergarten
Taylor Road Academy, AL

Santa's Visit

One Christmas
I saw a sack
It goes over Santa's back
It had a toy
That filled me with joy
The light is bright
As the moon's light
Lit the night!
Alex Merry, Grade 3
Fort Dale Academy, AL

Cloud

The puffy pink cloud
In the sunny sky
Floated through the air
Like cotton candy
In a child's hand at the fair.
Zoe Blackledge, Grade 3
Wellington School, FL

Winter

Winter is a time for snow.
This I really know.
I think it would be nice
If we would get more than ice.
When it is cold outside
I like to drink cocoa to warm me inside.
Kaitlyn Harris, Grade 2
Stone Academy, SC

Tiger the Cat

Tiger came to my house
And he tried to sneak in
When my mother was taking out the garbage.
Mom got him out with the broom.
We chased Tiger from the yard with a shovel
Because he was eating the flowers.
Harrison Levi, Kindergarten
United Hebrew Institute, PA

About Myself

want to read a lot
love to play sports more and more
I am half Chinese
Emilio Lau, Grade 3
Thelma L Sandmeier Elementary School, NJ

Trees

Trees are colors
Trees have bark
Trees are hard
Trees have leaves
They are colors
Trees are fun
Trees' leaves are green, red, and orange, too
Trees are pretty.
I like trees.
Trees have holes
Woodpeckers peck on the trees
The sun helps trees grow
Water helps trees grow, too.

Trees
Jace Douglas, Grade 1
Alvaton Elementary School, KY

Thanksgiving

Thanksgiving, Thanksgiving, it's almost here.
It's time to give some thanks and cheer.
It is a day we truly should share,
And show mothers we care.
We could thank people for the work they have done,
And then we can have some fun.
And most of all I am thankful it's here,
Because Christmas is near.

Steven LaRussa, Grade 3
Our Lady of Hope School, NY

Wintertime

Wintertime is here at last
Tree's lives are in the past.
Candy canes, snowballs, ice and more.
Decorations and snow galore.
Flakes flying left and right.
A blanket of white is a wonderful sight.
A figure eight upon a pond.
Of this season I am fond.
A snow globe filled with ice and snow.
Brilliant Christmas lights aglow.
Wintertime is so icy cold.
Make Christmas cookies with a special mold.
Licking your sticky candy cane,
Here comes Santa Claus down the lane.
Skipping merrily through the snow,
The wind is starting to blow.
Presents, toys, and a Christmas tree.
Everything is white around me.
Santa's little reindeer guide him on Christmas night.
That's why Rudolph's nose is so bright!

Bryn Manion, Grade 3
School Street Elementary School, PA

Music

Music is fun because I sing with everyone.
Music makes me feel happy.
I listen to the radio and my sister dances with me.
Music is a lot of fun.
I like music.

Viviana Maldonado, Grade 1
Mother Seton Inter Parochial School, NJ

The Floor and the Stairs*

Every floor loves stairs.
Every person loves pears.
Every seat sack loves chairs.
And I love you.

Adam Sullivan, Kindergarten
Eden Gardens Magnet School, LA
**Inspired by Jean Marzollo's*
"I Love You: A Rebus Poem"

Cole

C ole likes cats
O atmeal for breakfast
L ikes pizza
E veryone likes Cole

Cole Kramer, Grade 1
St Stephen's School, NY

Sarah Gray

Sarah Gray
Tall, smart
Football, baseball, tennis
Always funny with others
Gray Gray

Grant Hodges, Grade 3
Briarwood Christian School, AL

Lucky

Lucky
Messy, cute
Zooming, hiding, munching
Runs in snow
Puppy!

Elizabeth Nesbit, Grade 3
Mary Matula Elementary School, MD

Baseball

pitchers, strikers, batters
hit far, home run matters
mound, bases, bullpen
fun for our men
worried faces, sad faces, happy faces
run those bases

Luke Thomas, Grade 3
Broadway Elementary School, NC

My Pink Pig

I like the pig
Because he is big
My pig is pink
My pig will stink

Samantha Amaya, Grade 1
Northeast Elementary School, NY

Family

I love my family,
That is true.
I love to play with them too.
I love to color
With my mom
And she loves to color with me too.
I love doing
All things with my family.
And my family likes doing
Those things with me too.

Nina Tavarone, Grade 3
Our Lady of Hope School, NY

My Little Puppies

My little puppies are cute,
My little puppies play together,
My little puppies follow me.

I give them treats and milk,
And they quickly come to me.
But one day, I don't know when
My little puppies will grow.
And they will be
Just like their parents.

But for now,
They are my little puppies.

Barbara Cespedes, Grade 1
James H Bright Elementary School, FL

Seal-Ku

Jump out of water.
I like to watch seals jump high.
The seals are so cool.

Tanner Bradshaw, Grade 2
Paine Primary School, AL

Naptime Prayer

Jesus loves me and I love Him.
I am good and holy, like He is holy.
I see the stars that God made, and they are beautiful.
I like the animals that God made, and they are special.
God also made coal and rocks, and they are awesome.
God made me, and I am awesome, too.
I like everything, in the whole world, that God has made,
And I like me!

Aaron Burgmon, Grade 1
Home School, GA

American Girl Dolls

American Girl dolls are my favorite thing.
They make me laugh and make me sing.
They cheer me up when I am sad.
I read their books; it makes me glad.
I like Molly's name, because my name is the same.
My friends and I play pretend.
We pick our favorite girlfriend.
When we are having bad weather,
American Girls are the best ever.

Molly Taylor, Grade 2
Evangelical Christian School, TN

Jessica

J umpy
E nergetic
S weet
S tar-like
I ncredible
C urious
A dorable

Jessica Schlaen, Grade 3
Virginia A Boone Highland Oaks Elementary School, FL

Summer Days

Summer days are the best; there isn't any homework or any tests.
You can play basketball or soccer
and you don't have to worry about leaving stuff in your locker.
You can go to the pool, but there is one pool rule: NO DIVING!
But you can follow that rule, right?
So, as you know summer days are the best!

Olivia Barbacane, Grade 3
McKinley Elementary School, PA

Man O' Snow

I'm tall and proud.
Call me man o' snow.
I like to show off my design.
I have buttons for eyes
a carrot nose
and pebble mouth.
I throw snowballs
big and small.
If I melt don't be sad.
I'll be back next year.

Ryan Cook, Grade 3
Evergreen Elementary School, PA

The Basketball Shot

Basketball, basketball that is my sport.
I like to run up and down the court.
I dribble to my spot.
And I hit the winning shot.

Sean Nolan, Grade 3
Our Lady of Hope School, NY

Fall

F alling leaves,
A bove the breeze.
L ovely weather,
L ook! Here comes Heather.

P umpkins lighting,
O ctober sighting.
E vening's coming,
M idnight is humming.

Reese Regan, Grade 3
Birches Elementary School, NJ

The Toad

One day I was walking down the road,
When I saw a toad.
It almost hopped in the road,
But when it saw me it slowed
And almost got mowed.
My love for the toad flowed
As he hopped on across the road.

Logan Ruzic, Grade 1
Neosho Christian Schools, MO

My Dog Bingo

Bark bark wag wag
splish splash she's playing in the pool
while I'm in school.
Bark bark she's howling at the moon.
I hope to see it soon.

Grace Giles, Grade 3
Briarwood Christian School, AL

Penguins

Penguins swim.
Penguins waddle.
Penguins swim, swim, swim!

Kizuwanda Bailey, Grade 1
Northeast Elementary School, NY

I Like Dogs

I love dogs.
They are so sweet and fluffy.
If I had a dog, I would call it Muffy.
If my parents bought me another pet
then I will be very sad,
but if I could get a dog,
I'll be very glad.

Joshua Jaslow, Grade 3
McKinley Elementary School, PA

Winter Time

Winter, winter
What a wonderful time,
Snow falls so bitter
And I get chills inside.
It is like a blanket
That falls from the sky.

I make snow angels
And have a snowball fight.
Soon I am freezing
So I go in for the night.
I sip some hot cocoa
(What a chocolaty delight!)
And before I know it
I am out like a light.

Alexandra Hitchens, Grade 3
North Star Elementary School, DE

A Bird in the Sky

A bird in the sky,
A flower in the grass,
I'm in school learning,
All about mass.

Jason Dulberg, Grade 3
Virginia A Boone Highland Oaks Elementary School, FL

Clouds Above Me

The clouds above me look like a frog and a cat.
The clouds above me move like cars and rides.
The clouds above me might smell like cream and milk.
The clouds above me might feel soft and smooth.
The clouds above me might sound like wailing and wind.
The clouds above me might taste like milk and silk.
The clouds above me make me feel better.
Aren't clouds good to look at?

O'Raine Foster, Grade 2
Clover Street School, CT

Halloween

Scary movie, ghosts, goblins, witches too.
Lovely candy, caramel, chocolate, peppermint, too.
Halloween is made for you!

Melanie Stewart, Grade 2
Weston Elementary School, NJ

Birds

Birds fly in the sky
Every day birds eat earthworms
Birds are fantastic

Emily Palmeiro, Grade 2
Virginia A Boone Highland Oaks Elementary School, FL

Energetic Leaf

I'm greenish red
Like a hard, ripe apple.
I feel bumpy
Like a tall mountain edge.
I tremble like a tornado
With the strongest force.
I'm an energetic leaf.

Michael Zhou, Grade 2
Worthington Hooker School – K-2 Campus, CT

The Sparkling Isabella
Isabella
Cute, daughter
Loving, swimming, singing
I like to sing
Bella
Isabella Panepinto, Grade 2
St Stephen's School, NY

Fire Football
An egg
An oval
An "O"
A ball
You can throw it
right or left.
It's brown!
John Patrick Tynan, Grade 1
Holland Township School, NJ

Colorful Fish
A fish, a colorful fish
It looks like a
triangle.
A fish in my pond
An orange fish
I see it in the summer.
A fish might flip!
I feed fish.
I touch fish.
Kayley Brooks, Grade 1
Holland Township School, NJ

Astronaut
A wesome ways to discover
S aturn, Neptune, and Pluto
T ogether they make a team
R acing around the Sun
O rbiting in the galaxy
N ever stopping or pausing
A lways on the move
U nder the stars that twinkle
T hese planets are far away
Anshul Daga, Grade 3
Pride Elementary School, FL

When I'm Alone I…
Like to read a book,
Build things with Legos,
Practice my cartwheels,
Play chess to practice my skills,
Watch TV for a little while,
Get something to eat,
Construct a helmet,
Make a helicopter,
Fly a kite.
Nathan Yin, Grade 3
Madison Station Elementary School, MS

Life Is Like Shooting
Life is like shooting
you concentrate on something immensely
and can get overwhelmed by
something nerve racking
concentrating,
sweating,
focus,
aiming eyes on the bulls eye,
pulling back on the trigger
then — BAM
you release
he is eager but calm
the crowd waves to him
and he waves back.
Samantha Wheeler, Grade 3
Holland Township School, NJ

Christmas Day!
Me and my friends are going to the movies,
To see *This Christmas.*
It's Christmas! It's Christmas!
Let's go and have a snowball fight!
Today is Christmas day!
Christmas trees, gifts, and presents!
Christmas is fun, great!
Happy Holidays.
Ho! Ho! Ho!
Merry Christmas!
Peace.
Glory Seay, Grade 2
Narvie J Harris Traditional Theme School, GA

My Dad Mountain

The mountain is tall like my dad.
It is gray like my dad's hair
It is skinny like my dad.
My mountain is skin color like my dad.
It is stiff like my dad.
When my dad goes in the pool his hair goes in a triangle!

Sami Stamer, Grade 1
Sundance School, NJ

Landforms

Touring, touring, as I go, I see crops, animals, and farms. Oh, it's a plain flat as can be.

Touring, touring, as I go, riding my bike up the hill. Up, up, up it's hard as can be. Down, down, exciting and free with the wind kissing my face and my belly filled with butterflies.

Touring, touring, as I go, I see people hiking and camping on top of the mountain. As I look closer I see snow at the very top. Shall I climb it? Oh, no, no, no! At the top, it may be cold and hard to breathe. Oh, no, no, no, it's not for me!

Touring, touring, as I go, I think I see a giant sticking out its thumb with my bird's eye view. A closer look, I notice water nearly all around it. It's part of a larger land. Well, well, it's a peninsula I see.

Touring, touring, as I go, still in my bird's eye view, I see little spots of something. What could they be? Islands, islands, yes indeed.

Touring, touring as I go, plains, hills, mountains, peninsulas, and islands are very exciting things to see.

Tristan Regist, Grade 3
Public School 235 Lenox, NY

The Beach

It's early in the morning and it's hard to tell where the sea stops and the sky begins. The sand tickles the bottom of my feet while I walk toward the rocks but while I walk a clamshell stops me, it's broken. The shell is crusty gray outside pearly pink inside. As I walked up the salty tang of the water splashes my face. The cold water makes your skin feel like peppermint. Then I dry off in a nice snug towel. Then I lie on the sand, it feels like a soft cat covering you. Then the sky comes down to pink, orange, purple then black. I love the beach.

Caroline Doherty, Grade 3
Jeffrey Elementary School, CT

We're Together

We're together most of the time,
Even at the store, when we're in line.
Together for reading,
Together for eating.
It's better for your heart
Than being apart.

Jim Levri, Grade 2
Levri Home School, PA

Falling Leaves

Fall leaves flowing in the sky.
They fall in the green, green grass.
I see them when I go by.

Adam Gamba, Grade 1
East Dover Elementary School, NJ

Squirrels/Animals

Squirrels
Soft, nice
Climbing, rolling, digging
Cute, harmless, brown, funny
Animals

Mario Diaz-Montiel, Grade 3
Northeast Elementary School, NY

Santa

S anta coming in December.
A t Christmas Santa wears red.
N ose looks like a cherry
T hen he comes out the chimney.
A lways a friend.

Kolton Hanna, Grade 1
Small World Academy, WV

Day/Night

Day
Sunny, hot
Run, jump, ride
Light, nature, nocturnal animals
Sleep, eat, snore
Dark, windy
Night

Daniella Donado, Grade 1
Oliver Hoover Elementary School, FL

My Friend

Owen and I are very good friends
We play and laugh,
The fun never ends.
We go to the park,
We ride our bikes.
We also like to fly our kites.
We always like to help each other.
He's not just my friend,
He's also my brother.

Emma McClean, Grade 3
Our Lady of Hope School, NY

My Friend Zack

I have a best friend his name is Zack.
He moved away and isn't coming back.
He used to go to my school.
That was fun and so cool.
But, now I miss him so much.
I hope he keeps in touch.

Sean Clarency, Grade 2
St Anselm School, PA

On Christmas

On Christmas Eve
Santa will be
on his way.
I sat around the warm fire
drinking hot cocoa.
And then
we all go to bed
and get good sleepys.
And then
Santa comes.
He drinks my cold milk
and warm cookies.

Alexis Williams, Grade 2
Southside Elementary School, KY

Cake

I make cake.
With flour I bake.
To grandmother I take.

Mya Whitehurst, Kindergarten
Taylor Road Academy, AL

School Is the First Step for Life

School is cool
Whoever doesn't stay in school is a fool
School prepares you for your future job
Without school you'll probably be a future slob
I'm telling you to be smart and don't drop out
Because in the future you'll have regret without a doubt
And school brings you lots of fun
In the future you know you have won
So go to school and get the job done!

Vanessa Grullon, Grade 3
Marie Durand Elementary School, NJ

The Hornet School

Buses puffing like trains
Mrs. Anderson teaching pupils
Soft music is playing like lapping waves on an ocean shore
Drinking knowledge for our thirst
Soft smells of delicious foods drift through the room
My classroom smells of my teacher's perfume
Lollipops so strong in tasting it is bitter
My sandwich is soft and tangy
The desk is cold and hard
My heart is pumping with joy
I feel delightful and happy inside.

Caroline Jones, Grade 3
Bailey Elementary School, NC

Nature's All Around

Trees high in the sky
Grass so green in the brown dirt
Plants growing around.

Sofia Idone, Grade 3
Virginia A Boone Highland Oaks Elementary School, FL

I Am From

I am from my pretty bedroom
where my cozy blanket is there when I sleep in my room.
I am from my nice cozy mom's room
where I watch TV.
I am from my nice garden
where I smell flowers.

Karla Garcia, Grade 1
Berkeley Lake Elementary School, GA

Sofia

She is my little sister
she is messy like a pig and burps a lot
she throws her food on the table
it sounds like this ploop, ploop, ploop
we tell her not to drop her food
she ignores us and throws her food
then she burps so loud and then coos
Sofia, Sofia, we love you.

Daniel Lupercio, Grade 3
Public School 148 Ruby Allen, NY

Ice Cream

Ice cream, ice cream
It drips off my lips
When my tongue slips
Onto the ice cream
My brain freezes
Like Antarctica
Even though it gives me brain freeze
I still adore ice cream

Kristen Gibbs, Grade 3
Oak Ridge Elementary School, PA

September

S o energetic to start school.
E veryone likes fall.
P eople get ready for winter.
T ime to start school.
E veryone drinks apple cider.
M y favorite sport to watch is football.
B irds fly south.
E veryone eats apples.
R aking leaves.

Liam Carey, Grade 2
St Stephen's School, NY

School

School is
cool and rules
fun to learn
climbing to the top
attitude

Logan House, Grade 1
Broadway Elementary School, NC

Cake

I like cake.
Any kind of cake.
Yummy cake, tasty cake,
Juicy cake, funny cake.
Cake in my mouth.
Cake on my plate.
Cake with ice cream.
Any kind of cake.
I like cake.

Justice Michael, Grade 3
Landmark Christian School, GA

Bird

Birds fly
Birds sing
Did you know
They flap their wings?

Gianna Paul, Grade 3
Evergreen Elementary School, PA

Carriers

Big carriers in the sea,
Oh how strong they must be,
For the planes to land at sea.
Big carriers in the sea are
Very long indeed,
As there are many planes that are in
Need of landing in the sea.
Big carriers in the sea.

Austin Meis, Grade 3
Tri-County Christian School, MO

Rain

Rain, Rain
so fun,
so wet,
so cold.

Rain, Rain
big puddles,
big droplets,
big storm.

Jesus Nepita, Grade 3
Reidville Elementary School, SC

Nature

The birds are chirping
Blue birds are flying so high
I like birds the most

Adam Keller, Grade 2
Virginia A Boone Highland Oaks Elementary School, FL

Goldfish

Hi! I'm a goldfish.
My name is Jet.
My water smells like potato chips because my fish food tastes just like potatoes.
I like to go to the bottom of my tank,
because the rocks are so smooth.
I am really happy in my tank,
But I wish I was in the ocean with my family.

Lillian Tipton, Grade 2
Worthington Hooker School – K-2 Campus, CT

Early or Late?

Early or late, wouldn't it be great…
To mix up the day just for fun?
Breakfast for dinner, dinner for lunch,
Lunch for a midnight snack.

Early or late, wouldn't it be great…
To sleep through the day and stay up all night?
Snoring so loudly while others are working,
I could study at a midnight school.

Early or late, wouldn't it be great…
To play with the nocturnal creatures,
Games with bats and bugs and owls,
But you'd be sleeping, so rather than that…

I'D RATHER PLAY WITH YOU!!!

Hannah Berkowitz, Grade 3
Virginia A Boone Highland Oaks Elementary School, FL

Books

Books, Books, there are so many,
Each one with a different title.
They are all over the world,
Each one with a different writer!

Alex Palau, Grade 2
Virginia A Boone Highland Oaks Elementary School, FL

Blue

Water, sky
Blue Jays
Blue fireworks, blue pencils
A blue shirt, a sapphire
Blueberries, a blue fish.
Sean Flanagan, Grade 2
Sundance School, NJ

Spiderwebs/Silk

Spiderwebs
Silky, sticky
Webbing, spinning, sticking
Bugs don't see spiderwebs.
Silk
Johnny Romero, Grade 2
Consolidated School, CT

Santa

S anta giving gifts
A very nice man
N ever forgot a kid
T oo much fun
A lot of toys from Santa
Mikhaela Barnes, Grade 2
Small World Academy, WV

The Sun

Explosion!
It reminds me of
a twinkling star!!!
In space it floats and
keeps us warm!
Evan Baylor, Grade 1
Holland Township School, NJ

Maggie

M iss America
A mazing
G ood
G raceful
I like shopping
E veryone's friend
Maggie Couch, Grade 2
Park Elementary School, AR

Stars

S acrifice
T hey are thankful
A re good people
R espect
S ave our lives from danger
Brittany Graham, Grade 3
Bradford Township Elementary School, PA

Sweet Apples

Some apples are sweet, some apples are sour,
but all of them are good for an hour.
Some may be bitter, some may be fresh
but all of them are good for my flesh!
Alyssa V. Porcena, Grade 2
Coral Cove Elementary School, FL

Leaves Are Falling

Leaves are falling
Day or night
When I see them, I feel so bright.
Leaves are falling everywhere,
From the trees and the air.
But before I can notice it turns so white.
It happens to be snow.
So goodbye fall and goodbye leaves.
It is time for you to leave.
Kaitlyn Norris, Grade 3
Contentnea Elementary School, NC

Backward Town

I went to a town
Where everyone was a clown.
They all had a frown
And everyone wore a gown.

The children were tall
The adults were small.
And they like to run into the wall.

It was a funny sight to see.
Everyone was hanging from a tree.
After that they all got stung by a bee.
Austin Brown, Grade 3
Belfast-Elk Garden Elementary School, VA

Ice Cream

I ce cream is icy.
C ream is a good topping.
E normous scoops are delicious.

C an I interest you in taking me to Dairy Queen?
R eally good ice cream is hard to find.
E ating ice cream with my family is cool.
A ll flavors taste good to me.
M y favorite flavor is chocolate.

Marshal Hicks, Grade 3
Bensley Elementary School, VA

Bees in the Sky

Bees fly in the sky
They find all the sweet flowers
They take the honey

Daren Hirsch, Grade 2
Virginia A Boone Highland Oaks Elementary School, FL

Monster House

Dear Monster House,
You scare me!
I hate looking at you.
When I go trick or treating, I knock on your door.
Nobody comes,
I look through your window,
I see cracks in the floor,
It looks like a wooden mouth.
Then, Ah!
A face in the window scares me!
Then hands come out of the grass,
The sidewalk, the porch,
Ah! The hands grab me,
They pull me,
I try to tug them away,
They pull me under the porch.
I get on my feet,
I run all the way home.
I hide under the bed until Halloween is over.
I tell myself,
I am not ever going trick or treating again!

Justus Ray, Grade 3
Cool Spring Elementary School, NC

Gymnast

He is nervous,
The audience is impressed.
He is powerful.
His MUSCLES are keeping him up.
He is under a mat.
He is holding up his legs in the air.

Jessica Barosi, Grade 3
Holland Township School, NJ

My Family

My family is very special.
My family is very nice.
Every night when I go to bed,
They remain in my view and sight.

Keivlan Griffith, Grade 3
Joseph Pennell Elementary School, PA

The Gas Giant

Cassini explored.
Jupiter has a red eye.
I would like to go!

William Joseph Clifford, Grade 1
Clifford Home School, FL

Woof Woof

I like my dog.
He's black and white.
I love to hug him
With all my might.

He doesn't really have a name,
But I love him just the same.

My teacher says
His name is "Snoopy."
But I don't like that
Cause it rhymes with "poopy."

I want to keep him
'Cause he's a friend.
And I'll love him
To the end.

Laura Null, Kindergarten
The American Academy, PA

Black Horse

I like to eat…
Hay, grass, but not meat.
I can walk.
But I cannot talk.
I am Black Horse.

Jason Alvarenga, Grade 1
Northeast Elementary School, NY

Snow

I like snow.
I like it when it falls.
It is soft and cold.
My mommy likes it too.
How about you?

Angelina Brizuela, Grade 1
James H Bright Elementary School, FL

My Dog Sparky

Sparky likes to slide.
He climbs high for a silly ride.

He chases the four-wheeler very fast,
In our race I come in very last.

Sparky barked at a snake.
And I hit the snake with a rake.

Alisha Armer, Grade 2
Alpena Elementary School, AR

Sky

Sky is so blue, bluer than blue.
Sky is so nice, nicer than ice.
Ice is so clear, clearer than fear.
But sky is so blue, beautiful as you.

Sara Rivkin, Grade 3
Torah Academy, LA

Sport

My favorite sport is kick ball.
But it sometimes is hard to kick.
It is not easy at all,
But you have to be quick.

Daniel Molinsky, Grade 2
Yeshiva Ketana of Long Island, NY

Apples 'n Oranges

Apples 'n oranges and juicy blueberries.
Bananas 'n grapes, and delicious black cherries.
Apples 'n oranges, important and wise.
As soon as it is spring, the foods will rise.
Summer! Fall! Winter! Spring!
Rise and shine!
Let's eat! Let's eat!
Here's a fruit salad!
Bon Appétit!
Here comes the plants! Hurray! Hurray!
This will be a splendid day!
Apples 'n oranges, sour and sweet.
The taste of a grape cannot be beat.
Apples 'n oranges, a ton we shall eat.
Now I think our poem is complete.

Aleksandr Dopko, Grade 2
Collingwood Park SDA School, NJ

Best Friends

My best friends are so sweet. Candy is their favorite thing to eat.
We love to smell flowers. We talk ever hour.
They are small and tall and love to play ball.
We call each other every night.
Sometimes we even fly kites until they are out of sight.

Georgia Adams, Grade 3
Pike Liberal Arts School, AL

Candy

Candy candy is so sweet.
It's the sweetest thing you'll ever eat.
That's why candy is so neat.
So it will never ever be beat.
What a nice treat.

Noam Kleinman, Grade 3
Virginia A Boone Highland Oaks Elementary School, FL

What Is Pink?

A pink crayon,
A pink cotton candy roll,
A pink flamingo flapping its wings in the water,
Pink makes me happy and express myself,
Pink is a rose petal.

Brittney Winter, Grade 3
Scott Elementary School, MO

Moms

Moms are funny
funny as a comedian
Moms help with
our homework.
And our pencils
go scribble, scribble, scribble
across my paper. Moms make
our hearts go boom, boom, boom.
I'll give you my heart
(but not my very whole heart)
Mom you make
my heart
explode like
a bomb
going
boom you
throw a
bomb of
joy and laughter
at me!

Alesha Dunn, Grade 3
Public School 148 Ruby Allen, NY

Eiffel Tower

The Eiffel Tower
it's so big it might have power!
And if it crashed
on you boy, you would be mashed!
But the Eiffel Tower it's so pretty
I hope you get to see that city.

Olivia Hannum, Grade 2
Briarwood Christian School, AL

Fall

Fall is fun!
Oh, so fun!
I just want to
jump in the leaves — plop!
I do not want to stop.
I help my mom rake the leaves
So I can jump on top!

Taylor Lawson, Grade 2
Eagle's View Academy, FL

Pumpkin

Cookies are yummy
Parties are fun.
I like apple cider nice and hot.
Pie is like bread.
Muffins are too.
I like them both.
How about you?
Leaves will fall
Wind will blow
So where will you go?
Vines are growing.
Thyme is a spice.
Do you like ten sided dice?
Sugar is sweet.
Tarts are too.
I like muffins.
How about you?

Gregory Bell, Grade 3
Nativity Catholic School, FL

Butterfly

The big butterfly
sitting on an oak tree branch
looking to explore.

Makayla Brousse, Grade 2
Roseland Park Elementary School, MS

Fall

Apples fall.
Neighbors watch.
Deer call.

Ben Hill, Grade 3
Trinity South Elementary School, PA

The Cats

Meow, meow, purr, purr
The cats are sitting on the couch
and staring at the door
I hope they don't get bored.
They went out to play
they started to scratch the door
and it started to pour.

Natalie Crumpler, Grade 3
Briarwood Christian School, AL

Trick-or-Treat Halloween

Witches fly at night,
While children use light.
Halloween is so fun,
I just like to run.
When you see a skeleton, they are bony,
When you see me I am eating honey.
When children go trick-or-treating,
Look out I might give you a greeting.
So happy Halloween, but hold on to your bags tight,
I said that because I might give you a fright!

Shantavia Jones, Grade 3
Blakeney Elementary School, GA

Mr. Goofy

Mr. Goofy is a teddy bear.
He is brown and I love him and treat him with care.
He makes me feel bubbly.
I think it's because he's so cuddly.
He sits on my bed and I love him so much.
I want to keep him forever so don't you dare touch!

Natasha Garcia, Grade 3
Coral Cove Elementary School, FL

I'm a Little Girl…

I'm a little girl
In this great big world
I'm so spastic
It's fantastic
Do you like my style
I think it's very wild
My imagination
It's part of my creation

I'm a little girl
In my little world
When people say things
It just rings, rings
Can you come and play
You can have your way
My creations
It's part of your imagination

Aria Hartwell, Grade 3
Noonan Elementary Academy of Fort Myers, FL

Christmas!!!

C is for Christ
H is for HO, HO, HO
R is for ride
I is for I love the Lord
S is for Santa
T is for toys
M is for Mary
A is for angel
S is for Saviour

Mallory Conway, Grade 3
Fort Dale Academy, AL

What Is White?

A cloud,
A mystery Airhead,
A morning glory,
Soft like a pillow,
Quiet like water.

David Holder, Grade 3
Scott Elementary School, MO

Marines

My mom
Is special
Brown Eyes
Plays soccer
Fun mom!

Jeremy Espinoza, Grade 2
Marie Curie Institute, NY

My Horse

I have a horse.
My horse is brown.
It jumps over gates, of course.
My horse can ride to town.

Elise Jackson, Kindergarten
Taylor Road Academy, AL

Walking in the Jungle

Walking in the jungle,
I hear something in my ear.
Is it a snake?

Julian Foley, Grade 3
Tuxedo Park School, NY

A Happy Day

I was born on February 6, 1999.
I saw my hand print and my footprint.
When I was three,
I stuck my face in my birthday cake.
I was wearing my Lightning McQueen shirt.
I went swimming in the baby pool.
Then we went to the circus
and ate funnel cakes.
I was full.

Markel Whiters, Grade 3
Lee A Tolbert Community Academy, MO

Free

F reedom
R est
E verlasting
E veryone is safe

Tommy Hazel, Grade 3
Bradford Township Elementary School, PA

Leopards

Running fast
Like a leopard
Leaping through
The wet, misty forest
Jumping over
Branches and twigs

Naptime is coming
So I'm getting ready
To rest my body
And regain my energy
To pounce and growl

Zoë Neijna, Grade 3
Hunter GT Magnet Elementary School, NC

Basketball

I like basketball.
But it is not fun to fall.
It's really fun when you shoot the ball in.
Then you win.
I like basketball.

Casey Cornwell, Grade 3
Western Hills Elementary School, AR

The Color Blue

Blue is the color of my eyes
Blue is the pretty sound from a Blue Jay
Blue is a small blueberry which is soft and round
Blue is the round button on my coat
Blue is the candle on my birthday cake

Alexis Wassel, Grade 2
Sundance School, NJ

Autumn

A mazing birds fly like the wind.
U p to the colorful leaves on the tree.
T hanksgiving is a time you spend with your family.
U p I jump in the leaves, and they splatter everywhere.
M om makes good turkey on Thanksgiving.
N ice colored leaves fall from the tree, and I have to rake them into a pile.

Camryn Hambro, Grade 3
Central Park Elementary School, FL

The Funny Bunnies

There are funny bunnies
The funny bunnies were playing with me
The funny bunnies were laughing with their friends.

Frances Yu, Grade 1
Children's Village, PA

Wonderful Leaf

I'm bright yellow and black
Like a banana.
I feel as smooth
as a pillow.
I'm dancing
Like a ballerina
As I fall from the tree.
I'm a wonderful leaf.

Jiaxin Ying, Grade 2
Worthington Hooker School – K-2 Campus, CT

I Love Ice Cream

I love ice cream,
With a cherry on top.
My ice cream dropped,
So I have to clean it with a mop!

Ilana Hollender, Grade 2
Virginia A Boone Highland Oaks Elementary School, FL

My Sister

My sister is crazy
like a rock star she
likes music like a rock star
she loves to dance on
stage especially when there
is a loud audience clap, clap, clap
she can be as funny as a clown
no matter what she is she
will always be my sister
Penelope

Domenique Cifuentes, Grade 3
Public School 148 Ruby Allen, NY

Cats

C razy
A wesome
T alented
S mart

Jordan Wright, Grade 3
Pottsville Elementary School, AR

Flower

First you have to plant the seeds
and then you need to water
and you need sun to plant the seed
and then the seeds will grow to flower
and when the seeds get ready
you can take the seeds out
from the flower.

Anna Liu, Grade 1
Children's Village, PA

Fish

I like fish.
Any kind of fish.
Soft fish, bone fish,
Hot fish, cold fish.
Fish in my belly,
Fish on my line,
Fish with ketchup,
Any kind of fish.
I like fish.

Mason Frady, Grade 3
Landmark Christian School, GA

Spencer

S illy
P erseverance
E xciting
N ice
C hina
E xtraordinary
R ich

Spencer Jenney, Grade 2
Long Meadow Elementary School, CT

Clerk the Smirking Bird

Mr. Turb
had a bird
Its name was Clerk
He can Smirk.

Maddie Kidd, Grade 3
The Parke House Academy, FL

The Beach

Sandy Beach! Sandy Beach!
Sitting in a chair!
Sitting on the ground!
Reading a book!
Building a castle!
Brr!
Cold water!
Splash!
The waves go!
Boom! Crash!
The waves go!
On the beach!
Sandy Beach!
Sandy Beach!

Maggie Naughton, Grade 3
North Star Elementary School, DE

Pumpkins

Pumpkins round and fat
Growing lots of seeds
Carving, so much fun
Halloween just begun

Catherine Roxas, Grade 2
Somerville Elementary School, NJ

The Rose*

I see a red rose…wraps of beautiful red.
And inside the tiny wraps, I see tiny drops of water.
On the rose's stem, I see four tiny leaves.
They look as if it was raining.
They are looking very damp as water drips onto the side of the flowerpot and drops onto the moist grass.
As I write the poem down I will keep this poem in my memory as days, weeks, and months pass by.
I will remember this poem and I will pass it on to others.

Taylor Thompson, Grade 3
Robert Toombs Christian Academy, GA
**In memory of Kurt Jacobs*

My Dog

My dog is sweet and kind.
She's so cute and she's mine.
Her name is Fay Fay and she always obeys.
She would play with me every day.
I'm afraid she would bite, but I always hold on tight.
I loved her all the way until she passed away,
But I still remember her as of today.
It's sad to say but I didn't want her to go away.
I still love my dog even though she passed away.
Nobody can take my love for Fay Fay away.

Chloe Leung, Grade 3
John Ward Elementary School, MA

My Friends

My friends rock.
They're a lovely flock.
We laugh, play and shock our flock.
The boys all laugh without making noise,
But my friends laugh loud with joy.
If I get hurt it's not a problem today,
Because my friends will all make sure I'm okay.
When I take a walk with all my friends,
We have so much fun time quickly ends.
We miss each other when we're apart,
So much so it breaks our hearts.
The next time you see us in our pride,
Don't be shy and come say hi.

Michelle Myseros, Grade 3
Trinity Christian School, VA

Dripping, Dropping
Drip, drop
Down comes the rain
Down the path
Passing the playground
Going around, around and around
Getting dizzy and a little wet
On my way to school
All I feel is dripping and dropping
On my way to school
Things I pass
Quite exciting
Trains, towns, bridges and puddles
I splish and splash in the puddles
Samantha Mohr, Grade 3
Coram Elementary School, NY

One Day
One day I saw
A red ant on a big tree.
It sort of looked
Like a bumblebee
Then he crawled in a hole.
I think I will tell Mrs. Dole!
Owen Bitnun, Grade 2
John T Waugh Elementary School, NY

What Do I See?
I see a chalkboard.
I see windows.
I see an alphabet.
I do not see a mermaid.
Kenneth Escobar, Grade 1
Northeast Elementary School, NY

Farmers
Farmers
Farmers
Trying to catch a pig in a car
And they finally caught it
And when they saw their car
It was broken.
Jordan Sanchez, Grade 1
Southside Elementary School, KY

The Dog
The dog is good
The dog is nice
The dog eats food
The dog eats rice
Raquel Lopez, Grade 1
Northeast Elementary School, NY

Animals
Some animals are
big and some are small.
Some eat meat
some don't
Some are mean
some are nice.
Some sleep at night
some sleep during the day.
So watch out!
Look at the animals
before you pet them.
And stand your guard or they'll eat
you alive! And scratch you!
Alex Ramirez, Grade 3
Public School 148 Ruby Allen, NY

My Brother
M oney is good for him
Y es, he is a good brother

B aseball
R eally fun
O utstanding
T yler is his name
H ungry all the time
E ats a lot
R ough
Devon Conroy, Grade 3
McKinley Elementary School, PA

Bunnies
They are all so fast.
They all like to eat carrots.
They love to be loved.
Amanda Delaplaine, Grade 3
Miami Country Day School, FL

Myrtle Beach

Ocean waves are like rocks falling from the sky
Sand at the ocean is like spikes poking me
The ocean is like bears roaring in the forest
People are like birds chirping in your ears
The salt water is like the smell of pizza
Palm trees are like the smell of grass
The ocean tastes as nasty as spinach
The food is like receiving fresh water on a summer day
The waves are as rough as rocky cliffs
The sand is as smooth as an animal's fur
I feel happy and content.

Seth Whitley, Grade 3
Bailey Elementary School, NC

The Pig

The pig is a farm animal that is black or pink.
It likes fresh, clean water to drink.

It likes to roll in mud all day.
It also enjoys eating hay.

Its tail is curly and short.
It has a snout for a nose that it uses to snort.

A pig has short legs and hoofed feet.
Fruits and flowers are other foods they eat.

They are very smart and they have a great sense of smell.
They can sniff out food but they cannot spell.

A piglet is a baby pig that drinks its mom's milk.
The pig is round and its skin feels like silk.

Angela Viducich, Grade 3
St Alexis School, PA

Me

A shley's sweet like the fruit, apples and pears
S coops of ice cream on a cone,
H ops like a rabbit,
L oves a love song,
E ars like an elephant,
Y ellow like the sun.

Ashley Haynes, Grade 2
Public School 152 School of Science & Technology, NY

Fall Fun

I like fall
Best of all.
When it's noon
There is no moon.
But when it's night
It's very bright.
The wind blows
Against your nose.
The leaves fall down
Without a sound.

Zachary Moore, Grade 2
Eagle's View Academy, FL

Christmas

When I see the night
The stars look so bright
When I see the toys
It fills me with joys
When I see my treat
It looks so sweet!
When I see the tree
It feels me with glee!

Tori Simmons, Grade 3
Fort Dale Academy, AL

My Camping Trip

The skunks are stinky
The bears are really hungry
They eat our lunches

Lauren Perillo, Grade 3
Tuxedo Park School, NY

Christmas

Christmas is coming,
Do not be crying,
Do not be pouting,
Because Saint Nick is coming.

Christmas is near,
Do not fear,
Stocking are hanging,
The trees are shining.

Susie Stell, Grade 3
Pike Liberal Arts School, AL

What is Light-Blue?

Light-blue is a sky on a sunny day,
It is delicious like blue gummy bears,
It smells like a blue scented marker,
Light-blue is hard construction paper,
Light-blue sounds like a blue jay chirping.

Kayla Farrill, Grade 3
Scott Elementary School, MO

Spring Baseball and Winter Basketball

Baseball in spring is lots of fun
Because you get to run in the sun.

You must run fast to the base
And try not to fall and hurt your face.

I could play every day
And if my team wins, hip hip hooray!

Basketball is great fun, too.
I hope I don't need to tie my shoe.

I can play when it is cold
On the court the ball to hold.

"Pass, pass," I always say
And if my team wins, that makes my day!

David Matej, Grade 2
The American Academy, PA

Ice Cream

Ice cream, ice cream —
Vanilla on the top
How many toys do I have?
I've got a lot!

Sean Lynch, Grade 3
St Joseph Catholic Grammar School, NJ

Pretty Leaves Fall

Leaves fall on the ground
All colors red, orange, and yellow
Kids play in the leaves
Kids say "I can't wait till fall comes again!"

Toni Jo Castelucci, Grade 3
Concord Elementary School, PA

Dancing

D ancing is my hobby!
A t home and at school.
N ow I want to dance on T.V.
C an my teacher dance?
I know "I" can dance good.
N ow that I'm out of school I can do it again.
G o dancing!

Allure Hayes, Grade 2
Dr Martin Luther King Jr School Complex, NJ

Stay in School

School is fun, under the sun.
We play in the hay all day.
The teacher acts like a preacher.
She preaches, and preaches until we reach lunch.
School is cool so don't be a fool.
Keep your cool and stay in school.

Ashanti Bailey, Grade 3
Western Hills Elementary School, AR

Halloween

Halloween is scary and kids say
"Trick or treat"
Dressed like scary monsters
Super heroes that are fake
'Cause everybody knows
They are only people dressed like them
Some people are not scared only little kids are scared
Halloween is the time to have fun with families and friends

Sergio Hernandez, Grade 3
Public School 131, NY

Teachers

T utor
E xam
A pple
C lassroom
H elp
E xchange
R eport Card
S ubject

Kdeja Correa, Grade 3
Virginia A Boone Highland Oaks Elementary School, FL

My Mom

Beautiful, warm, sweet
Helping, loving, sleeping, snuggling
Comfort, togetherness, family
Gina

Ava DelForno, Grade 2
St Mary's School, NJ

I Love October

October is great!
When will Halloween be here?
Fall colors are nice.

Shannon Cholak, Grade 2
Wanamassa Elementary School, NJ

Snow!

Snow
looks like a pale face.
Snow falls
d
o
w
n
from the sky lightly.
Snowmen never end
Snowballs are thrown
Look out! Boom!
Snow is the best!

Benjamin Pracht, Grade 3
Reidville Elementary School, SC

The King Married the Queen

The king loved the queen
so he gave her a ring.
She sat on a bee
and it gave her a sting.

Reed Eason, Kindergarten
Northeast Baptist School, LA

Things I Love Outside

The grass is so green
I smell the great outdoor air
When I go outside

Spencer Britt, Grade 3
The Parke House Academy, FL

My Pet

Cat
Does back flips
Meows
Sits in my lap
Purrs
Drinks milk
Kitty

Leanna Boggs, Kindergarten
Broadway Elementary School, NC

My Favorite Color

I like red.
The fire truck is red.
The lipstick is red.
The apple is red.
I like red.

Hailey Sanchez, Grade 1
Northeast Elementary School, NY

Spencer

Spencer
smart, tall,
football, basketball, baseball,
always nice to others,
Pop

Lily Cooper, Grade 3
Briarwood Christian School, AL

Fish

I caught an orange fish he went
gulp, gulp, gulp
and tried to get
away he moved a lot
splish, splash, splish, splash
the fish and he got away
Oh no, I said
"Come back, come back"
he jumps out of
the pail swims
quicker than a snail
My fish got away.

Giselle Avila, Grade 3
Public School 148 Ruby Allen, NY

One Boy

There once was a boy whom was quite witty,
He got up one day and went to the city,
He gave up a big sneeze
I think he got the flu,
Oh what a pity
I hope he gets well quickly.

Jedidiah Armstrong, Grade 2
Public School 152 School of Science & Technology, NY

My Best Friend

My best friend is shy and sweet.
Mac and cheese is one of her favorite things to eat.
She has a cute smile and dresses cool.
She is one of the best students in school.
My best friend has short chubby fingers, blonde hair, and big eyes.
She can get her feelings hurt and easily cries.
She calls me every night when we get home.
We like to talk about what we'll wear tomorrow on the phone.
My best friend's name is Bailey Black.
She's just like me and that's a fact!

Savannah Hollis, Grade 3
Pike Liberal Arts School, AL

Fall

In the fall, I taste sweet, striped candy corn at the hay ride.
In the fall, I hear blowing leaves in my front yard.
In the fall, I smell delicious, incredible hot chocolate at my house.
In the fall, I feel big, round pumpkins on my porch.
In the fall, I see hot, bubbly pumpkin pie baking in the oven.
In the fall, I don't see lemonade, people with shorts, sleeveless shirts on,
or leaves hanging on trees.

Dakota Younger, Grade 3
Watsontown Elementary School, PA

Starry Night

Look up in the night,
You might see a bright light.
That is a star like a firefly,
Up so high.
It is happy to brighten our night.
The stars shine so right,
The night would not be the same without them.

Laura Ellen Gray, Grade 3
Evangelical Christian School, TN

Simple Pleasures

Ice cream is like ice cold memories
The feeling never goes away
Cake is like slices of daylight
you can never get enough
Frosting is like big blobs
Of things to do

Meghan Hurley, Grade 3
Lincoln Elementary School, PA

Carleigh

C ute
A wesome
R eally good student
L ovable
E xciting
I love my family
G irl
H elpful

Carleigh Kaczmarski, Grade 2
Park Elementary School, AR

Dress-up

We dance to music.
We pretend we are princesses.
We go to movies for pretend.
I dress like Jasmine,
But my belly sticks out!
I have a red and purple crown.
The cookies said our name.
Dress-up is fun.

Saraea Kaplan, Kindergarten
United Hebrew Institute, PA

Matthew

M agnificent
A greeable
T alented
T errific
H elpful
E ager
W ell-mannered

Matthew McGrath, Grade 2
Long Meadow Elementary School, CT

My Cousin

Her name is Michelle.
She is so smart
like a scientist
Her luscious black wavy hair
moves fast as a monkey swishing
from tree to tree
swish, swish, swish
when she is running to me.
Although we don't see each other
we will still meet somehow.
She knows how to bake and cook.
She is from Colombia.
When she sees me
I have to look way up high
whoa, whoa, whoa.
We still love each other
even if we're 25, 50, or 75.
This is the poem to describe her.
She is my cousin Michelle.

Alejandro Ruiz, Grade 3
Public School 148 Ruby Allen, NY

Cat-Ku

Fluffy yellow striped
Soft meow purr purr purr purr
Has four legs is good

Katie Bailey, Grade 2
Paine Primary School, AL

Penguins

Penguins hop.
Penguins hide.
Penguins pip, pip, pip!

Miguel Santiago, Grade 1
Northeast Elementary School, NY

Bunnies/Fur Balls

Bunnies
Cute, furry
Hopping, playful, munching
Soft, cuddling, loving, happy
Fur balls.

Marissa Rondinone, Grade 3
Wapping Elementary School, CT

UAW-Ford 500

The UAW-Ford 500 took place in Talladega, Alabama.
Zoom, zoom, the race has begun.
Go! Cheer! The fans are cheering on their favorite driver.
Boom, boom, smack, pow, the big one takes out nearly 7.
Bam, the little one takes out one.
Go! White flag! Almost the final lap.
One lap away.
Yaaa! Checkered flag. Jeff Gordon, the restrictor plate king wins.

Tony DiTaranto, Grade 3
Wolcott School, CT

All Year Round

Fall is when there are many colors
Fall is when there are leaves twirling off trees
Winter is when there are white snow flakes falling from the sky
Winter is when snow covers the green grass
Spring is when red flowers bloom in the flower patch
Spring is when bluebirds sing sweet tunes
Summer is when you swim in a cool pool
Summer is when you ride your bike on the street

Destiny Green, Grade 3
St Charles Homeschool Learning Center, MO

The Words That Speak My Poem

The words come out of my mouth and onto my paper
Without moving a muscle.
Some people think it is not possible that I get all the answers right.
I do this without writing a single word.
I just have to think and it will happen.
The teacher tells everyone I'm whiziriffic!

Nina Sone, Grade 3
Wolcott School, CT

Dear Pumpkins

Dear Pumpkins,
You are so orange and ripe,
You scare me sometimes during the night.
That scary face of yours and that light that shines,
Scares me each and every time.
When it turns Halloween,
You come out and make me scream.

Mojanika Daye, Grade 3
Cool Spring Elementary School, NC

Mrs. E.

My teacher
Perfect smile
Teaching math
Reading stories
Best teacher.

Tyler Frolke, Grade 2
Marie Curie Institute, NY

Ruby

Ruby
Generous, tall
Swimming, singing, playing
I like to sing
Scooby

Ruby Benz, Grade 2
St Stephen's School, NY

My Family and Me

We bake cookies.
I get a Christmas tree.
We wrap presents.
My family and me.
I open presents.
We play with toys.
I play with my dog.
Jesus loves girls and boys.

Gabriella Selby, Grade 1
Westlake Christian School, FL

Santa

No fear
Santa is here.
He has toys
For girls and boys.
Balls for boys
Dolls for girls.
His belly
Jiggles like jelly
His sack that
Lays on his back
Is full of toys
For girls and boys.

Meagan Davis, Grade 3
Fort Dale Academy, AL

The Umbrellas

Smells like McDonalds
So we stop to get French fries
There are a lot of cars starting up
Vroom! Vroom!
We like the smell of gas
Pine trees everywhere
Purple, red, blue, yellow and pink umbrellas
We're on our way to school
We hear our teacher's call

Cheyenne Flood, Grade 3
Coram Elementary School, NY

Grandma's House

The white snow fall
My cat's purr
The slippy slidy snowboard
Hot gingerbread cookies

Morgan Green, Grade 3
Bradford Township Elementary School, PA

A Visitor

I woke up in the night.
I saw a frightening sight!
But wait, it was Old Saint Nick.
My present he was about to pick!

Riley Dodd, Grade 1
St Vincent De Paul Elementary School, MO

My Next Door Neighbor's Dog Teddy

Bark bark he's playing in the creek.
He is so annoying he makes me go ink.
But he is so sweet.

Grace Madeline Harris, Grade 3
Briarwood Christian School, AL

If I Were a Pizza

If I were a pizza,
I'd have pepperoni, sausage, cheese
And little bits of bacon on me
I would feel yummy
And taste good in someone's tummy
If I were a pizza

Emma Kolb, Grade 2
St Charles Homeschool Learning Center, MO

Thanksgiving

T he time of year to be thankful.
H olidays are about being together.
A ny time you can be together with your family.
N ever doubt your family.
K now your family everywhere around the world.
S ave all of the memories spent with your family.
G iving thanks and love to your family.
I nvest all of time and love with your family.
V ery good and thankful wishes for you and me!
I magine spending the holiday with your family!
N ever stop loving your family!
G ive love to your family!

Delano Hendrix, Grade 3
Dr Martin Luther King Jr School Complex, NJ

Soda

The bubbles and the fizzing in the popping soda
sound like an instant alarm going off.
The nice sweet smell of soda is like vinegar,
sugar and sweetness combined together
to make a nice, cool soda
on a smooth cocoa colored table
and soft cotton tablecloth.
The bubbles and the fizzing have slowed down
and I take a big sip and swallow it all down.
The cool, nice drink is gone
but I can still feel the soda inside me.

Mong Zhang, Grade 3
Lincoln Elementary School, PA

Spring Things

The first yellow, blue, red, and green frog of spring
A big blue lake with fish swimming all around
A giant yellow and black puffy bumblebee
The first chestnut brown squirrel of spring
The big puffy clouds and a yellow bright sun
A colorful rainbow high in the sky
Puffy white bunnies running all around
The leaves on the trees are finally growing back
The snow is melting! Yay!
I see pink and yellow roses growing in my garden.
Whoa! It's spring!

Sarah Davidson, Grade 3
John T Waugh Elementary School, NY

Ghosts/Terrifying
Ghosts
Soft, white
Whooing, flying, scaring
Sneaky invisible spooky spirits.
Terrifying
Randy Nunez, Grade 2
Consolidated School, CT

Rain
R ain falls from the sky
A raindrop is cold
I like rain
N ice for trees
Taylor Cross, Grade 1
Annie Belle Clark Primary School, GA

Halloween
Last Halloween I was a witch,
But this Halloween I am Tinker Bell.
And I hope it goes very well.
Chug a chug a choo choo,
Many children go through.
I feel like I am spinning,
But really I am winning.
But my mom pushes through,
And I get more candy too!
Haley Miller, Grade 2
Watsontown Elementary School, PA

Penguins
Penguins pip.
Penguins dive.
Penguins slip, slip, slip!
Taina Saez, Grade 1
Northeast Elementary School, NY

The Fastest Dog
I am fast.
I am never last.
I like to jump.
I never bump.
I am the fastest dog!
William Guevara, Grade 1
Northeast Elementary School, NY

My Mouse
My mouse eats cheese
And not bees
I play with my mouse
He goes on my blouse
Veronica Flores, Grade 1
Northeast Elementary School, NY

My Body
I have eyes that blink and wink,
I have a mind to help me think,
I have hands to clap for fun,
I have feet to jump and run,
I have ears to hear a song,
I have lips to praise Jesus all day long,
I have a body strong and good,
To use it for Jesus as I should.
Madison Yon, Grade 3
Trinity Christian School, VA

What Do I See?
I see a flag.
I see desks.
I see books.
I do not see a dragon.
Leah Talon, Grade 1
Northeast Elementary School, NY

My Shoes
My
Shoes can
Climb
On
My
Room
And my
Mom
Said
What
Are
You doing?
Nothing.
Gerson Solis, Grade 1
Southside Elementary School, KY

Ashley

A wesome
S hy
H appy
L ovely
E ffortless
Y oung

Ashley Tacher, Grade 3
Virginia A Boone Highland Oaks Elementary School, FL

Military

M ilitaries train soldiers.
I am proud of the military for fighting for freedom.
L et's support our troops.
I have an aunt in the military.
T he soldiers are important.
A captain is in charge.
R eal people have died fighting for our country.
Y our country needs the military for protection.

Malia Bell, Grade 3
Bensley Elementary School, VA

Halloween

One of my favorite holidays
Lots of decorations
Some monsters are scary, some are nice
Lots of costumes
Some are witches, some are vampires
It's fun to go trick-or-treating on Halloween night
Under the Halloween moon

Abigail Gorun, Grade 3
St Mary's School, NJ

Clouds Above Me

The clouds above me look like whipped cream.
The clouds above me move like a car.
The clouds above me might smell like silk.
The clouds above me might feel soft.
The clouds above me might sound quiet like a bunny.
The clouds above me might taste like milk.
The clouds above me make me feel happy.
Aren't clouds smooth?

Sean Harrington, Grade 2
Clover Street School, CT

The Fly That Likes to Buy

There once was a fly
shicka boom boom boom
that liked to buy
shicka boom boom boom
He bought a pair
shicka boom boom boom
of new wings for the air
shicka boom boom boom
He flew so high
shicka boom boom boom
That he didn't come back
until the Fourth of July
shicka boom boom boom

Harrison Neville, Grade 2
Briarwood Christian School, AL

Pink

I am an eraser.
I am a crayon.
I am a pig.
I am pink.

Esther Hernandez, Grade 1
Northeast Elementary School, NY

Fall

Fall is fun.
You better get done.
All the leaves turn different colors.
You better get working
Before you're too late
To see the colors
Fall leaves make.

Noah Gibson, Grade 2
Eagle's View Academy, FL

My Favorite Color

I like black.
The Halloween cat is black.
The shoe is black.
The hat is black.
I like black.

Natalie Rivas, Grade 1
Northeast Elementary School, NY

Clouds

C an be gray or white.
L ive in the sky.
O ut in the open.
U mbrellas, no need.
D ark when they are rain clouds.
S urvive the winter.

Meera Sumukadas, Grade 3
Wolcott School, CT

Apples

A pples are green
P ie is great
P leasant to smell
L ike to
E at
S weet apples

Roberto Penate, Grade 3
Bensley Elementary School, VA

Penguins

Penguins dive.
Penguins hop.
Penguins sing, sing, sing!

Sabrina Zuniga, Grade 1
Northeast Elementary School, NY

Socks, Clocks, Blocks*

Every shoe loves a sock.
Every watch loves a clock.
Every shelf loves a block.
And I love you.

Hailey Ammons, Kindergarten
Eden Gardens Magnet School, LA
**Inspired by Jean Marzollo's*
"I Love You: A Rebus Poem"

Kracken

Kracken
Big, scary
Destroys, eats people, crushes ships
I like the Kracken.
Giant squid

Josh Tegarden, Grade 3
Clinton Christian Academy, MO

Clothes

You can wear different clothing every day.
We have SPECIAL clothing for the Summer, Fall, Winter, and Spring.
I like Summer clothing.
A pretty pink blouse and shorts is just GREAT for me.
When I go shopping I can see the different colored shirts, pants, and dresses.
On Sunday, I love to wear MY church clothes.
My mother picks them out and she's really good at it.
I sit in the front row of my church. I like for everyone to see my church clothes.
I LOVE looking GOOD.
I LOVE pretty DRESSES.

Stachell Santemore, Grade 3
New Orleans Free School, LA

A Hot Sunny Summer

Summer is so hot,
I hate the wind in my face.
Flowers blooming,
All over the place!

Samuel Kates, Grade 2
Virginia A Boone Highland Oaks Elementary School, FL

Candice

Caring
Smart
Loving
Funny
Wishes to get anything for Christmas
Dreams of becoming a fashion designer
Wants to get an iPod for Christmas
Who wonders how many stars are in the sky.
Who fears tigers
Who is afraid of haunted mansions
Who likes gifts
Who believes in God and Jesus
Who loves family and friends
Who loves my house
Who loves gifts
Who loves people
Who plans to go to college
Who plans to accomplish my year in third grade
Who plans to live in a mansion.
Whose life is going to be great.

Candice Joseph, Grade 3
Central Park Elementary School, FL

Winter/Season
winter
snowy, icy
sliding, rolling, sledding
I think it is the best season.
season
Cameron Knowlton, Grade 2
Wells Central School, NY

Cat
Cat
Soft, shiny
Meowing, scratching, purring
I like my cats.
Cute!
Tionni Robinson, Grade 2
St Andrew School, NY

Shining Fish
Green and blue.
Swimming in the water.
It seems so fast!
John Sessock, Grade 1
Holland Township School, NJ

My Birthday
My Birthday, my birthday
Is a special day for me.
I will get lots of presents.
So come and see.

I will also invite
A couple of good friends,
I might even invite
Some of my other best friends.
There will be ice cream, cake
and candles that are blue.
We will have lots of fun too.

My Birthday, my birthday is a
Special day for me.
It has always been special
Since I have been me.
Gage Brady, Grade 3
Pike Liberal Arts School, AL

Fall
Fall
Colorful, cold
Raking, playing, jumping
I really like fall,
Season
Mackenzie Thayer, Grade 3
Chestnut Street Elementary School, PA

Baby My Baby
Baby my baby,
She is a good baby.
She has blue eyes.
Yes, my baby is 7 pounds and 19 inches.
I am glad that God made my sister.
Her name is Mary Lynn.
Boys and girls, I will tell you,
You might have to change the baby's diaper.
God has made my family and my baby.
I am glad that God made my sister!
Will Fisher, Grade 2
Evangelical Christian School, TN

North Pole
Lots of cold white snow on the ground
The freezing winds blowing on my face
Stinky rotten fish blowing up on the ice
Frosty snow in the air
Thayne Morgan, Grade 3
Bradford Township Elementary School, PA

The Fireplace
Warm and cozy, it brings us light,
My family sits around the fireplace tonight.

The fire is the sun that floats into our hearts,
That brings us a feeling where memories start.

All of us come together to share,
A memory that will always be near.

The warm feeling the fire gives me at night,
Makes me feel so thankful and bright.
Taryn Barnabei, Grade 3
Jeffrey Elementary School, CT

Veteran's Day

V ery special day
E xcellent time for thanking veteran's
T ime to thank people for serving our country
E veryone has to thank veterans
R emember to write letters
A round the world they go
N ice for serving our country
S ee your family again

D ad travels to other countries
A rmy guys
Y es for my dad

Lacee Hodge, Grade 3
Susquehanna Community Elementary School, PA

Life at the Sea

I am Sylvie. I live in the sea.
I am Ariel's daughter and queen to be.
Yes you heard me.
Yes you heard me right.
I am a queen to be.
But being a princess is not all that.
I go to etiquette class, protocol class, even diction class.
I even go to royal galas and fancy dinners in other kingdoms.
When I am outside and I may dance to my hearts content for a few moments that is.
I love who I am.
I also know that I will be a great queen.

Sylvie Cherry, Grade 3
McKinley Elementary School, PA

I Play Hockey

Last year I played hockey on a team,
when our team scores our fans let out a scream.
When I score I beam,
and when I am playing I never daydream.
Hockey takes good coordination to play good,
Should I play next year? I think I should.
When we win a game I am so thrilled,
my coach thought my team was skilled.
I did not care if we lost or won,
I just played for fun.

Colton Tincher, Grade 3
Ellicott Road Elementary School, NY

Rain

Rain
Pouring
Down on me
Will the rain stop
When?

Gabrielle Lopez, Grade 3
A L Burruss Elementary School, GA

Halloween

Scary costumes
Jack-o-lantern pumpkins
Tasty candy
Frightening tricks
Yummy treats
Halloween

Anthony Bizarro, Grade 2
Weston Elementary School, NJ

Tigers

Tigers
Very noisy
Roar a lot in the zoo
Tigers are wild inside the cage
Feline

Thomas Gonzalez, Grade 1
Oliver Hoover Elementary School, FL

Pink

I am a pig.
I am a heart.
I am a tongue.
I am pink.

Angie Cornejo, Grade 1
Northeast Elementary School, NY

Snakes

S limy is nasty
N o touching of snakes for me
A snake is very bad
K inds of snakes are poisonous
E at a snake and you might get poison
S nakes are not cool!!

Tavaris Perry, Grade 3
Bensley Elementary School, VA

Snowy Night

The snowy night is soft
quiet and peaceful
You can hear the sounds
of wolves howling near the moonlight
And the moon is as white
as the milk
in a cereal bowl

Charlie Falbo, Grade 3
Lincoln Elementary School, PA

My Favorite Place

Disney World
because there are water rides
I see High School Musical People
because Grammy and PopPop come
and my cousin Brynn

Jillian Brennan, Grade 1
Sundance School, NJ

A Cheetah

A cheetah is very fast,
And it has sharp, sharp teeth.
The girl cheetah could bite me.

Geula Brownstein, Kindergarten
United Hebrew Institute, PA

My Favorite Place

El Salvador
many pools
sleeping in bathing suits
coconuts, YUM!
fun

Ashley Alvarenga, Kindergarten
Sundance School, NJ

My Favorite Color

I like red.
A fire truck is red.
An apple is red.
A car is red.
I like red.

Garis Martinez, Grade 1
Northeast Elementary School, NY

Autumn

The sun is bright like the light.
And the leaves are shaped like fans.
The owl makes its hole
And sap is sticky like glue.
I hear the crunchy leaves.
It is autumn.

Lance Fillmore, Grade 2
Worthington Hooker School – K-2 Campus, CT

My Dirt Bike

My dirt bike was green,
My dirt bike was black.
I put on my helmet,
It was tight, but it was a good sight.
I rode it back and forth on the big, gravel road.
"Crrrr."
It was so fun that my daddy bought one.
It was just like mine.
I put some decals on.
It made me more excited.
I rode and crashed,
Bang!
I got up and rode it more.

Sam Strickland, Grade 3
Briarwood Christian School, AL

Thanksgiving

Thanksgiving
Happy Food
Eating tasting drinking
I smell turkey and every time they give us turkey we say thank you
it tastes so good
dinner

Tanisha Muniz, Grade 3
Marie Curie Institute, NY

My Pet Dog

Her name is Jade,
We love each other.
We are both the same
That is why I love her
And she loves me the same.

Jasmin Spiers, Grade 2
Public School 152 School of Science & Technology, NY

Sarah

S its a lot
A rt
R uns
A ctivity
H ugs

Sarah Johnson, Grade 2
Wisdom's Way Academy for Girls, PA

My Eyes

I look through my helmet.
I am nervous.
I wait for the snap.
Do I hand off to the running back
Or pass to the receiver?
The defense comes through the line.
No wide receiver.
No running back.
Forget it.
I'll score the touchdown myself.

Nick Iannone, Grade 2
St Peter the Apostle School, GA

Yellow

I am the sun.
I am a star.
I am a banana.
I am Yellow.

Karen Vasquez, Grade 1
Northeast Elementary School, NY

Toys

I like toys.
I like boys.
My toys are boy toys.

Daniel Meyer, Grade 2
Yeshiva Ketana of Long Island, NY

Penguins

Penguins hop.
Penguins dive.
Penguins waddle, waddle, waddle!

Monica Paredes, Grade 1
Northeast Elementary School, NY

Snowflakes

Snowflakes are falling all around
Some are falling to the ground
Snowflakes, snowflakes everywhere
Snowflakes are light when in the air
Snowflakes are falling on her nose
Some are as pretty as a rose
Snowflakes are white
And they make the sky bright
Snowflakes are cold
Some are very bold
When snowflakes are in sight
They are very bright
Now the snowflakes are out of sight
Because now it is night

Nicole Sprague, Grade 3
Heron Pond Elementary School, NH

Butterfly

B eautiful
U nique
T ravel
T here to here
E njoyable
R est on
F lowers
L ike nectar
Y ellow, black, orange

Caroline Ayers, Grade 2
Broadway Elementary School, NC

Winter Is Near

Welcome to winter
Santa's sleigh bells are coming near
Flying all the way

Kristen Gotsis, Grade 3
Tuxedo Park School, NY

Purple

I am a flower.
I am grapes.
I am jelly.
I am purple.

Linda Mejia, Grade 1
Northeast Elementary School, NY

A Scary Monster

I see a scary monster,
And it is really freaky.
When it looks at me,
It looks really creepy!

Joshua Klein, Grade 2
Virginia A Boone Highland Oaks Elementary School, FL

Seasons

Summer, fall trees are tall. Winter breezy.
Yellow, orange, gold and brown everywhere in town.
Everywhere hooray hooray.
We are having fun today.
Come to the left come to the right
Leaves everywhere all in sight.
I love Autumn. I love Spring.
On Christmas let's put popcorn on string.
Summer oh summer.
Summer is not a bummer.
I love this. I love that but
I don't love bats.
Autumn on Halloween night
Bats flying everywhere in sight.
Scary this, scary that.
A beautiful leaf fell on my hat.
Ha Ha Ha Ha Ha I love the seasons!

Cierra Smith, Grade 3
Concord Elementary School, PA

The Howler Monkey

Swinging from a vine, it must be easy with a spine.
I heard he eats fruit; man, this monkey is a hoot!
I heard his loud howl; his smell is very foul.
He eats like a monkey; that is very fine.
He eats plants and leaves and grapes from a vine.
He lives in a tropical rainforest.
It's the environment he likes the best.
In the morning with his stomach growling,
He joins his friends in a round of howling.
To the tree tops to find food, to put him in a good mood.
He spends most of his day resting in a tree.
This makes him seem very lazy.

Sam Randig, Grade 3
St Alexis School, PA

Christmas Is Cool

I like Christmas.
The children unwrap the toys.
I drink hot chocolate.
Christmas bells make noise.
My mom opens her presents.
Christmas is cool.
We love Jesus.
We decorate at school.

Christopher Howe, Grade 1
Westlake Christian School, FL

Joseph

Joseph
Fast, tall
Playing, running, talking
Likes to watch TV
Joey

Joseph Pappano, Grade 2
St Stephen's School, NY

King

I dress as a king.
I wear my new ring.
I dance and sing,
And I swing.

Megan Arant, Kindergarten
Northeast Baptist School, LA

Life Is Like Snowboarding

In the air
people think
I'm flying.
They feel
the strong
wind blow.
Sometimes,
people think
I'm a bird
Some days,
it's sunny
but very
cold.

Ava Boethig, Grade 3
Holland Township School, NJ

October/Month

October
Cold, fun
Exciting, trick-or-treating, walking
People are raking leaves
Month

Joseph Newton, Grade 3
Chestnut Street Elementary School, PA

Pumpkin

Pumpkin, pumpkin,
You glow in the night.
But tomorrow morning,
You will be out of sight.
Pumpkin, pumpkin, you were carved out
And well made,
But tomorrow morning,
You will totally fade.
Pumpkin, pumpkin, I will miss you so!
And I don't want you to go.
But next Halloween,
I'll put you by the door,
So we can talk and chat some more!

Nassim Davila, Grade 3
Coral Springs Elementary School, FL

Shelby

Wishes to run like a horse
Dreams of making schools a better place to be
Wants to be sisters with all of my friends
Who wonders if I would get a big pool
Who fears very big heights
Who is afraid of the dark
Who likes dogs
Who believes in people who I know
Who loves to go on field trips
Who loves the color red
Who loves pizza
Who loves going camping
Who plans to go to the movies on Friday
Who plans to go to the park
Who plans to go to Target
Who believes in God

Shelby Davis, Grade 3
Central Park Elementary School, FL

Ode to My Stuffed Tiger

Oh tiger, how I love you.
When we met
I was happy as could be.
When we snuggle
You're as soft as a cloud.
Your eyes look like
Waves of blue,
And your black stripes
Are like the midnight of the moon.
You smell like a jungle tiger
Spying through the grass.
Oh tiger, how I love you.

Jonaya Muse, Grade 2
Worthington Hooker School – K-2 Campus, CT

Who Wrote This?

Lillian is nice, Lilian's smart,
And they are also good at art.
Kaitlyn, Caitlin, Briggs in summer,
Since you have them it is not a bummer.
Marquez, Bryson, Peyton, Sam,
These people can read like I can!
Quanace, Ava, Abigail, William too,
Well, they're good at pasting glue!
Halie, really WOW, and Reynolds, OH!
If you didn't have them you would not say "Wee Hoe!"
Sarah, Oliva, Sydney, Nykia,
These cool girls are really prettiya!
Thomas is nice
Elliott and Eli are cool with "E"
But the person who wrote this is actually ME!

Shona Fitzer, Grade 2
Stone Academy, SC

Fall

In the fall, I hear black and white Canadian geese honking
while they're flying south for the winter.
In the fall, I see long, old firewood stacked on the ground for a winter fire.
In the fall, I smell delicious pumpkin pie at my neighbor's house.
In the fall, I taste incredible corn, mashed potatoes, and turkey
on the Thanksgiving table.
In the fall, I don't feel the hot sun burning my back while playing in the yard.

Raymond Hauck, Grade 3
Watsontown Elementary School, PA

Spooky

S uper times
P lay all day
O ver at last
O ther days
K ind times
Y ou are scary for Halloween

Jake Curran, Grade 3
McKinley Elementary School, PA

Valley

Oh to be in the valley
To walk in the valley
Along the river
Watching the grass sway
Moving gently on a summer day
Trees bright and green
Waiting to be seen
Oh to be in the valley
Just one more day

Arik Armstead, Grade 3
Public School 235 Lenox, NY

Matthew

Matthew
active, fast
baseball, football, hunting
helps others when needed
Matt

Baylee Hill, Grade 3
Briarwood Christian School, AL

Black Cats

Black cats cross the road.
Halloween if fun to me.
October is cool!

Jake Benner, Grade 2
Wanamassa Elementary School, NJ

Santa Claus

Reindeer paws
Pull around
Good Santa Claus.

Michelle Biksey, Grade 3
Trinity East Elementary School, PA

Baby Brother

It is fun to have a baby brother.
You can feed him.
You can hug him.
You can bathe him.
But when your mom changes him,
Back away and hold your nose!

Lindsay Fullerton, Grade 3
McKinley Elementary School, PA

Noisiest Day

The noisiest day began…
The doors go bang.
The ghosts go boo!
I ran home that very day.
I could not sleep.
My dad was snoring
What a long day!

Toni Cullop, Grade 2
Annsville Elementary School, NY

Christmas

Christmas is a time of giving.
Just like Thanksgiving.
Christmas I rest and
It is the best.

Rosheeka Williams, Kindergarten
Collingwood Park SDA School, NJ

My Secret Hiding Spot

When I was little
I used to hide myself
In the fog,
Up in a tree,
In the closet
Or
Somewhere
I can't tell you about
But I can tell you this
No one
Has found me there
Yet

Lauren Guthre, Grade 3
Oak Ridge Elementary School, PA

Birds

When it is winter
The wind blows and the birds hide
Then the blizzard stops

Daniel Nash, Grade 2
Virginia A Boone Highland Oaks Elementary School, FL

Leaves

Leaves are colorful and they are wonderful.
They float in the air and blow in the breeze.
Leave sometimes swing in the trees.
There are brown leaves, green leaves, orange leaves, too!
So many leaves in the months of fall. I run outside where leaves are everywhere.
So many leaves!!!
I love them.
The world needs leaves!!!

Wil Johnson, Grade 3
Reidville Elementary School, SC

Fall

Fall is a good season for many reasons.
It is not too hot or cold.
It is just right for playing outdoors.
Leaves are pretty when they change colors and fall from the trees.
I love to jump and play in them.
These are the reasons fall is a good season.

Austin G. Miller, Grade 1
Thomas Jefferson Elementary School, VA

Thanksgiving Dinner

We watch the Macy's parade,
Since the dinner is getting made;
We sit down for dinner,
Our turkey is always a winner.
We pass the bread stuffing,
This was made with mom's loving.
We pass the red cranberry,
It's always fun for Aunt Mary.
We pass the creamy potatoes,
We don't serve them with tomatoes.
It's time to eat pumpkin pie,
Then we say our long good-byes.

Lauren Ruiz, Grade 3
Virginia A Boone Highland Oaks Elementary School, FL

My Favorite Color

I like white.
Santa's beard is white.
Paper is white.
Snow is white.
I like white.

Christian Odom, Grade 1
Northeast Elementary School, NY

Animals

Animals are in a forest
Animals can be in the woods
Animals can be in the mountains
Animals can be in the barns
I like animals!

Animals

Kara Massey, Grade 1
Alvaton Elementary School, KY

Pat Had a Cat

Pat
had a cat
to chase a mouse
out of the house

Viktoria Lien, Grade 3
The Parke House Academy, FL

My Silly Nose

My silly nose is just as great
As any other one.
I love my nose
Because it's fine with me
To have a different nose.
My nose can sniff.
My nose can run.
It is just as fine as every one.
My nose eats lunch
In his own room.
He drops his crackers
All over the floor.
I have a silly nose.

Anna Kirsanov, Grade 3
John Ward Elementary School, MA

My Mom

I have a mom.
She is calm.
We hug.

Alexander English, Kindergarten
Taylor Road Academy, AL

Recess

Recess, recess,
So much fun,
Cheers me up
When I am glum.
I hit the ball
Into the stands,
I hear fans yell
When it lands.
Then I tag
Someone out.
The umpire gives
An excited shout.
Oh no!
What's that?
Do I hear the bell?
Back to class,
I don't feel so well.

Max Josef, Grade 3
John Ward Elementary School, MA

Carpool

Carpool
Run, drive
Walking, running, driving
Parents are picking up their children
Dismissal

Emily Clasen, Grade 3
Briarwood Christian School, AL

Halloween

Very dark
Scary houses
Spooky costumes
Awesome candy
Happy Halloween

Ryan Loften, Grade 2
Weston Elementary School, NJ

Sun

Sun is an oven so hot it burns you.
Sun is like a yellow basketball going wherever you go.
Sun is like a volcano shimmering down at your face.
Sun is fireworks in the sky so shiny and beautiful.

Hana Chabinsky, Grade 3
Hunter GT Magnet Elementary School, NC

I Have a New Cell Phone

I have a new cell phone,
It has a new ring tone;
It hurts my parents' ears,
And brings them to tears;
My sister likes it a lot,
So I keep it in a pot.

Aaron Albert, Grade 3
Virginia A Boone Highland Oaks Elementary School, FL

My Apple

I see green and brown spots
I hear baseball players hitting a ball with a bat.
I taste apple juice in the sun.
I smell the wet ground by a tree.
I feel bumps like on a road telling you to slow down.

Alba Falcon, Grade 2
Arlington Elementary School, MA

School

S chool is sometimes very boring or very fun you see
C oming every day is what we do
H ome should really be a place for me and you
O h how I wish I wasn't also at school
O h how I wish this wish to come true
L earning and knowing is what we do.

Alana N. Baum, Grade 3
Blakeney Elementary School, GA

The Teacher Gets Paid

There was a teacher of second grade.
Who thought long after the sun did fade.
Lots of money she was paid.
They all hoorayed.
In honor of our teacher of second grade.

Joshua Timblin, Grade 2
St Mary of the Assumption Catholic School, PA

My Favorite Place

Texas
born there
hot days
good food
warm mornings

Ananya Sankar, Kindergarten
Sundance School, NJ

I'm Shannon

Shannon
Nice, tall
Swimming, dancing, playing
I like to jump
Shani

Shannon Klein, Grade 2
St Stephen's School, NY

Candy Corn/Halloween

Candy corn
Sweet, triangular
Eating, smelling, tasting
White, orange, and yellow.
Halloween

Rachael Albertson, Grade 2
Consolidated School, CT

Christmas Spirits

Christmas gifts lay
under a sparkling tree
love hot chocolate

Laura Yordán, Grade 3
Tuxedo Park School, NY

My Heart

It looks like lips.
Lips are red.
I see it at the store
when it's Valentine's Day!
It's beautiful!
It's a heart.
It looks like an apple.
You can give it.

Sarah Febre, Grade 1
Holland Township School, NJ

Fall

Fall looks like birds flying across the sky
Fall looks like smoke from a fire
Fall tastes like pumpkin pie
Fall tastes like apples
Fall feels like chilly
Fall feels cold
Fall smells sweet
Fall smells fresh
Fall is sweet!

Jaron Burr, Grade 1
Alvaton Elementary School, KY

What If?

What if my grandma died?
I might cry my eyes out.

What if she didn't go to Heaven?
I could never see her again.

What if she hadn't died?
I would still be with her.

What if nobody ever had to die?

Gabrielle Hannum, Grade 3
Byrns L Darden Elementary School, TN

When I Was Little

When I was little
I wanted to grow up and be a teacher.
I wanted to teach kindergarten.
I would teach them their alphabet
And hand writing.
I would give them praise when
they did a good job.
Each person would have a job to do
Like clean the toys.
I would let them have recess
For forty minutes until PE time.
I would teach them about colors,
Shapes and size.
The children would have fun and do
centers and journal writing after nap time.

Ca'lin Anderson, Grade 3
Lee A Tolbert Community Academy, MO

Basketball

The team runs through the tunnel, onto the court.
They take practice shots.
They meet the other team.
They practice the two teams.
They play the game.
There is a winner and a loser.
They shake hands.
Everyone goes home.

Jordan Kasimow, Grade 3
Virginia A Boone Highland Oaks Elementary School, FL

Fastpitch Softball

F riends, females, fans, facemasks
A AU, aches, all-stars, applause
S ponsors, sweat, swinging, shortstop
T rophies, team, tans, throws
P itcher, ponytails, players, pain
I cepacks, infield, innings, instructions
T ags, third base, timeouts, tournaments
C heers, cuts, coaches, cleats
H igh fives, homeruns, handshakes, hustle

S unflower seeds, score, sunglasses, squeeze play
O utside, outs, outfield, opening day
F ouls, fences, fly balls, flexible
T hirsty, t-shirts, training camps, talent
B uddies, bases, bunts, bats
A nxious, athletic, aggressive, attitude
L ine-ups, laps, losses, leftfield
L eague, laughter, loaded bases, leaders

Janna Moore, Grade 3
Contentnea Elementary School, NC

Ms. Dong

M anages class 2-236
S haking her body and dances

D iva
O utstanding
N eat
G reat in reading

Giovanni Thompson, Grade 2
Public School 152 School of Science & Technology, NY

Fall

The leaves are fun,
I play in the sun.
The leaves turn brown.
I won't make a frown.
I see a brown tree.
It's such a sight to see.
I see a leaf fly,
In the blue sky.

Kyle M. Lucero, Grade 3
Birches Elementary School, NJ

Red, White, Blue

Red, white, blue.
When it waves it makes me feel good!
I like it, it makes me feel nice.
I say the Pledge of Allegiance.
It is popular because it is beautiful.

Kaitlyn Bodder, Grade 1
Holland Township School, NJ

I Am From

I am from my warm bedroom
where my little lightning lamp is
and where my warm bed is.
I am from my lovely TV room
Where my little TV is.
I am from my beautiful yard
where the leaves are falling down.

Yvonne Au, Grade 1
Berkeley Lake Elementary School, GA

Catching Bubbles

Bubbles fly in the air
Sometimes it isn't fair
Because sometimes
They just get in my hair.
So if you go bubble catching
And when they get on my skin
I suddenly start scratching.
Now if you go bubble catching
Just beware
Of getting bubbles in your hair!

Brittney Ortiz, Grade 3
Marie Durand Elementary School, NJ

Holiday

Christmas, family fun,
spending time together,
Santa comes tonight,
gift giving, family visiting.

Kelly Ostruszka, Grade 3
Coral Cove Elementary School, FL

Fall

Yellow apples
Nuts crunching
Apple pie baking
Wet leaves

Jasha Leonhardt, Grade 1
Northeast Elementary School, NY

Sahara and Me

Sahara and me
like to snuggle
lots of times we might cuddle
Sahara and me
like to play outside
sometimes Sahara likes to hide
Sahara and me
like to eat meat
we really don't like to eat wheat!
Sahara and me
like to sleep
when we're not together we will weep
Sahara and me
My bestest dog
She'll love me more than a frog
Sahara and me!

Andrea Escobar, Grade 2
Coral Cove Elementary School, FL

My Favorite Color

I like purple.
My bike is purple.
A grape is purple.
My room is purple.
I like purple.

Natalie Peralta, Grade 1
Northeast Elementary School, NY

My Dog

My dog has spots on his
back when he fights he
sounds like a bat!!! "Eeek, eeek, eeek!!!" His name is Bebe
it's pronounced baby in Spanish.
The other dogs are all around
the window barking, "Woof, woof,
woof!" Bebe begins to howl
"Oooooooooooo." I can't sleep
Bebe, Bebe calm the noise and go
to sleep. My little Bebe.

Adonis Pujols, Grade 3
Public School 148 Ruby Allen, NY

It's Time for Costumes

October is the time to get your Halloween things out.
Halloween is the time to get your costumes and your candy
And go trick or treating and eat some candy.

Hunter Grill, Grade 3
Concord Elementary School, PA

November Fun

November days are full of play,
We rake the leaves and run away.
Leaves of gold, red, and green,
Are very beautiful to be seen.
We jump into leafy piles with happy smiles,
Gobbling turkeys will make a feast for me and my family to eat.
I'm not shy for pumpkin pie,
Today is the day to say,
"Hooray for Thanksgiving Day!"

Brynn Morgado, Grade 3
Middlebury Elementary School, CT

Thanksgiving

Thanksgiving, Thanksgiving, Thanksgiving!
Let's take time to praise the wonderful Lord Almighty
For all He has done for us.
Let's be thankful on this wonderful day.
Get your family, get your friends.
Come all you people, let's celebrate the amazing Lord.
Come let's show Him we're thankful
For all He has done.

Bailey Ross, Grade 2
Evangelical Christian School, TN

Snow

S now is cold
N ew snows too
O r so white
W ow snow

Abbi Toews, Grade 1
Annie Belle Clark Primary School, GA

Raccoons

With a blindfold over its eyes,
Knocking trash cans over,

The neighbors don't like raccoons,
They think raccoons are a pest,

But raccoons are smart,
And they will get them back one day.

Danielle Brown, Grade 3
Pike Liberal Arts School, AL

Trees, Trees, Trees

Trees, Trees, Trees
So full of life and green beauty.
You stand so tall as the rain and
Snow falls as you wait for a sunny day
As your fresh air escapes
We breathe life.
Trees, Trees, Trees
How would we live without them?

Alexia Grant, Grade 3
Public School 235 Lenox, NY

Leaves Everywhere

Leaves are all in the air
And they might fall in your hair
They spin around
They fall on the ground
And they are falling everywhere
Leaves are big and small
And change into different colors
They also burn well in fires
And they make tiny leaf piles go higher!

Bruno M. Costanzo, Grade 3
Marie Durand Elementary School, NJ

Michaela

M arvelous
I nteresting
C alm
H elpful
A wesome
E xciting
L oving
A musing

Michaela Quinn, Grade 2
Long Meadow Elementary School, CT

Summer

I go outside
A temple of heat
Surrounds me in the meadow
I vanish in the rose garden
With a butterfly
In the garden.
A kind spirit
Came over my friend when
He saw me
On the ground.
I climb up an apple tree on
The hillside.
The heat slowly goes
In the darkness
With one dim
Summer star
I say
Goodnight
Summer
Day.

Christopher Taylor, Grade 3
Oak Ridge Elementary School, PA

Rabbit

R an in a race
A te carrots
B eat the turtle at first
B ragger
I n last place
T urtle won!

Beatriz Alvarez, Grade 2
Broadway Elementary School, NC

Seeing Character

Brown Bear, Brown Bear, what do you see?
I see a dolphin looking at me.

Dolphin, Dolphin, what do you see?
I see children looking at me.

Children, children, what do you see?
I see respect looking at me.

Respect, respect, what do you see?
I see responsibility looking at me.

Responsibility, responsibility, what do you see?
I see the right to learn looking at me.

Right to learn, right to learn, what do you see?
I see Mrs. Leveillee looking at me.

Mrs. Leveillee, Mrs. Leveillee, what do you see?
I see a great school looking at me.

Paris Brown-Carter, Grade 3
Mary Matula Elementary School, MD

I Wonder Why

I wonder why the dog went by
Did he need a bone to say goodbye?

I wonder why the cat went by
Did she need a toy to play and sigh?

I wonder why the rabbit went by
Did she need carrots to hop so high?

I wonder why the bird went by
Did he need the seeds so he could fly?

I wonder why the horse went by
Did he need some oats from that old guy?

I wonder why these pets went by
Did they need a home? I will always wonder why

Shelley Kaleita, Grade 3
Binks Forest Elementary School, FL

The Bratz Fashions
I like all four Bratz
Because I like their fashions.
Their fashions are cool!
Brooke Lieberman, Grade 1
United Hebrew Institute, PA

My Favorite Place
Florida
there's a river
Grandma
lots of houses
my vacation
Samira Issa, Grade 1
Sundance School, NJ

Gymnastics on Bars
I felt
TWISTY
FLEXIBLE
POWERFUL
as I hopped up
on the bar and
flipped as powerful
as a tiger:
gymnastics on bars
Tabitha Liucci, Grade 3
Holland Township School, NJ

Deer
Deer
herds, meat
jumping, running, eating
Men hunt for them.
Animals
Brian Sacco, Grade 2
Consolidated School, CT

My Dog
Owwwwww!
Bark, scratch, whimper.
Scratching on the door.
What a dog, Oreo!
Ben Fraley, Grade 2
Clover Street School, CT

On Our Way to School
Splish, splash, raindrops go,
Vroom, vroom, the train goes,
On our way to school
Beep, beep cars go
When we walk across the street
Round and round
We dance around the fountain
We feel dizzy
On our way to school
Pretty colors
Red, blue, green, yellow, black and pink
Looking up
Raindrops spinning
And dripping and dropping
On our way to school
Finally we're at school
All of those umbrellas left
Now it's just me
Alexandra Houvener, Grade 3
Coram Elementary School, NY

School
Going to my school is fun,
Because my teacher makes it number one.

I like reading,
As much as eating.

Language is the best,
Of all the rest!

If you want to stay on the right path,
You have to study your math.

Some people say it's outlandish,
One of our subjects is Spanish.

The class that won my heart,
Is my all-time favorite, ART!

The main reason I can't stay away,
I love to chat with my friends every day!
Addyson Bryan, Grade 3
Pike Liberal Arts School, AL

Washington D.C.

The White House is white as a lamb
Squirrels are as brown as a tree trunk
The traffic is as loud as a train whistle
People are talking in the city as loud as crows squawking
Hot dogs attracting many people fast
Ice cream luring kids to the corner stand
The pizza stands so busy filled with hungry customers, I can't even get one slice
Popcorn so buttery makes me feel warm inside
At the Air and Space Museum you can touch the moon
A sensitive plant says good night to me when I touch it.
I feel happy and free!

Kimberly Smith, Grade 3
Bailey Elementary School, NC

Playful Leaf

I'm reddish brown
Like a fall flower.
I look like a petal
Shining in the sun.
I'm twirling in the wind
Like a dancing ballerina.
I'm a playful leaf.

Camilla Beeley, Grade 2
Worthington Hooker School – K-2 Campus, CT

Sunlight

The morning sun awakens me.
I will play today at the bay with my friends Haley, Tawny and Emanuel.
I will play the pillow game.
I will leave to eat lunch at home.
While I go to my house, the sunlight shines on me.
And I am happy all day now.
And everybody else is happy today.

Kaelyn Wood, Grade 3
Robert Toombs Christian Academy, GA

Toys

Toys are fun to play with,
Hot wheels go very fast,
Toys can be Nerf that you throw,
Dinosaur toys have very sharp teeth,
There are many kinds of toys all over the world.

Marcus Nieuwkerk, Grade 2
Marie Curie Institute, NY

Football

run, throw, pain
Please don't rain.
cheers, helmet, armor
I don't want to be a farmer.
cleats, shirts, pants
Watch out for those ants!

Jacob Hickman, Grade 3
Broadway Elementary School, NC

The Olympic Sport of Volleyball

The players are
d
r
i
p
p
i
n
g
with sweat because of the heat.
I can see from my seat.

Mackenzie Bundt, Grade 3
Holland Township School, NJ

Season

Winter
Winter is cold and a time to play
Winter is a time for Jesus's birthday

Spring
Spring is a time for cool air
playing outside feeling the breeze

Summer
Summer is going around the world
getting hot in the sun
getting in the pool every day

Fall
Fall is feeling cool breezes
Jumping in the leaves
Raking the leaves one by one

Madison Giles, Grade 3
Reidville Elementary School, SC

Penguins

Penguins swim.
Penguins hop.
Penguins sing, sing, sing!

Daphne Rosado, Grade 1
Northeast Elementary School, NY

Penguins

Penguins walk.
Penguins pip.
Penguins sing, sing, sing!

Justin Diaz-Montiel, Grade 1
Northeast Elementary School, NY

Spring and Fall

Spring
Bright, warm
Growing, popping, flying
Park, baseball, leaf, jump
Jumping in leaves, playing, running
Hot, leafy
Fall

Brendan Wheeler, Grade 3
John T Waugh Elementary School, NY

Okapi

Love onions and leaves
Is part horse, zebra, giraffe
Head small and long tongue

Rebecca Fulford, Grade 3
Miami Country Day School, FL

I Am From

I am from my soft bedroom
where my fluffy birds sing and
they wait for me.
I am from my cozy living room
where my hot chocolate is still hot
for me with marshmallows.
I am from my beautiful front yard
where my green tree waits for me
to climb it and the chipmunks see me.

Allison Lopez, Grade 1
Berkeley Lake Elementary School, GA

Cookies

C hocolate chip
O reo cookies
O ccasional cookies
K inds of cookies
I love all cookies
E aten every day
S weet cookies

Dan Berlfein, Grade 3
Virginia A Boone Highland Oaks Elementary School, FL

Dolphins

Dolphins swim beneath the sea.
They are like an elegant butterfly swaying unto me.
Eeee! Go the dolphins you shall hear.
You may hear them loud and clear.
As you walk on the beach they are such a pretty sight.
As they will entertain you all night.
Although I write about dolphins, I have never seen one before.
I cannot wait for the day when I will see them from the shore.

Katie Mier, Grade 3
Briarwood Christian School, AL

Halloween

When it was Halloween,
I heard a scary noise that sounded mean.
It sounded scary,
I saw something in the woods that looked hairy.
Then I got creeped out,
And it had a snout.
Then I hear a noise,
I found out it was a couple of boys.

Elyssa Synor, Grade 3
Ellicott Road Elementary School, NY

My Pumpkin Cat

Oh Pumpkin you are round and you have a stem.
When I put the colors pink and blue on you,
You will look like an animal
I will make you into a cat.
You will look so cute with pink and blue,
What do you think about that?

Julia Osorio, Grade 3
Coral Springs Elementary School, FL

Christmas

C aroling
H oliday
R eindeer
I nvitations
S anta Claus
T urkey
M erry Christmas
A te too much turkey
S now

Jeffery James, Grade 3
Reidville Elementary School, SC

Christmas

When Santa comes on Christmas Day,
He gives you presents then goes away,
He goes away on a sled,
And then I guess he goes to bed.

Vivian Li, Grade 1
Afton Elementary School, PA

Mountains

Up high, touching the sky,
Capped with snow, most people know.
Taller than valleys,
Reaching below space.
When it shines through the sun,
Its power will embrace
It still lives very high,
Still with the beautiful sky,
Those big beautiful…
Mountains

Jetoye Andrews, Grade 3
Public School 235 Lenox, NY

Baseball

strike, foul, ball
make that call
home run, runs, out
hear the team shout
sport, watch, fun
great under the sun

Conley Hunter, Grade 3
Broadway Elementary School, NC

Squirrels

Squirrels are playful.
Squirrels are excellent climbers.
Squirrels eat nuts.

Danny Shpigler, Grade 3
Tuxedo Park School, NY

Ladybug

The little ladybug sits on a leaf
looking at the bees
who are sipping
the flowers so sweet.

Lena Ann Brodauf, Grade 3
Cool Spring Elementary School, NC

Civets

Some live in burrows.
Spotted skunks are called civets.
They have cat faces.

Noah Dutcher, Grade 3
Clinton Christian Academy, MO

Nature and Me

Trees are green
Trees have roots and leaves
Stems are brown
Trees have to have water
I love trees on the ground
Trees are green
Trees are beautiful
Trees are big
Trees can be bigger than a building
Trees can be everywhere
You cannot take away the trees!
I love trees.

Tyler Hayes, Grade 1
Alvaton Elementary School, KY

Puppies

Happy, playful, fun
Playing, chewing, walking, running
Sweet, lovable, cuddly
Puppies

Hailey Enrique, Grade 2
St Mary's School, NJ

Nature

Blossoms spring open
And birds fly high in the sky
While the sun travels

Jack Gottlieb, Grade 2
Virginia A Boone Highland Oaks Elementary School, FL

Wind and Rain*

I see a green wolf running in the sky.
His tail is made of lightning and his crest is shining.
A blue fire rock is flying in the darkness.
A blue jay's head is glimmering in the dark; its beak is as cold as a coin.
A shallow, light blue rainbow looks like a spirit rising from the sun.
In the distance I see an evil black evening sky.
The shadowy, bright light looks like a candle burning in the sky.

Francesco Spirli, Grade 2
Worthington Hooker School – K-2 Campus, CT
**Inspired by a piece of artwork by Georgia O' Keefe*

Happy Spring

A rainbow with all different colors all around me,
Roses, pink and white,
Spring up from the ground.
Blue jays blue and white are flying all around
In the warm spring sky.
Clothes in spring colors, like yellow, blue, and lavender,
Eyes deep blue, chestnut brown, emerald green,
Looking all around.
I love colors! Happy spring!

Kendra Guenot, Grade 3
John T Waugh Elementary School, NY

My Cool School

It's cool, it's fun, and it's school.
School teaches you a lot.
How cool is that? I go to art, computer, and aces.
We study about lots of places.
It's a lot of fun.
Trust me, it's also terrific.
We read books. The teachers are really nice.
I win lots of prizes for being good.
Come on, admit it.
The best part is recess!!!!!!!

Luna Elortegui, Grade 3
Miami Country Day School, FL

Fox-Ku

Furry, red, big tail
Very very sharp sharp teeth
Howl, bark, bark, howl, bark

Joshua Dale, Grade 2
Paine Primary School, AL

I Wish I Were

I wish I were
A baseball player
On the baseball field
Hitting a HOME RUN
Proudly!

Nathan Salopek, Grade 3
Ross Elementary School, PA

Shawnee

S imple person
H elpful
A ngel
W onderful
N iece
E xciting
E merald to my dad

Shawnee Boyd, Grade 2
Park Elementary School, AR

Octupus-Ku

Eight legs, smart and cute
Blu blu blu blu blu blu blu
Has a smushy head

Alex Mueller, Grade 2
Paine Primary School, AL

My Great Star

The stars are in the
sky where GOD lives,
He is very important.
He makes
the stars at night
and the stars come
out and light up the world.
So pretty!

Alexa DeWire, Grade 1
Holland Township School, NJ

Christmas

C ool toys
H olidays are so fun
R ipping wrapping paper
I s so fun
S oiled in gifts
T iny presents for my new born sister
M other likes watching me open my stuff
A lways excited
S anta

Gavin Starr, Grade 3
Bradford Township Elementary School, PA

My Sister Debora

I love my sister.
She makes me laugh so much.
We play hide and seek.
My mom takes us to the lake so we can skate.
We play with my dog as I trip on a log.
We love playing together!
Now we need to take a nap!!

Abigail Maldonado, Grade 2
Mother Seton Inter Parochial School, NJ

Ballet

B allet is very fun.
A ll classes start with barre.
L ines are what you dance in.
L aces are what you wear.
E veryone does the same.
T eachers help you

Anna Shepard, Grade 3
Madison Station Elementary School, MS

My Kitty

Lucy is my kitty
I think she is so pretty
I picked her out special off the internet.

She zips around the house
And snoozes in the chair
I love to pet her soft fur
And cuddle to make her purr.

Lexie Rook, Grade 3
Evangelical Christian School, TN

Ice Cream

I ate chocolate ice cream for dessert.
C an I have strawberry now?
E verybody in my family likes ice cream.

C ream is good in ice cream.
R aspberry sherbert is awesome.
E veryone should try ice cream.
A man was eating some at the park.
M y class might have an ice cream party if we behave.

Dana Colin, Grade 3
Bensley Elementary School, VA

Halloween

I hear scared children running away from a house.
I smell cooking pumpkin seeds.
I feel slimy oozing worms.
I taste candy going down my throat.
I see scary ghosts and zombies.

HALLOWEEN

Luke Markus, Grade 3
Wellington School, FL

Wintertime

The snow is very, very high.
Sometimes it falls from the sky.
I am loving the color white
but no one gets into a fight
because everyone agrees that winter time is best.
I want to play in the snow but today there is a test.

Amy Priest, Grade 3
School Street Elementary School, PA

The Autumn I Saw*

The autumn I saw was the greatest I've seen, but everything else was in between.
I saw the first autumn leaf, and then my mom told me to brush my teeth.
When I woke up it was Halloween, but this was the best day I've ever seen.
My friends and I go trick-or-treating,
we saw more candy than the people we are meeting.
Then we are done for today, after that we will play.

Dairyus John Cox, Grade 2
Melwood Elementary School, MD
**In remembrance of all the days I celebrated Halloween with my friends.*

My Dream

I wish I were
An All Star left fielder
Catching fly balls over my head
Soaring in the air to grab a homerun
Gladly

Jarod Rozanski, Grade 3
Ross Elementary School, PA

Cars

I love the cars of blue
And the cars of red.
Some cars are fast.
And some cars turn your head.

Djimon Boggs, Grade 3
Joseph Pennell Elementary School, PA

Afraid

Don't be afraid
I am just your imagination
so start thinking
happy thoughts
so don't
be afraid
I am always here
to listen
to you
So don't be
afraid
I am
always here

Margarita Reyes, Grade 3
Public School 148 Ruby Allen, NY

Rain

I love the rain!
Watching it fall on my window pane
Is such a beautiful sight
So clear and white
It is very wet
But I don't fret
I can still have fun
It just won't be in the sun

Sophia Testo, Grade 3
Sacred Heart School, NY

Red

RED
Red is bright
Red is hot
Red is the most beautiful at sunset
Red is a bright and most elegant rose
Red is the shiniest rock, a ruby
Red is the brilliant planet Mars
RED

Aditya Gollapudi, Grade 1
Sundance School, NJ

The Kiss

One summer day
I saw a girl
named Theresa
I had a crush on her
I was happy and nervous
at the same time
I was so nervous
I couldn't talk to her
She looked at me
I could not move
She walked past
I froze
so I talked to my big bro if
he thought I should
bring her flowers
So I did
eeem, eem yes,
said Theresa
I gave her the flowers
and she gave me a kiss
I was so excited

Sharif Thomas, Grade 3
Public School 148 Ruby Allen, NY

Flowers

I like the flowers
The flowers are red like the fire
Flowers are white like the snow
Flowers are beautiful!

Sage Cowles, Grade 1
Alvaton Elementary School, KY

Autumn All Around Us

Have you ever tasted the fresh autumn air?
It seems to follow you everywhere.
Have you ever felt an acorn, smooth as polished wood?
Maybe you could. Maybe you should.
Have you ever heard the rustling of leaves?
Sometimes they're caused by the breeze.
Have you ever heard the crowing of a big, black crow?
Do you think they'd do the same in the snow?
Have you ever smelled the fresh scent the autumn leaf brings?
The very big leaves look just like wings.
Have you ever noticed why squirrels run so fast?
No wonder they fly by so fast.
Have you ever seen how thin a pine needle can be?
It's so sharp, you can sew with me, you see.
Have you ever noticed how some holes open in a tree?
It seems like they want to talk to you and me.
Autumn's all around us. Take a look and see.

Laura Rosado, Grade 2
Worthington Hooker School – K-2 Campus, CT

Moon and Sky

The moon in the sky shines so bright.
So, that we can see with all his moonlight.
Every 29 days he comes and disappears.
It takes forever for him to appear.
Sometimes he hides in the clouds.
He stays there silent and doesn't make any sounds.
We often wonder what happens to him in daylight.
He's there but we can't see him with our sight.
All of this happens to the moon, the mysterious moon in the sky.

Meghana Bhimreddy, Grade 3
Mendenhall Elementary School, FL

Noise

My little sister played with a jacket,
I woke up and said, "What is all the racket?"
My mom told me "Don't yell at the baby, Rob!"
Then the baby started to sob.
I really need to go to bed!
I put the pillow over my head.
I only got an hour of sleep.
I better not hear another peep!!

Robert Fashano, Grade 3
Ellicott Road Elementary School, NY

Christmas

Christmas, Christmastime is near
What joy it brings!
Santa will be here.
Choirs sing,
Bells ring,
My favorite time of year.

Fabiana Gagliardo, Grade 3
Our Lady of Hope School, NY

My Dog

Funny, weird, nice
playing, licking, running, obeying
friend, protector, kind
Rupert

Casey Londene, Grade 2
St Mary's School, NJ

Snowmen

Snowmen are so cool
I make a lot of snowmen
They are cute to me.

Coby Samuels, Grade 2
Coral Cove Elementary School, FL

Santa Comes Down the Chimney

My family takes a picture,
In front of the Christmas tree.
Gracie holds the baby,
We like the Christmas lights we see.
Santa comes down the chimney,
He comes when we sleep.
He puts presents under the tree,
He doesn't make a peep.

Lauren King, Grade 1
Westlake Christian School, FL

The Floor

The people step on me.
Dirt falls on me.
I do not shine.
It is sad to be a floor.

Joseph Menjivar, Grade 1
Forest Street Elementary School, NJ

Penguins

Penguins hide
Penguins hop
Penguins pip, pip, pip!

Joshua Garcia, Grade 1
Northeast Elementary School, NY

A Big Heart

Love
Happiness
Care
That's a mom,
That's a dad,
Sisters, brothers, aunts, and uncles
Everyone gives a thought,
Puts it up,
Keeps it there,
They lock it and throw away the key.
A special box called a
HEART.

Jasna Janikic, Grade 3
McKinley Elementary School, PA

My Brother

His name is Ethan
He likes to paint
He likes TV
My brother has black hair
He likes to play with me
My brother is nice as a rose
I love him

Daniel Lopez, Grade 3
Public School 148 Ruby Allen, NY

Son Mountain

As bright as fire
warming a home for children.
As tall as a giraffe.
Filling the hot desert with warmness.
Son Mountain is as
hard and solid as an emerald rock
It's grass covers
the whole desert with bright green

Elias Korpela, Grade 3
Sundance School, NJ

I Wish I Had a Rabbit

I wish I had a rabbit
that would hop in the woods
And run up under my bed.
Her name would be Mandy.
She would grow to be six feet tall.
She would leave rabbit footprints
on the carpet.
She would jump really high with me on her shoulders
And listen to me read.
She would try to sing to me,
But she couldn't.
When she went to sleep,
she would snore.
I dream about her every night.
I dream I would count to three
and she would come out to play.
I hope my wish comes true.

Airrion Wright, Grade 2
Lee A Tolbert Community Academy, MO

Robot Rap

Robot's
Are nerdy nice and pleasant but they get nerdy
Dirty
And mean
And when you're eat'n chips they'll call chip the robot and
He
Makes you
A
ROBOT by putting a chip in your brain.
AND THAT'S HOW EVIL THEY ARE!!!!!

Collin Preston, Grade 2
Southside Elementary School, KY

Thankful

Thank you God for my family.
This is what Thanksgiving means to me.
Toys and video games are nice
but life without my family would not be right.
Every night I tell God "thank you" for giving me
my mom, dad and sister, who light up my life.

Trajan Diaz, Grade 3
Mother Seton Inter Parochial School, NJ

Nicole

N ice
I nspiring
C aring
O ctober birthday
L oving
E xciting

Nicole Gilmore, Grade 2
Park Elementary School, AR

Red Hearts

Red hearts
remind me
of love.

Hearts keep us alive,
and hearts beat.

Morgan Makarick, Grade 1
Holland Township School, NJ

Thanksgiving

Eating turkey
Drinking tasting smelling
Thanksgiving is fun
Fiesta

Lynoska Morales, Grade 3
Marie Curie Institute, NY

Halloween Cat

My cat is
Black like a bat
It gives me a
Fright at night.

I got it
For a buck
But I did not know
It was bad luck.

A black cat is
Often very hairy
It can also be
Very scary!

Kaitlin L., Grade 3
St Alexis School, PA

Fat Cat

My cat has not got a name
But she likes to play a game.

She feels so very soft and furry
But when she scratches, I start to worry.

On my arm I have a scar
And I won't let her go too far.

I chase my cat under the bed
Where it's dusty my mom said.

"Get out from under there
Or you'll get dirty and then you'll care!"

Catherine Lyon, Grade 1
The American Academy, PA

Sharks

Fast, powerful, large
Jumping, swimming, eating, conquering
Predators, hunter, killer
Sharks

William Louis Syslo, Grade 2
St Mary's School, NJ

I Am

I am a person who is capable to do anything.
I am someone who is beautiful.
I am someone who has talent.
I am someone who is worthy.
I am a person who is helpful.
I am someone who takes care of my dreams.
I am someone who is lovable.
I am someone who is powerful.
and I am an angel.

Milan Watson Small, Grade 3
E. Rivers Elementary School, GA

Tyler

funny, sneaky, fun
crazy, cool, friendly, active
awesome, fast and wild

Tyler Stoeckle, Grade 3
Thelma L Sandmeier Elementary School, NJ

Twilight

The cerise, electric orange and deep yellow sun is going down in the mysterious town where the lights flicker on and off in the misty pitch black night. You can hear the owls and you can see the electric bright yellow moon floating in the glittering deep black night. You can see the dew spangled webs move up and down from the frigid wind covering you. You can hear the wolves find food. I saw the steaming, floating sun. I saw the glittering silky orange and yellow fish. I saw the green seaweed sticking on the gray-black scallops. As the sun came up, the birds were singing a beautiful sound. Everybody was going to work or school. All the nocturnal animals fell asleep.

Alexander Bondarchuk, Grade 3
Jeffrey Elementary School, CT

Ireland

Ireland
Green fields
Lots of cousins
Colorful dancers
Soft music
Old castles
Many good memories

Fiona Sweeney, Grade 3
Noonan Elementary Academy of Fort Myers, FL

The Awful Egg

The awful egg is rotten,
It is now yellow.
I really mean it too,
Because I'm not a lucky fellow!

Marley Katz, Grade 2
Virginia A Boone Highland Oaks Elementary School, FL

I See

I see friends
Blue jays flying all around
The sun filled sky
Bright red roses are blooming in people's gardens
Fuzzy black bumblebees buzzing around my head
Beautiful blue skies surrounding me
Red breasted robins are flying around,
And mother spider is spinning her sparkling web in the sun
The little spiders of red, blue, yellow, black, with some red
Hatch from the egg sack.

Connor Kwilos, Grade 3
John T Waugh Elementary School, NY

Snowmobile/Suzuki

Snowmobile
Fun, fast
Freezing, falling, snowing
Exciting, tired, sweaty, happy
Suzuki

Jonathan Caccomo, Grade 3
Wapping Elementary School, CT

Santa Is Coming!

Christmas is Jesus' birthday.
We have cake and it is fun.
We get presents.
And we play in the sun.
We count the days till Christmas.
We read a Christmas book.
Santa leaves presents.
Santa is coming! Look!

Matthew Wakefield, Grade 1
Westlake Christian School, FL

Cupcakes

Cupcakes
Yummy, small
Bake, icing, eating
Happy, good, fat, hungry
Sweets

Kiyah Sweatt, Grade 3
Woodland Elementary School, KY

Oh, Birds!

Oh, birds, I love you!
You sing the best songs, so sing!
Sing to Jesus Christ!

Emily Balke, Grade 3
Clinton Christian Academy, MO

Sasha

S illy
A greeable
S hy
H elpful
A mazing

Sasha Nerney, Grade 2
Long Meadow Elementary School, CT

Twilight

Twilight star, twilight star
Twinkling high above so far.

Shining light, shining so bright
Will you grant my wish tonight?

Olivia Jackson, Grade 3
Reidville Elementary School, SC

My Mom

My mom is gorgeous
She has black brown hair
Her smile always makes me
Feel good inside
She is lovely
Every time I see her
I feel happy
I love my mom

Paul Contreras, Grade 3
Public School 148 Ruby Allen, NY

Orange

When I think of the color orange
I see a ripe orange sitting
On my kitchen counter
I imagine the sun
On a burning hot day
And remember toasting
marshmallows
Over a campfire

Emma Wagner, Grade 3
Memorial School, NH

Pizza

Pizza is my favorite food,
It puts me in a good mood.
I like the crust.
The sauce on top, is a must.
I like pepperoni on mine.
It is hot and right on time.
I also like the cheese.
I want some now please!

Nathan Castilloux, Grade 3
Ellicott Road Elementary School, NY

Spiderman

S piderman is my favorite televisions show.
P erfect describes Spiderman.
I t's fun to watch him.
D ecide for yourself, Spiderman is the best!
E xcellent superhero.
R un fast.
M an, he is strong.
A lot of people enjoy watching him.
N ame your favorite superhero *now.*

Darrius Harris, Grade 3
Bensley Elementary School, VA

Out of the Park

I hit the ball out of the park.
It goes through a wall.
I hit the ball out of the park.
I call 911 they say…I hit it out of the park and it busted through a wall.
Boom!

Logan Miller, Grade 3
Reidville Elementary School, SC

Siblings

So annoying you want to scream.
And sometimes they're so mean.
You always want them to stay out of your room.
But, if they're little, when they're asleep
don't scream or take a peek.
They'll slobber all over your clothes.
And sometimes you won't be able to move.
The twos are trouble, you never want those.
But watch your attitude with those rascals.
And they're spoiled rotten.
They're real meanies and brats!!!

Essence Morris, Grade 3
Madison Station Elementary School, MS

Seasons

Leaves go side to side in fall.
Little flowers grow so big and bright in summer.
In spring the grass is ripe.
Winter is very snowy.

Janessa Wilkinson, Grade 3
Cool Spring Elementary School, NC

Autumn

A pples are good to eat at harvest time.
U p in the tree, I pick an apple.
T hanksgiving is when I eat turkey.
U p, the birds fly south.
M ashed potatoes are exciting to eat!
N oisy birds leave the trees.

Julian Salowe, Grade 3
Central Park Elementary School, FL

Fall

Fall looks like dead trees
Fall looks like crunchy leaves
Fall feels like good wind
Fall feels like cold winds
Fall tastes like yummy pumpkins
Fall tastes like cut apples
Fall smells like apple pies
Fall smells like pumpkin pies
Fall sounds like birds singing
Fall sounds like crunching leaves
Fall is fun!

Connor Hartis, Grade 1
Alvaton Elementary School, KY

I Love Flowers

I see flowers every day,
I watch them grow in every way.
They are pretty and bright,
Some are pink and some are white
I love flowers don't you too?
Here's a flower just for you!

Sage O'Brien, Grade 2
Briarwood Christian School, AL

Rachel

R ose
A wesome
C olorful
H ats
E xciting
L oving

Rachel Donovan, Grade 2
Long Meadow Elementary School, CT

Beach

I love to
go to the beach
I walk
on the sand
It feels warm
like a fire
I love to
go in the water
I splish and splash
water on my face
The water is
cold like ice.
I feel the goose bumps
on my feet
What a treat
I love the water

Ashley Cena, Grade 3
Public School 148 Ruby Allen, NY

Playing Baseball

Burning hot attention
Swinging the bat with great force
Making a home run

Apaar Anand, Grade 3
Tuxedo Park School, NY

Baseball

I hear baseballs
Hitting bats
All over my head
All day and night
All through the season,
Click, clack
Day and night

Carson Ruffing, Grade 3
Reidville Elementary School, SC

Rainbows

Rainbows are so pretty.
You can see the colors like blue,
yellow, red, and purple.
Rainbows are so pretty.

Joshua Alvarez, Grade 3
Mendenhall Elementary School, FL

Five Little Pumpkins

Five little pumpkins sitting on a fence
The first one said, "I see something coming"
The second one said, "I see him running"
The third one said, "He is carrying something"
The fourth one said, "We should be hiding"
The fifth one said, "Hurry, let's jump off the fence, and run inside."

Rishi Gandhi, Grade 2
Hunter's Green Elementary School, FL

My Hamster, Jester

I have a little hamster, his name is Jester. He just met a new friend, but I think he is a monster, because he has a green face, sharp teeth, looks very ugly, his mouth is sideways, and yesterday he went fishing and caught a fish and ate it without even cleaning it, and the eyeballs were still in it. So I told Jester not to play with him anymore and then he got mad and went to sleep on my master bed, and I went to bed in his tiny bed.

Shania Donaldson, Grade 3
Coral Cove Elementary School, FL

Autumn

A pples are good to eat.
U p in a tree, there are apples.
T urkey is good for you to eat.
U p down all around leaves are falling on the ground.
M y family and I like turkey and mashed potatoes.
N ice pumpkins to carve. That is my poem. How nice you all are.

Christopher Geschwill, Grade 3
Central Park Elementary School, FL

My Snowman Named Boardwalk

I will build a snowman, and his name will be Boardwalk.
He will really move, and he will really talk.
He will have a starfish nose, and a shell for a smile.
He will be friendly, but it will take awhile.
I have done it! I finally built my friend,
but now I am really tired, and my joints can barely bend.
He has three sections, bottom, top, and middle.
He isn't very big, but surely pretty little.
He is very nice, and also really tame,
but our friendship only lasted, until a big wave came.
But we're still friends, although we're far apart.
When a friend leaves, they are still in your heart.

Jimmy Touey, Grade 3
McKinley Elementary School, PA

Fall Leaves

Fall leaves fall.
You have to fall
So the other leaves can grow
Big and strong.

Tyler Anderson, Grade 2
Eagle's View Academy, FL

Struggling to Hit the Ball

Hands sweating…waiting.
Nervous to get a strike out.
Hit the ball — HOMERUN

Joshua LaDuca, Grade 3
Holland Township School, NJ

Pizza

Pizza
Crunchy, spicy
Eating, tearing, munching
I love pepperoni pizza.
Tasty

Jaylon Mull, Grade 2
St Andrew School, NY

Birds/Robin

Birds
colorful, feathered
flying, eating, chirping
Fly south for winter.
Robin

Alison Hodge, Grade 2
Consolidated School, CT

A Present for Me

Christmas, Santa.
A square.
A shirt inside.

Birthday.
Wrapping paper.
Ribbon, bow.
Very colorful.
I like to get presents.

Eric Schaible, Grade 1
Holland Township School, NJ

Welcome Seasons

Welcome, Welcome, Welcome Fall!
You're the greatest season of all,
I love the way your leaves change color
When it comes to Fall, I'm such a lover!

Welcome, Welcome, Welcome Winter!
You're so cold you make me shiver;
Sometimes I'll skate on a frozen river!

Welcome, Welcome, Welcome Spring!
Aren't you just the cutest thing?
Spring is when the flowers grow,
Spring is when I wear a bow!

Welcome, Welcome, Welcome Summer!
Without you it's such a bummer!

Sage Jenne, Grade 3
Evangelical Christian School, TN

When I Get Mad

When I get mad, I get an attitude.
I don't feel like giving any gratitude.
When I get mad, I really behave bad.
When I get mad, you don't want to be near me
'Cause I get really mad.
I guess I need to change my attitude.
And not be so mad at the world.
Maybe I can learn from people
Who don't get mad like me.

Allan Saari, Grade 3
Public School 131, NY

Soldiers

Soldiers, soldiers, I hope you know
That when I think about you
I want to pray
And this is what I say,
Dear Lord, I hope You let the soldiers know
How brave I think they are
To hear and see the guns and bombs
And let them know if they get hurt or killed
I keep them in my heart.

Josie Sullivan, Grade 3
Pike Liberal Arts School, AL

Soldiers of America

You die for your country.
You fight and never stop.
You think of your loved ones far away.
I wish I could be brave like you, maybe I'll be you some day.
To be a soldier is hard work.
So when you see a soldier, salute them.
It will make you and him feel good inside and swell with pride.

Emery Thomas, Grade 2
Briarwood Christian School, AL

My Pretty Hair

My hair is long and black it falls straight down my back
It feels like fine silk because I wash it with milk

I wake up early every day to comb all my tangles away
I always want to be certain that my hair falls like a curtain

Mom thinks my hair is a mess Dad said my hair is too stressed
My brother said I am too vain I don't want them to complain

Last week, I cried my eyes out after coming back from my hair cut
I cried all day and all night my short hair just doesn't feel right

Now, I'm happy to say I'm glad my hair is this way
I can brush my hair in a jiffy till it is nice and spiffy

I like my hair fluffy just like my dog Muffy
I like my hair just fine it is totally divine

Kristin Chan, Grade 3
Infant Jesus School, NH

Christmas Things

People singing holiday songs.
Warm sugar cookies.
Nice and toasty around the fire.
Eating warm ham.
Gathering around the table for food and Christmas songs.
Celebrating the Lord's birthday!
Old Saint Nick giving presents to girls and boys.
What a joy to the world.

Samantha McKenzie Dixon, Grade 3
Bradford Township Elementary School, PA

Michael

Michael
small, dangerous
toys, art, baseball
Does what others want
M.D.B.

Katie Howard, Grade 3
Briarwood Christian School, AL

In the Dark

In the dark
The mountain lions creep around
Camden, Rome, Taberg
If you go out at night
You might see one
And if you do…
You might want to go inside.

Gabrielle Hayden, Grade 2
Annsville Elementary School, NY

Horses

Galloping,
Jumping,
Trotting,
Walking

That's what horses do.
They're walking and trotting
here and there
eating delicious
hay and grass.

Getting bigger and bigger
they grow up so fast.

Regan Anderson, Grade 3
Reidville Elementary School, SC

Christmas Tree

Tree
Big, pretty
Shining, decorating, twinkling
Christmas trees are pretty.
Christmas

Sean Morse, Grade 3
Landmark Christian School, GA

Drake

Nice
Cool
Friendly
Smart
Wishes to be a MLB player.
Dreams of my family.
Wants to go to New York.
Who wonders about my brother.
Who fears the dark.
Who is afraid of bad people.
Who likes my family.
Who believes in God.
Who loves my brother.
Who loves my aunt.
Who loves my family.
Who plans to be a good kid.
Who plans to be a good person.
Who plans to be nice.

Drake Henriksen, Grade 3
Central Park Elementary School, FL

Mom

Mom, Mom, Mom
I love my mom
She has short black hair
She is sweet like chocolate
Even without mints
her breath smells
sooo good!
She loves me
as much as
I love her
Everybody says
we look like twins
mom, mom, mom
I love my mom
her favorite color
is baby blue
She is forty-one
My mom, my mom
I love my mom

Alexandra Altamirano, Grade 3
Public School 148 Ruby Allen, NY

My Brother

My brother is a nerd; he can type a fifty page essay
My brother is a genius; he knows how to do algebra
My brother is a geek; he can fix any computer problem
My brother is an athlete; he can play any sport you name
My brother is a leader; he is always leading me and others
My brother is a historian; he can name you all the 50 states
My brother is a scientist; he knows the elements in the periodic table
My brother is a writer; he writes stories and reads them to me
My brother is my hero; he is always there to help me
My brother is my teacher every day; he teaches me new things
My brother is my brother; he will always remain in my heart and soul
My brother is my life; I can never live without him

Pranab Das, Grade 3
Public School 131, NY

They Rock

My family is caring and loving to all.
They raise money for homeless people.
They protect me from danger.
They always hug me when I come back from school.
They're the best.
They rock.
I love them.

Megan Osorio, Grade 3
Miami Country Day School, FL

Bees Buzz

Bees buzz all the time
Whoosh, whoosh, bzz, bzz all around
Up, down, left, right, whoosh!

Aaron Kredi, Grade 2
Virginia A Boone Highland Oaks Elementary School, FL

Clouds Above Me

The clouds above me look like cream.
The clouds above me move like a turtle.
The clouds above me might smell like butterscotch.
The clouds above me might feel like silk.
The clouds above me might sound quiet like the ocean.
The clouds above me might taste like cotton candy.
The clouds above me make me feel like a cotton ball.
Aren't clouds nice?

Grace Heersping, Grade 2
Clover Street School, CT

Who Has Seen Pluto?

Who has seen Pluto?
Not William, not you
But, when the moon sets down and
You see Pluto behind you,
The planet Pluto is passing through.

Who has seen Pluto?
Not you, not me
But, when the sun sets again
The planet Pluto is passing by.

Eero Korpela, Grade 2
Sundance School, NJ

My Friend

My friend LiLi we go to the park
and swing on the swings we both
love ice cream
but
she likes strawberry and I like
vanilla we jump through the
sprinklers
and we get wet
we slide on the slide
we go down so fast that we
fall down on the floor
and then
we laugh
we will be best friends forever

Adeliris Gonzalez, Grade 3
Public School 148 Ruby Allen, NY

Deer

Deer are brown
Deer live everywhere
Deer are all around
Deer blend in with the grass
Deer have four legs
Deer hunters wear camo clothes
Deer can give you good meat!

Deer

Canaan Scruggs, Grade 1
Alvaton Elementary School, KY

My Dog

My dog likes to play fetch
with me,
She likes to lay on me, too.

Will Clontz, Grade 1
Cool Spring Elementary School, NC

Penguins

Penguins slide.
Penguins pip.
Penguins sing, sing, sing!

Alanys Vasquez, Grade 1
Northeast Elementary School, NY

Christmas

Christmas is a good season,
It is also really fun!

It is a good holiday
And it is on the way.

There are always happy endings,
And happy beginnings too.

Jesus was also born on this day,
But some say no way.

Bailey Garrett, Grade 3
Pike Liberal Arts School, AL

Things

I have a favorite thing
And it is to sing
I have a special ring
I wear it on my wing.

Kallan Mulhearn, Kindergarten
Northeast Baptist School, LA

Hunter

Hunter
funny, tall
football, soccer, baseball
Always helpful to others
Thorny devil

Emily Hanrahan, Grade 3
Briarwood Christian School, AL

October

Fall is here.
The leaves have changed colors.
It's starting to be cold in the morning.
Halloween is coming.
Everyone is getting ready for Halloween.
People are getting costumes and candy.
Children are going to be trick-or-treating in a little while.

Lindsay Redmond, Grade 3
Duncan Elementary School, SC

Costumes A to Z

A ngel, **b** aby, **c** at, **d** evil
E lephant, **f** airy, **g** host,
H orrible Harry
I guana, **j** aguar, **k** ing,
L ion, **m** odel, **N** emo, **o** n/off switch,
P irate, **q** ueen, **r** eindeer, **S** cooby Doo,
T iger, **U** nderdog, **v** ampire, **w** itch, **x** -ray machine,
Y oyo, **z** ipper.

Brittany Redfern, Grade 2
Weston Elementary School, NJ

Brave Leaf

I'm green and brown
Like the Earth.
I'm as soft
As a fluffy bed.
I am flying
Like an eagle.
I'm a brave leaf.

Kyle Godfrey, Grade 2
Worthington Hooker School – K-2 Campus, CT

Archery

Archery is lots of fun.
Hit a target without a gun.
I pull the string hard with my hand.
I hit my target on a stand.
When I hit the center I yelled, "yes!"
With lots of practice I'll be the best.

Aaron Sykes, Grade 3
Noonan Elementary Academy of Fort Myers, FL

Winter World
Winter is fun.
We decorate a Christmas tree.
We give presents.
Alex Vasseghi, Grade 3
Tuxedo Park School, NY

Jesus' Birthday
I love Christmas.
I love my toy.
Santa is the best.
Christmas is joy.
I love reindeer.
I love the snow.
We eat ham.
Santa says, "Ho! Ho! Ho!"
Jack Kennedy, Grade 1
Westlake Christian School, FL

My Favorite Place
Disney World
Peter Pan ride
saw Minnie Mouse
bunk bed
begging to go back
Alanna Redwood, Grade 1
Sundance School, NJ

5 W's
I
love to watch tv
in the afternoon
in my mom's room
'cause I am tired
Isabelle Weldon, Grade 1
Sundance School, NJ

Thanksgiving
Thanksgiving
Friendly happy
Playing feasting smiling
I love Thanksgiving
Fun
Genesis Morales, Grade 3
Marie Curie Institute, NY

Football
Crack! The helmets hit,
The quarterback goes down.
Hut! Hike! The quarterback has the ball.
He gets hit in the backfield,
Time is running out.
He lobs up a pass,
The wide receiver jumps,
He has it! Touchdown!
They win! They win!
Barrett Tindall, Grade 3
Briarwood Christian School, AL

Butterflies
We could catch them.
I want to keep them.
I like the gold, colorful
Rainbow butterflies.
I like when they fly on the flowers
Because I catch them easily.
They spread their wings out and fly very fast.
They fly very high and very low.
Olivia Roth, Kindergarten
United Hebrew Institute, PA

Things That Never Die
Mummies wrapped in gauze,
A polka dotted blanket,
Jesus the son of God,
Big gray statues,
America discovered in 1492,
Dirt that is really brown
The Bible, God's word,
Water very clear,
King Tut 3,000 years old,
Our healthy bones.
Sarah Bartley, Grade 3
Madison Station Elementary School, MS

Winter
As the snow falls down
I love to make a snowman
It is so much fun
Krista Ortenzi, Grade 3
Catherine A Dwyer Elementary School, NJ

My Ball

Up the hill and down the street
What do you think I have to seek?

It is shining, it is round, it bounces all around.
It is hiding it is peeking, and wondering where I am going.

My ball my ball I am right here —
What do we do and where do we go?
Be it may we finally got to play?

Sara Sheward, Grade 1
Childrens House Montessori School, MS

Spring

The first blue jay flies in spring
I see green buds growing on trees
And green grass growing from sprouting underground,
Yellow sun, fish swimming, and red apples in the bag in the grocery store,
Gray fuzzy squirrels running around,
Looking for chestnuts.
Happy spring!

Zachery Ballowe, Grade 3
John T Waugh Elementary School, NY

I Am From

I am from my wonderful bedroom
where my colorful books are waiting for me to read.
I am from my warm computer room
where my computer is waiting for me
to play at my house.
I am from my soft backyard where my
slanted hill is waiting for me to roll down.

Andrew McKay, Grade 1
Berkeley Lake Elementary School, GA

The Pumpkin Patch!

I went to a pumpkin patch.
There were so many pumpkins!
I picked one that had a face.
Not a mean face,
Not a scary face!
The face that I picked was a happy faced pumpkin!
He had a huge happy smile!

Kyle Reiking, Grade 3
Coral Springs Elementary School, FL

Autumn

I see brown squirrels
Pumpkins are growing right now
Squirrels are pretty

Gracelyn Ely, Grade 2
Wellington School, FL

Volleyball, Volleyball, Volleyball

Volleyball, Volleyball, Volleyball
It is so sweet,
I hit the ball hard,
Then we win,
Yea! Yea! Yea!
Our coach is proud.

Haley Compton, Grade 3
Cool Spring Elementary School, NC

Class

I like class,
Any kind of class.
Science class, Art class,
Weird class, funny class.
Class in a school,
Class on the green pad,
Class with a teacher,
Any kind of class.
I like class.

Kaitlyn Stonecash, Grade 3
Landmark Christian School, GA

Rain

R ain is when it is cloudy
A rain jacket will keep us dry
I like to play in the rain.
N ice for me

Joshua May, Grade 1
Annie Belle Clark Primary School, GA

Brown

I am a dog.
I am chocolate.
I am a bear.
I am brown.

Angel Rivera, Grade 1
Northeast Elementary School, NY

Ramone

Ramone is a dog who
Likes to play fetch.
He is black and white.
He likes to sleep in bed.
I like to pet him.
He is small.

Matan Fox, Grade 3
John Ward Elementary School, MA

I Am

I am a niece, a sister, and a daughter.
I wonder why trees are green.
I hear loud sounds like a tiger roaring.
I see the jungle and vines all around.
I want to be a world famous rock star.
I am a niece, a sister, and a daughter.

Lacey Rhodes, Grade 3
Stone Academy, SC

Beautiful Fall Leaves

Leaves fall and blow from tree to tree.
Red, yellow, and green I see.
Coats zipper. Winds blow.
Gray wind hangs down low.
It is night time but early now.
It grows darker as we lay to sleep.
Tomorrow, another tree I will see.

Jordon Clibbens, Grade 3
Concord Elementary School, PA

Fall

Oh fall, oh fall,
Why do your leaves fall?
Oh fall do you know why
your leaves fall?
They land on the wall.
I love when they
f
 a
  l
   l on my head.

Savannah Jewell, Grade 3
Cool Spring Elementary School, NC

In the Fall

In the fall, I taste a soft, crunchy, juicy apple under a tree.
In the fall, I taste the fluffy, mushy, mashed potatoes at dinner.

In the fall, I smell warm, crispy pie waiting on the table.
In the fall, I smell small, toasty, warm pumpkin seeds cooling on the counter.

In the fall, I see my large, red, smoky wood stove in the kitchen.
In the fall, I see white, noisy geese floating on a frosty pond.

In the fall, I hear dry, rough leaves swishing through the air.
In the fall, I hear my dad's old, rusty leaf blower
trying to start up outside in the garage.

In the fall, I feel the damp, cold frost on the windows.
In the fall, I feel the fast, breezy wind blowing at me in the yard.

In the fall, I don't feel the hot, sticky sun above me
while I'm swimming in our pool.
In the fall, I don't taste cold, frosty ice cream at the ice cream shop.

Rylie Urbanski, Grade 3
Watsontown Elementary School, PA

Sisters

Sisters are clean and very kind,
but my sister can only be mine.
My sister is cool, nice and awesome
When you smell her, she smells like cherry blossom.
Sisters are sweet like sugar candy.
When you need help, sisters come in handy.
Sisters are helpful and also thoughtful
when I'm sick she coaxes me to feel hopeful.

Gianni Burnside, Grade 2
Coral Cove Elementary School, FL

My Apple

I see goosebumps and I see yellow and green mixed together. I see seeds
I hear an owl at night saying, "Hoo, hoo."
I taste sour and sweet and it tastes like candy.
I smell green bubblegum.
I feel a basketball, squishy.

Ivinson Batista, Grade 2
Arlington Elementary School, MA

My Horrible Birthday
It was my birthday
When came a fright,
My friends were nowhere in sight.
I thought they would come,
But boy what a bum
When I had to play
Laser tag with my dad.
"Zzzz."
Man, that is sad
That I was beaten by my dad.
Connor Martin, Grade 3
Briarwood Christian School, AL

The Angels Shine on Me
Santa Claus is on his sleigh,
Rudolph's nose shines at night.
He is so cute!
His nose is so bright!
My ornaments are shining,
I love my Christmas tree.
The angels are cute,
The angels shine on me.
Veronica Scott, Grade 1
Westlake Christian School, FL

My Sister and Brother
I have a lovely sister and brother.
I talk to her and him.
I want them to know that I love
Both of them.
Cache Walters, Grade 3
Joseph Pennell Elementary School, PA

Why Carl Bugs Me
Carl bugs me!
He's weird,
He's tiny,
He's a nerd,
He always follows me around.
He laughs too much.
And he runs around with no shirt.
Mark Gómez, Grade 3
Mary Matula Elementary School, MD

The Horse Dreamer
I know a horse named Dreamer.
She is beautiful and fun,
She likes to play and run.
She likes sweet honey too.
Linley Green, Grade 2
Briarwood Christian School, AL

My Pet
Fish
Take care of it
Lives in water
Swims around
Likes to play
In a fish bowl
Blows bubbles
Flips its tail
Fishy
Yasmine McNeill, Kindergarten
Broadway Elementary School, NC

The Sport of Olympic Shooting
Still as a statue
Aiming and focusing while
Recharging at once
Gabriel Smith, Grade 3
Holland Township School, NJ

Thanksgiving/Family
Thanksgiving
Fun, turkey
Cooking, eating, praying
Loving, hungry, starving, tiring
Family.
Amber Driscoll, Grade 3
Wapping Elementary School, CT

Anna Fay
Anna Fay
happy, joyful
soccer, volleyball, tennis
She cheers people up
Fay Fay
Bryant Gilson, Grade 3
Briarwood Christian School, AL

Angels

Angels are watching over me.
Watching so patiently, angels, peacefully.

Sensitive angels are so nice.
I like angels that are giant,
Adorable, responsible, enormous angels,
Plan ahead angels, ridiculous, excellent angels,
Tardy angels, yo-yo angels.
Angels are so pretty, they make me silly,
I like angels.

Angels are watching over me.
Watching so patiently, angels, peacefully.

Camille Jones, Grade 2
Narvie J Harris Traditional Theme School, GA

Friends

Friends mean happiness both good and bad,
You can tell friends your secrets without feeling sad,
Friends come and friends go as happy as can be,
But true friends are ones that you don't need to see.

Lexi MacPherson, Grade 3
A L Burruss Elementary School, GA

Autumn's Arrival

When autumn leaves begin to fall,
they rustle down a chilly hall.
The hall is a big forest trail,
and when leaves fall, they never fail.
When autumn's arrival is in the air,
the leaves all fall, they're everywhere!
When autumn comes the kids all go,
to school to learn what they need to know.
When Halloween comes, it's almost the end of fall,
but it is fun for one and all.

Adam Ziccardi, Grade 3
Ellicott Road Elementary School, NY

Lizards

They run and play games
All the lizards hide in trees
One of them jumps off.

Teddy Abrams, Grade 2
Virginia A Boone Highland Oaks Elementary School, FL

Cara

C aring
A wesome
R ose
A mazing

Cara Johnson, Grade 2
Park Elementary School, AR

The Kitten

I got my mitten
And I found a kitten.

It was cold,
So the kitten I did hold.

I took him to my house
He found a little mouse.

Victoria Salerno, Grade 3
Penn-Kidder Campus, PA

Stacey

Nice mom
Brown eyes
Cooks dinner
Goes trick or treating
Very sweet!

Brian Guilder, Grade 2
Marie Curie Institute, NY

Stars

Stars
Twinkly, diamond
Glowing, sparkling, glittering
Stars look very beautiful.
Twirl

Jada Hooker, Grade 2
St Andrew School, NY

School

My school is so cool.
The teacher is so great.
My school has many rules.
I love Our Lady of Hope!

Nick Macchia, Grade 3
Our Lady of Hope School, NY

Growing Beautiful

Growing,
With bright feelings,
Starting small and weak,
As a bud,
But then growing,
Growing in a life cycle,
Weakness into strength,
Colors going wild,
Swaying in a meadow,
Making the world more and more beautiful,
Until the time comes,
When you regain your weakness,
Then you curl up,
And you are gone forever.

Carlie Gasia, Grade 3
Hunter GT Magnet Elementary School, NC

My School ECS

I love my school, they teach me so much.
Math and science and such and such.
We learn Reading and Writing too.
We have fun in P.E. with the things we do.

Bayley Smith, Grade 2
Evangelical Christian School, TN

Fluffy Puppy

There once was a puppy,
Her name was Fluffy,
She broke her leg,
Now it's a peg,
Her last name was Muffy.

Haley Rossi, Grade 3
John H Winslow Elementary School, NJ

My Hamster Fudgey

Zoom goes Fudgey on his wheel.
Whom has entered my territory?
Doink is the noise when he falls doink, crash.
Nibble nibble chew chew.
That is the noise when he eats his food.
With his little arms and little feet,
He runs on his wheel and I can't go to sleep.

Charlie Campbell, Grade 3
Briarwood Christian School, AL

Clouds Above Me

The clouds above me look like fluffy ice cream.
The clouds above me move like turtles.
The clouds above me smell like vanilla ice cream.
The clouds above me might feel like fluffy bunny fur.
The clouds above me might sound quiet like the ocean.

Sydney DePaulo, Grade 2
Clover Street School, CT

Snakes

S nakes sense their prey with their tongues
N ice snakes like people
A snake opens their jawbones very wide
K inds of snakes can hear their prey
E ven a man cannot stop the snake

Jaikale Logan, Grade 3
Bensley Elementary School, VA

My Dog, Gucci

G reat
U nusual
C ute
C uddly
I ntelligent

Samuel Gotsman, Grade 3
Virginia A Boone Highland Oaks Elementary School, FL

Twilight Comes Twice

Dusk's hands erase the stars on the blackboard of night.
The moon hits the sun and disappears into the glowing starry night.
Pale twilight touches the sky.
The shimmering moon lights up the sky like a brand new night light.
Drinks up night's leftover darkness.
The stars shimmer like a polar bear's big shiny eyes.
Dew spangled webs spread out on newly cut grass.
In the morning the big blistering sun rises up above sprayed evergreen trees.
The crescent moon glows with the stars.
The beautiful shining sky is like ten huge carnival lights.
Light that ushers in a brand new day.
The lemon drop colored sunbeams shine down on the ground covered in topless and topped acorns.

Madalyn Perrotti, Grade 3
Jeffrey Elementary School, CT

My Love

you are my sweetheart
you are my love
you are my candy
you are my mug

you are my dream love
you are my hug
you are my true love
you are my snug

you are my baby
you are my cube
you are my princess
you are my rose

Kiana Boyd, Grade 3
Blakeney Elementary School, GA

Thanksgiving

Thanksgiving is
family fun.

Thanksgiving is
hunting for turkey.

Thanksgiving is
eating corn, green beans,
corn bread, and turkey!

Blaine Dempsey, Grade 3
Reidville Elementary School, SC

Darkness

Darkness covers the sun
and its light
It is blank and wondrous,
soothing and soft.

Darkness is not shame,
but beauty
I lay in bed
look up at the sky
and slowly drift away
into my dreams.

Gabriella Owens-DeMarco, Grade 3
Lincoln Elementary School, PA

Letter to Sky

Dear Sky,
You are very bright.
I like to talk to you.
What does the sun do to you?
The stars are so bright,
They are beautiful.

Ashley Nicholas, Grade 3
Cool Spring Elementary School, NC

Super Horse

I can run.
I eat buns.
I am brown.
My feet are black.
I am Super Horse.

Veronica Castillo, Grade 1
Northeast Elementary School, NY

My Fish

When he swims
he goes
glob, glob, glob
He is like a crayon
that squeaks
very loud
He is like a
car that goes
vroom, vroom, vroom
when he drinks water
he goes
blub, blub, blub
My fish
Carlos

Enzo Mateos, Grade 3
Public School 148 Ruby Allen, NY

Love

I love my mom
I love my dad
I love Miss Truppo
I love, love God

Bridgett Sona, Grade 1
Three Bridges Elementary School, NJ

The Beautiful Nature Preserve

Happy, excited filled the room like water overflowing with dripping tears.
Mrs. Chenault is taking us to the nature preserve to pick some really neat nature like leaves, acorns and branches.
I just can't wait to see the beautiful nature preserve. When the sun shines down it is as beautiful as a butterfly flying in the air.
Now we are getting ready to go to the nature preserve to pick some neat items like, leaves, acorns, and other nature.
Excited and cheerful, I felt as if I was running as fast as a cheetah having fun.
I was standing at the entrance of a beautiful nature preserve and it was so beautiful. The plants were too.
Right outside of the nature preserve it was a pretty as a colorful garden.
While everybody was standing outside of the nature preserve, I heard birds chirping and I can smell the very old, tall trees.
When we were walking around we found some really neat stuff.
My eyes are looking all around the nature preserve watching the birds chirping in the tree.
I found a rolly polly crumbling up trying to roll away from me, tweep-tweep.
When I picked it up it felt like there were holes in it, but there wasn't. It was hard though.
He looked like a little bug and I didn't know what is was. I was excited.
My eyes are looking all around the nature preserve watching birds chirping in the tree.
I found an acorn that was brown, and I found some berries. I put them in my bag and they were dripping red juice.
When I picked the berry up it felt as slimy as a goose and my acorn, it was cool too.
Let's keep moving forward! Looking for stuff.
Blue — mad now we have to leave all the little rolly pollies and the sunny nature preserve.
No more of the smelly flowers or hearing birds chirping way up in the trees.
Now we have to go back to enter the building to work.
I hope I get to go back to the nature preserve.

Katelyn Moreland, Grade 3
Woodland Elementary School, KY

The Leaves Are Still Green

Here we are in Halloween.
And, actually the leaves are still green.
Even though they should be red, orange and yellow,
The green ones should go to bed.
Here we are in Halloween.
I wonder why the leaves are still green?

Isabel DeVito, Grade 1
Sundance School, NJ

My Family

i have my family
i like my family
they take me everywhere
i have 2 sisters
they are really funny
my family makes me happy
i like my family.

i love my mom
i love my dad
they take good care of me
i take good care of them
they want me, to be a good child
i always help my family
i like my family.

i love my sisters
i love my relatives
i love my friends
i want my family to be happy
because, i love my family
i like my family

Bismah Zia, Grade 2
Coral Cove Elementary School, FL

Snowman

I put on a hat
I put on a scarf
I put on arms
I put two feet
He looked in my window
And broke my gameboy.

Nino Harris, Grade 1
Southside Elementary School, KY

My Friend

Jacob
cool, good
playing TV games
eating popsicles with me
Jacob

Daveona Lowery, Grade 2
Bensley Elementary School, VA

Molly

M agical
O utgoing
L ovely
L ively
Y outh

Molly Doyle, Grade 2
Long Meadow Elementary School, CT

My Jack-o'-lantern

My pumpkin is orange.
It has a light in it.
It is smiling.
It is very shiny.
It has eyes and is glowing at night.
It looks scary.
It has a nose.
A candle is inside.
The pumpkin has yellow eyes!
I love Halloween!

Kyreek McKee, Grade 2
Newton Elementary School, MS

I Love NASCAR

I love NASCAR.
Jeff Gordon is a star.
He came in second in the chase!!!
He's really good in a race!
He's my favorite driver!
He is a survivor!

Zechariah Copeland, Grade 2
Saving Kids Academy, NC

Beautiful Nature

Have you felt the wind blow?
Have you seen a sky
Bluer than the sea?
Golden pine needles fall
On you and me like a dream.
Drops of water on leaves
Look like tiny fairy eggs.
Have you noticed what's outside?
Take a look and you'll see.

Merle Curran-Ackert, Grade 2
Worthington Hooker School, CT

Goldfish
Goldfish goldfish
In a creek
Hearing creepy noises
That sound like a fish.
Cherish Skelton, Grade 1
Southside Elementary School, KY

Roses Are Red
Roses are red violets are blue
Why are you looking at my shoe?
What do you see in the clouds so high?
What do you see in the deep blue sky?
William Woodley, Grade 3
Western Hills Elementary School, AR

Connor
C urious
O utstanding
N ice
N eat
O wn a Gameboy
R ap
Connor Santoro, Grade 2
Long Meadow Elementary School, CT

Angela
My mother
Brown hair
Plays games
Rides bikes
Hugs a lot.
Carlie Marie Bennett, Grade 2
Marie Curie Institute, NY

I Love You, Mama*
Every bottle loves a top.
Every car loves a stop.
Every weed loves a crop.
And I love you.
Lacee Maggio, Kindergarten
Eden Gardens Magnet School, LA
**Inspired by Jean Marzollo's*
"I Love You: A Rebus Poem"

3-Wheel Mike
There once was a boy named Mike
Who rode on a very small bike
He got a new wheel
And now he can feel
What it feels like to ride on a trike.
Allard Williams, Grade 3
Perrywood Elementary School, MD

Winter
W arm inside
I cy
N o school
T oasted marshmallows
E xcited about Santa
R iding down a hill on a sled
Jarred Sareault, Grade 3
Reidville Elementary School, SC

My Cat
Cat
Fluffy, gray
Meowing, sleeping, playing
Loves to come inside
Simba
Karissa McFadden, Grade 3
Landmark Christian School, GA

Maui/Hawaii
Maui
Beautiful, flowers
Boogie boarding, swimming, crashing
Wet, strong, happy, excited
Hawaii
Justine Barnett, Grade 3
Wapping Elementary School, CT

The Rat
Eak went the rat.
The rat is being chased by a fat cat.
The very fat cat can track the little rat.
Up went the rat, darn that cat
the rat must have gotten away.
Daniel Darwin, Grade 3
Briarwood Christian School, AL

Baseball

Clap, clap, snap
Pop, pop, cheering
The Red Sox Win!
The Red Sox are great!
Kaylee Duran, Grade 2
Clover Street School, CT

My Favorite Place

Bow craft
hits the bear
Pirate Boat
ice cream
love it
George Pappas, Grade 1
Sundance School, NJ

My Football

It looks like an oval.
It looks like an eye.
It looks like lips.
It looks like a head.
It flies at a football game.
I cheer for the flag
football team.
Clare Nugent, Grade 1
Holland Township School, NJ

A Colorful Day

Brightly colored leaves
Gently falling to the ground.
It's like a rainbow.
Lindsay Romano, Grade 3
Tuxedo Park School, NY

William

W orthy
I nspiring
L oyal
L istening
I nside a lot
A pple eater
M ad at school
William Colburn, Grade 2
Park Elementary School, AR

My Backyard

My backyard is big with lots of land
I like to play in my box of sand
I like to swing and slide and do handstands

My backyard can be a ton of fun
I like to jump and run
I like to play in the snow and the sun

My backyard is bright and colorful
My backyard is splendid and playful
My friends and family thinks it's wonderful

My backyard can play a tune
When the trees are whistling in June
I like to play from noon till I see the moon
Zachary R. Uhler, Grade 2
Roosevelt Elementary School, NJ

The Scary Rain

It seems like it rains every day
Morning, afternoon, and night
I put the TV loud
So it won't give me such a fright
The lightning makes a flash
The thunder makes a boom
The scary rain makes me run to my room
When the rain stops I go out and play
And I hope that the rain stays far, far away
Jason Rivera, Grade 3
Coral Cove Elementary School, FL

Things That Make a Rainbow

Red for the stripes on the flag,
Orange for pretty sunsets,
Yellow for the bright sun,
Green for growing grass,
Indigo for water,
Purple for flowers,
Pink for cotton candy,
Roy G. Biv discovered it.
It has really bright colors.
It's the prettiest thing I've ever seen.
Kaitlin Joshua, Grade 3
Madison Station Elementary School, MS

Trees

Now what shall I do with the trees?
The day said the day said
Strip them bare, strip them bare.
Let's see what is really there.

And what shall I do with the sun?
The day said, the day said, Roll him away 'til spring.

Genesis Luciano, Grade 3
Mendenhall Elementary School, FL

My Little Birds

My little birds are cute and they sing to me every day.
They are blue and yellow and fly high in the tree.
I call them to come back to me.
They are sweet and they go tweet tweet.

Catherine Reyes, Grade 1
Mother Seton Inter Parochial School, NJ

Twilight Comes Twice

Night and day stand whispering secrets.
Night and day stand quietly whispering secrets in each other's ears.

Dusk gives the signal for night to be born.
Dusk frees out the signal that the night time sky is near.

A crack opens between night and day.
A slanted crack slowly pulls apart between night and day.

Dusk deepens the colors.
Dusk takes over the sinking glowing afternoon light.

Pale twilight touches the sky.
Pale twilight catches the electric pink sky.

Hayley Akel, Grade 3
Jeffrey Elementary School, CT

Stars

I wish upon the sun.
I don't have to wait for the stars to come out.
Oh, shooting stars are very special
But I think I'll wait for the stars to come out.
You can wish upon the sun, which is a star but really close.

Andrew Marks, Grade 2
Hurlbutt Elementary School, CT

Lost in Love

lovely pink
sweet small
light fluffy

Sydney DeSimone, Grade 1
Hilton Head Christian Academy, SC

Monkeys

Monkeys hop all around
They like to play on the ground
They are so, so silly
and they think they are too
People think they are cute
but when they're grumpy
they are not
When they smile they are
good once again!

Graham Williamson, Grade 3
Pike Liberal Arts School, AL

I Can See

I can see the door closing
eek, eek, eek, eek,

I can see the dog barking
whoof, whoof, whoof,

I can see the frog flying.

I can see the alligators eating
people saying aaaaaaaa!

I can see the be
buzzzzzzzzzzzing.

I can see the horse saying,
hee, hee, hee, hee

I can see the train saying
choo, choo, choo, choo,

I can see the wind whooshing
What do you see?

Katherine Vasquez, Grade 2
Public School 148 Ruby Allen, NY

My Pet

Horse
Gallops
Trots
Leaps over fences
Champion
Has nice hair, mane
Long tail for swishing flies
Pony

Tanner West, Kindergarten
Broadway Elementary School, NC

Night

Night night
As frightening as
Tigers at night
The crocodiles mean
Business
The lions are mean
They eat you
But more dangerous is us.

Kevin Palacios, Grade 2
Southside Elementary School, KY

My Skateboard

Skateboard let's ride.
Fill me with pride,
in the park,
until dark.
Let's have fun,
till Mom says I'm done.

Joshua Sanchez, Grade 3
Coral Cove Elementary School, FL

Hot Chocolate

Smooth and creamy
My taste buds sing with joy
It travels down my throat
Like a calm river
And into my stomach
And then I say yum
And ask for more

Zachary Benavage, Grade 3
Oak Ridge Elementary School, PA

The Book

Roses are red, violets are blue
I like reading, do you too?
If you do, come to me then you will see what to read.
I go to the librarian and get a book each day
Yay!

Keaston Hampton, Grade 3
Reidville Elementary School, SC

Baseball

Baseball
Sweaty, hot
Running, throwing, hitting
Balls, bats, bases, gloves
Catching, practicing, playing
Fun, exciting
Baseball

Tyler Goguen, Grade 3
Noonan Elementary Academy of Fort Myers, FL

Science

The solar system's biggest planet is Jupiter.
Though the people who watch too much TV get stupider.
I like to study about the planet Saturn.
And its rings all have a pattern.

Benjamin Smith, Grade 3
Pike Liberal Arts School, AL

My Little Brother

He has brown eyes and brown hair
He likes to have fun and play fair
When we go outside to play
He wants to stay all day
He likes to play tag and baseball
Especially in the cool fall!
When it comes to hunting and fishing
This little guy does some really big wishing!
Even though we get on each others' nerves and fight
In the end we try to make it all right
I am glad we do because he is like no other
I love him and am proud to call him my little brother

Jeremy Hall, Grade 3
Anacoco Elementary School, LA

Cute Dog
I can bite
I sleep at night
I can run
I like to have fun
I am Cute Dog.
Wendy Gomora, Grade 1
Northeast Elementary School, NY

Mitah and the Cheetah
My grandfather's name is Mitah.
He once met up with a cheetah.
He loved it so much,
He gave it a munch,
When they were at a famous pizzeria.
Aaron Soibelman, Grade 3
John Ward Elementary School, MA

Acorns/Nuts
Acorns
Dark, brown
Falling in November
From Autumn colorful trees
Nuts
Shannon Doherty, Grade 3
Northeast Elementary School, NY

Sheep
Sheep leap.
Sheep eat.
Sheep go baa.
In their sleep.
Andy Toxtle, Kindergarten
Forest Street Elementary School, NJ

Threes, Keys, Ts*
Every two loves a three.
Every door loves a key.
Every S loves a T.
And I love you.
Alexis Taylor, Kindergarten
Eden Gardens Magnet School, LA
**Inspired by Jean Marzollo's*
"I Love You: A Rebus Poem"

My Mom and Me
I like my mom. My mom likes me.
We like each other as you can see.
I love my mom that is right.
My mom is really out of sight.
Cassie Roach, Grade 3
Duncan Elementary School, SC

Woodfrogs
Woodfrogs jump so high
Woodfrogs eat snails and insects
Some woodfrogs are green
Zvi Shleifer, Grade 3
Yeshiva Ketana of Long Island, NY

Fall
It is warm and cold.
I like the color of the leaves:
orange, red, yellow, pink.
And it is darker when I sleep.
I like it when the wind shivers
and the leaves twitter.
As the owls hoot and the moon shines,
I stay inside — sometimes.
Emma Mires, Grade 3
Virginia Beach School, VA

Fairy Tale
Nice
A princess
A Girl
Married
Sweet
Cinderella
Shivani Samlal, Grade 1
Northeast Elementary School, NY

Super Kid
I can eat everything.
But I don't like meat.
I like to jump.
But I don't like to bump.
I am Super Kid!
Celvin Nunez, Grade 1
Northeast Elementary School, NY

The Twilight Zone

The crows finish their last minute gossip
Communities of crows cackle, cawing for help
Flushes out an army of mosquitoes
The mosquitoes get chased by peacefully flying bats
Celebration of night
The lightning bugs fly like little floating, shimmering lights
Fading light, the break of dawn
Shows off its orange skyline
In the park, in the park
The light green shimmering grass sparkles upon the sun
Sopping for breakfast worms
The beautiful flying robin
Was gracefully looking for breakfast
Pale twilight touches the sky
Pale orange skyline rises over the cerise brown houses
The glimmering shine of the baseball diamond reflects into eyes
Dusk pierces the syrup of darkness
Into the forest
Dusk arrives in the redwood forest
With moonlight shining
Upon the stars

Kyle Kuhn, Grade 3
Jeffrey Elementary School, CT

Clouds Above Me

The clouds above me look like vanilla frosting.
The clouds above me move like a fan.
The clouds above me might smell good.
The clouds above me might feel like a pillow.
The clouds above me might sound quiet.
The clouds above me might taste like a Frosty.
The clouds above me make me feel like a feather.
Aren't clouds as beautiful as a pillow?

Shawn Banks, Grade 2
Clover Street School, CT

Good Old Friend

Chihuahua
Peaceful and fun
Loving, running, growling
Miniature creature
Good old friend

Alexander Coman, Grade 2
Worthington Hooker School – K-2 Campus, CT

Thanksgiving
Thanksgiving
Fun thinking
Baking, cutting, eating
Buy the turkey
Feast
Morgan Durinick, Grade 3
Marie Curie Institute, NY

Football Player
Football player —
Throw!
Touchdown!
Win.
Play games.
Pull off a flag.
Seven points to
touchdown!
Rams are awesome!
Heath Trainor, Grade 1
Holland Township School, NJ

5 W's
I
love to play
in the night
in my yard
'cause the moon is out
Ethan Harriz, Kindergarten
Sundance School, NJ

Autumn
Squirrels climbing trees
Squirrels are burying nuts
Crows are on wires
Tyler Sawyers, Grade 2
Wellington School, FL

God Is Good
God is good
He gives us food
Everyone loves Him
If they would
Amaya Steele, Kindergarten
Taylor Road Academy, AL

My Doodle Monster
My doodle monster is my favorite toy.
His name is Jr.
Sometimes he wants to sleep with me.
He is card of Slappy, a very scary puppet,
I am afraid of him too!
Luis Aguiar, Grade 2
Mother Seton Inter Parochial School, NJ

Cheerleading
Cheerleading is my favorite sport.
I can do cartwheels around the court.
You would love to do it because it's very fun.
So try it!
If it doesn't work out just try again next year.
Don't just fall down and burst into tears.
You go to games and even competitions.
Cheerleading is my favorite sport!!!!
Nikita Hemans, Grade 3
Forest Street Elementary School, NJ

Pet Snake
I want a pet snake
So it can eat all the mice in my house.
It will look mad when it sticks out its tongue.
It will make hissing sounds,
And stare at me for a long time.
It will feel scaly and I know
That its tongue will help it smell things.
I don't want to be a snake
Because hunters will try to hunt for me.
I have pet my friend's big snake
And look up snakes on my computer
With my dad.
My dad was in the army,
So he is not scared of snakes.
Derrick Dale, Grade 3
Lee A Tolbert Community Academy, MO

Surya
Black hair, tall, glasses
Glasses make me different
I don't like glasses
Surya Makkar, Grade 3
Thelma L Sandmeier Elementary School, NJ

The Field

Colorful water splashing in cracks
Big rocks as old as my pa
Birds singing louder than a yell
Leaves soaring toward me
Trees waving in the wind smelling like flowers
In the pond fish are swimming faster than lightning
The scent of rain filling my nose
Dirt with worms filling my shoes
The wind blowing my hair into tangles
The water's mist covering me up
I feel warm and fuzzy inside.

Rebecca Whitley, Grade 3
Bailey Elementary School, NC

Rockets

10, 9, 8, 7, 6, 5, 4, 3, 2, 1 Blast Off!
up went my dad in the rocket way up high. Is something coming down?
Yes, it's part of the rocket. What's that — another rocket part?
My mother explained that father would be back soon.
So we stood and stood. Then out of the blue we saw it. The pod was down.
I ran to them and father ran to me.
He explained what he saw. It was wonderful.
I'm glad he's not going back, at least for now.

Abby Fancher, Grade 3
First Wesleyan Christian School, NC

A Halloween Mean Witch

On a hill there was a haunted mill,
There was a cat on a mean witch's spooky black hat,
Oh, how that witch will travel here and there,
But she really doesn't travel anywhere
That witch was stirring brew,
When a ghost jumped out and cried, "Boo!"
Coyotes are howling, and spiders are springing,
That witch was frowning,
A clown was dead to the ground,
On a hill there was that haunted mill,
There was that cat on a witch's spooky black hat!
You know that witch isn't so mean after all!
Happy Halloween!

Paula Goodgame, Grade 2
Wellington School, FL

Summer Camp

I like summer camp
In summer you play soccer
In soccer you kick

Daniel Goodman, Grade 3
Yeshiva Ketana of Long Island, NY

My Uncle

My uncle is a very nice man
he takes me everywhere
he has green eyes
and brown hair
everyone says he looks like me
he is my dad's brother
his name is Haver
every time he buys something
I jump
up and down
again and again
we go everywhere together
he takes me to Manhattan
to buy me toys
Wow!
I love him
so much
hope I see him
hope I see him

Natalie Tascon, Grade 3
Public School 148 Ruby Allen, NY

Penguins

Penguins walk.
Penguins dive.
Penguins waddle, waddle, waddle!

Zien Banuchi, Grade 1
Northeast Elementary School, NY

Grass

G reen grass lies upon the ground.
R esting animals rest in the forest.
A bird is humming.
S un is shining.
S ee the deer everywhere.

Nate Donaldson, Grade 2
Broadway Elementary School, NC

Tennis

Tennis fun, hit and run
one on one in the sun
all day long we play
you hear the crowd cheering
and see the clouds coming
nearer and nearer.
Hurry home
have some fun
tennis will come
but don't be sad or glum,
blue or sad
I promise tennis will
come again and soon.

Calypso Peraticos, Grade 3
Miami Country Day School, FL

Isabella

I ncredible
S weet
A wesome
B rilliant
E xciting
L oving
L aughable
A mazing

Isabella Pasqualucci, Grade 2
Long Meadow Elementary School, CT

Blue

I am Blues Clues.
I am a crayon.
I am the ocean.
I am blue.

Celine Carrion, Grade 1
Northeast Elementary School, NY

The Sun

The sun is yellow.
The sun is bright.
I love the sun.
It gives us light.

Ayana Hicks, Grade 3
Joseph Pennell Elementary School, PA

I Love My Brother

I love my brother
because he comes to visit.
He's smart.
He cares for me.

Deja Lopez, Grade 2
Robert E Lee Expressive Arts Elementary School, MO

My Apple

I saw red and green and brown polka dots.
I heard a heart beating inside of you.
I tasted apple pie and apple cookies walking to you.
I smelled green bubble gum that you chew.
I felt goosebumps as if the apple had been out during a cold night.
My apple.

Lidyanette Gonzalez, Grade 2
Arlington Elementary School, MA

Pumpkin

You might be old and sandy,
But I can wash you off.
You will look so neat standing by my door!
But at the end of the day, you will become my dessert.
Pumpkin pie or something more!

Matthew Hines, Grade 3
Coral Springs Elementary School, FL

Animals

Animals have fur on their big or little bodies,
and when they look for food they are greedy and naughty.
They have big or small paws and have pointed claws,
and like to climb on walls.
They sleep in the ground during winter,
and look for food in the fall and sleep in the winter.
Animals have lots of food,
and are not in a very good mood.

Kalen Houston, Grade 3
Western Hills Elementary School, AR

Flying Birds

The birds are flying
They fly up high in the sky
They fly together

Amit Siama, Grade 2
Virginia A Boone Highland Oaks Elementary School, FL

Pink

I am an eraser.
I am a pig.
I am a cherry.
I am pink.
Britney Concepcion, Grade 1
Northeast Elementary School, NY

Fall

I want to be raking leaves today
And making pies another day.
Eating corn blowing a horn
that's what I want to do today.
I also want to carve pumpkins
and sell muffins,
then bake all kinds of cakes.
Why I had a busy day,
but God really did lead me
through my way.
Neetthu George, Grade 3
Nativity Catholic School, FL

Green

I am a frog.
I am on trees.
I am grass.
I am green.
Abel Sanchez, Grade 1
Northeast Elementary School, NY

Friends

help you
you can trust them
they make you happy
they don't lie
to you
they will be with
you forever
you'll stay together
friends
what would we
do without them
Mayra Ramos, Grade 3
Public School 148 Ruby Allen, NY

I Love School

I love my teacher,
We like to talk at carpool,
When you're through with this poem,
You'll know I love school.
I love all my friends,
At school the fun never ends.
I love my principal,
Like I said,
I love school.
I love my headmaster,
School helps me learn faster.
If I did not have school,
That just wouldn't be cool.
If I didn't have school,
I would not write this poem,
'Cause those phonics rules,
I would not know 'em.
Some others think that school is cruel,
But not me, no way,
I love school.
Soledad Green, Grade 3
Trinity Christian School, VA

Christmas

To the Parents:

C hristmas is for caring.
H ooray! I got my presents!
R udolph the red-nosed reindeer
I s it snowing?
S anta Claus
T oys and more toys
M rs. Claus
A ngel on top of the tree
S weet! Santa! I'll go to the North Pole!
Christian De Angelis, Grade 3
Birches Elementary School, NJ

Dog

The big happy dog
Lives in a blue wooden house.
The dog likes to play.
Conner Sanders, Grade 2
Roseland Park Elementary School, MS

Perfection

People aren't perfect you know.
Not like a play or show.
Nobody can be a pro at all the things they know.
Mistakes are okay.
I make one every day.
No one is perfect inside.
Some people think it's something to hide, that they're not perfect you see.
If you and I were perfect life wouldn't be fun.
So God decided to make none, as perfect as can be.
Not even a cherry tree.
Now you know no one or nothing is perfect.

Maya Shenoy, Grade 3
North Star Elementary School, DE

Flag

F ree forever
L ove the red, white, blue
A ny day and every day you see those colors
G ood for me and you

Taylor Sharp, Grade 3
Bradford Township Elementary School, PA

My Friend

My friend and I play games and do wild and crazy dances.
We work together on school projects.
We talk on the phone and at each other's houses.
We sit together on the bus and watch everyone make noise.
We listen to our bus driver, when she says "Sit down and be quiet."
We visit each other every day.
We share candy and treats.
My friend is everything to me.
My friend is nice to me.

Iyanna Brooks, Grade 3
New Orleans Free School, LA

Jumping

They are GLIDING in the air like birds,
they are RISKY like a squirrel crossing the road,
they are PROUD when they jump
in the air with the snow.

Zoe Mirabella, Grade 3
Holland Township School, NJ

My Favorite Place
Disney World
Buzz Lightyear Ride
animal safari
helper on the train
love it there
John Sierant, Grade 1
Sundance School, NJ

Apple Cider/Apple Juice
Apple cider
sweet, delicious
drinking, pouring, smelling
I like apple cider.
Apple juice
Matthew Leach, Grade 2
Consolidated School, CT

We Gather Together
I love Christmas.
Jesus loves girls and boys.
That's when Jesus was born.
I like my toys.
I like hot chocolate.
We get a Christmas tree.
We hang ornaments.
We sing with glee!
Julia LaPierre, Grade 1
Westlake Christian School, FL

What Is Green?
A green house,
Icing on a cake,
Like a pepper,
Carpet in a store,
A green car passing by.
Blake Bauer, Grade 3
Scott Elementary School, MO

Summer
Beauty in the sun
As bright as a ripe orange
Floating in the sky
Alessandra Ietta, Grade 3
Tuxedo Park School, NY

Tiffany
Is my best friend
She is a cute girl
Her eyes are like two moons
She is as bright as a star in the sky
Her hair is like a waterfall rushing down
She is cute as a teddy bear
I am so glad she is my best friend.
Yesenia Rojas, Grade 3
Public School 148 Ruby Allen, NY

After the Rain
Dandelions shining like the sun.
Grass crunching under my feet.
The rain is splashing in the pond.
Colorful rainbow is splitting the ground.
Mushy clouds floating like sailboats
Taking the summer away.
Arnas Naujalis, Grade 3
Wolcott School, CT

Autumn
Leaves falling and changing colors,
Orange, yellow, and rusty brown
Wind blowing at my face
And owls hooting, "Hoo, hoo, hoo"
Pumpkin pie cooking, fresh air blowing,
Cinnamon applesauce, Mmm!
Bark on a tree, bumpy pumpkins glowing,
Apples, apple pie, apple cider tastes so good!
Tyler Jackson, Grade 2
Wellington School, FL

The Christmas Dream
It was Christmas Eve night
When I turned off the lights,
I was snuggly and cuddly in my bed.
I heard a jingle jangle on his big, red sled.
I felt Santa laugh a booming, "Ho, ho, ho!"
I listened to a crash above, click, clack!
I got out of my bed
Realizing it was all in my head.
"Merry Christmas!" my family said.
Mrs. Fields' Third Grade Class, Grade 3
Briarwood Christian School, AL

The Funny Bunny

The funny bunny likes to jump on his rope.
I like my friends because they always play with me.
I like my kitty because my kitty is cute.

Jessie Liang, Grade 1
Children's Village, PA

Train Game

My brother and I play with toy trains
And sometimes we have to use our brains.

We put the train onto the track
And sometimes we have to go on back.

At the siding we have to stop
Or one of the trains might fall and drop.

Each train has been given a name
So they don't all sound the same.

Once "Thomas" got his own branch line.
But "Murdoch" is my brother's favorite, and "Emily" is mine.

Hannah Master, Grade 1
The American Academy, PA

Animals of the World

Animals, animals here and there,
Animals, animals everywhere.

Some are near and some are far,
Some can even be really bizarre!

I like the cute and cuddly ones,
Animals can be lots of fun.

But when the day is done,
I can't wait till a new day has begun.

My animal friends have to go,
And they're going with their heads low.

It's time to say goodbye to each other,
We'll play again tomorrow, the next day, and another.

Caitlin Champlin, Grade 2
Stone Academy, SC

My Notebook
I take my notes in it for school
I write a lot of notes in it for writing
I go all around with it
Oh, good idea I should jot it down
But I have no space in my notebook
I will do it on my laptop
Going around town listening for ideas.
Taylor Smith, Grade 3
Public School 131, NY

The Cloud
The light puffy cloud
in the morning, bluish green sky
bounced like a monkey swinging
through the jungle in the afternoon sun
Olivia Drexler, Grade 3
Wellington School, FL

The Lovely Tree
lovely green
bright cool
nice funny
light colorful
nice tall
pretty beautiful.
Caroline Murray, Grade 1
Hilton Head Christian Academy, SC

Trampoline
We jumped so high,
We touched the sky.
We saw the birds fly by.
We had so much fun.
We made the squirrels run.
Ali Ogletree, Grade 2
St Peter the Apostle School, GA

Wood Fun
Whittling the wood.
While the wind blows,
My papa watches me very closely,
As I whittle the wood.
Tucker Traub, Grade 2
St Peter the Apostle School, GA

Spring Things
The trees are green.
The grass is green.
What else can I say?
It's spring!
Lauren Stichweh, Grade 2
Stichweh Family Home School, GA

Fall
Fall flies in with
school bells ringing
and wonderful memories
on a cool and windy night
with my dad taking out pumpkin seeds
Mikayla Cooke, Grade 3
Wellington School, FL

I Love Christmas
Christmas is a pleasant day
To celebrate in every way.

Leave milk and cookies on a tray,
For Santa comes upon his sleigh.

Christmas is my favorite day
To celebrate in every way.

Christmas is a family day,
I love Christmas, hooray, hooray!
Nora Madaras, Grade 3
Webster Montessori School, NY

My Pet Turtle
I have a turtle his name
is Honda like the car brand he likes
to sleep in his shell he's fifty
years old and is very big He runs
as fast as a kitten he climbs
like a snail his shell is hard
as a crab turtle, turtle show
your face in and out of your
shell turtle, turtle show your face
Omar Badawi, Grade 3
Public School 148 Ruby Allen, NY

Fall

In the fall, I see red, brown, yellow, falling, crunchy leaves in my leaf pile, as I am jumping into them.
In the fall, I taste pumpkin, apple, and boysenberry pie at the dinner table.
In the fall, I hear wild, plush squirrels hiding in the trees.
In the fall, I smell crunchy, juicy apples falling from the trees.
In the fall, I feel cold, white frost on my mom's car window.
In the fall, I don't feel steamy when I'm running around outside.

Bryce Kessler, Grade 3
Watsontown Elementary School, PA

October Greatness

In the oven I smell pumpkin pie.
Outside I see jack-o'-lantern lights.
On my tree I see red and orange leaves.
My mom is making pumpkin cake.
How come when I go outside it seems like pumpkin bake?
Scarecrow, acorn, harvest, everything is autumn.
Apple cider, roasted seeds, pumpkin tarts, yummy!
Carving pumpkins is really funny.
Candy corn is fun to eat.
Pumpkin cookies are yummy treats!

Emma Janus, Grade 3
Nativity Catholic School, FL

My Dog, Comet

Comet is my dog.
I play with him a lot.
He fetches anything I throw.
I chase him until he stops.

Colin Krings, Kindergarten
St Mary of the Assumption Catholic School, PA

What I Dream

I dream of a place that is magic.
It's a very nice big castle.
It's name is mlantic corpantic
I like to go there a lot with my friends.
They say wow, woah, cool, awesome and sweet.
I love the place and like to go there all the time.
And that's what I dream.

Anna Grace Browning, Grade 3
Madison Station Elementary School, MS

Penguins

Penguins swim.
Penguins waddle.
Penguins slip, slip, slip!

Jaheim Commisso, Grade 1
Northeast Elementary School, NY

Eraser

Feeling smooth,
as a pencil.

Sounds like,
smooth sandpaper.

Smells like,
smokey fire.

Looks like a pink rose
beginning to bloom.

Kyle Perry, Grade 3
Reidville Elementary School, SC

Letter to Cat and Miss Bear

Dear Cat and Miss Bear,
You help me to not get scared at night.
Dear Serene,
Why do you come in my room
And jump up on my bed?
I love you.

Brianna Adkins, Grade 1
Cool Spring Elementary School, NC

Sea Monster

I see some glowing eyes
They're glazing
They're shiny and red
It's a sea monster I see
Scaring me
And
Pulling me in
What should I do?
Should I whip him with a broom?

Lydia Houser, Grade 2
Annsville Elementary School, NY

Tornado

T ornado
O ver the barn
R ains from the sky
N ot coming
A fter us.
D o tornados go
O ver you?

Landon Bateman, Grade 1
Annie Belle Clark Primary School, GA

Christmas Tree

Oh Christmas tree, Oh Christmas tree
Your color shines so bright
The colored lights glow through
The snow filled night.
Decorations on the tree
Added very carefully
Oh our hearts are filled with glee
As we merrily dance around the tree.

Zachary Beauregard, Grade 3
Tri-County Christian School, MO

My Pet Speaks

Woof! Woof!
Come and play with me.
Let's go take a walk,
Give me a bone.
Woof! Woof!
Let's play,
Let's jump together.

Kayla Thapvongsa, Grade 3
Cool Spring Elementary School, NC

Winter

Snowmen being made
Snowballs everywhere
having fun all winter
It is the idea
It is no care
have no worries
Winter is here

Sergio Sanchez, Grade 3
Coral Cove Elementary School, FL

I Am From

I am from my pretty bedroom
where my goldfish is waiting for me
after school to play.
I am from my warm playroom
where my bright Christmas tree has presents under it.
I am from my hilly backyard
where I sled down my hill in winter
and yell YAHOO!!!

Bret Hazen, Grade 1
Berkeley Lake Elementary School, GA

Veteran's Day

V eterans
E ven the odds
T hey serve America
E very shot counts
R eload
A great country
N avy
S ave our country

D efeat the enemy
A badge for some
Y ells "Move Out"

Austin Chisek, Grade 3
Susquehanna Community Elementary School, PA

New York's Subways

Wait, wait, wait for the subway to come,
Stuck underground with no where to run.
Hate, hate, hate when the roaring subway is here,
Stand back from the edge; no reason to fear.
It comes so fast and goes in a blast.
However does it do it? No clue at all,
Let's just get to it.
There's all different places to go,
On one small speeding bullet train,
You can hitch a ride uptown or go across over to Main.
We took it over to the Museum of History,
How we got there so fast is still a mystery.
I love New York City and all that it holds,
I love the subway, especially when it's cold.

Madison Gamble, Grade 3
North Star Elementary School, DE

My Favorite Place

Long Beach Island
really cool houses
cousins and uncles
look for shells
love it

David Fromm, Grade 1
Sundance School, NJ

The Jungle

A hay house
The man is coming out of
the hay house
Another man building a
triangle house
Flowers blooming
Trees shaking
Tall grass and blue sky
Birds saying tweet tweet

Kyria Santa, Grade 1
Stone Academy, SC

Turkey/Chicken

Turkey
Juicy, yummy
Starving, eating, cooking
Roasting it is fun!
Chicken

Tommy O'Donnell, Grade 2
Consolidated School, CT

Turkey

Turkey
Biting chewing swallowing
take off the feathers

Johan Barquero, Grade 3
Marie Curie Institute, NY

On Christmas Night

On Christmas night,
The chimney shakes as
Santa comes,
And I hear presents

Patrick Donaghy, Grade 3
Tuxedo Park School, NY

On Christmas Day!

On Christmas day, Jesus came.
The Earth would never be the same!
On Christmas day we see His star.
We know He is with us and is never far.

Nash Lochmann, Grade 1
St Vincent De Paul Elementary School, MO

Bad Luck with Pets

My fish died.
My neighbor's cat ran away
After she gave it to me.
I used to have a rabbit.
When I took it out to exercise,
It gave me a love bite.
It hurt and I cried.
Its name was Hoppy.

Devin Roberts, Grade 3
Lee A Tolbert Community Academy, MO

Thanksgiving

T hanksgiving!
H appy days!
A ham and turkey, "yum!"
N ever stop eating!
K eep having lots of fun!
S oda and water that's all we get.
G iant plates of food
I love Thanksgiving.
V ery, very much!
I will always love it,
N o matter what!
G ood old Thanksgiving!

Siani Alicea, Grade 3
Dr Martin Luther King Jr School Complex, NJ

The Park

The park is a good place to play it's fun.
The park is a playground.
It's a beautiful place to be.
You can relax and renew.
When the sprinklers turn on they go
Whoosh, Whoosh, Whoosh.

Karen Castro, Grade 3
Public School 148 Ruby Allen, NY

Lucky Rainbows and Pots of Gold

There is a pot of gold at the
end of every rainbow so we're told.
So if you see a leprechaun walking along the way
make sure to follow him, it might be your lucky day.

Emily Foley, Grade 3
Concord Elementary School, PA

A Dirty Sock

I have a revolting yet lucky sock.
Its smell was enough to make you gawk,
And yell "Oh my gosh!"
I never want it in the wash.
And because of that I hide it away.
In a place that I will never say.
And if you ever find it,
I will snatch it and again hide it.
In a different place this time.
In a place you will have to climb.
And if it ever gets found,
An alarm will make a loud sound.
From that dirty, smelly, lucky sock.
That will even make make a million chickens squawk.

Kevin Collette, Grade 3
Infant Jesus School, NH

Winter

Winter is cold.
We all feel very bold.
It is snowing,
And the ground is turning into a white blanket.
The trees are turning gray.
But the colored lights are very bright.
You just can't wait till Christmas Eve.
You want to see Santa Claus,
But you know you need to be asleep.
Winter.
Sweet, sweet,
Winter.
Winter is cold.
We all feel very bold.

Kendall Adkins, Grade 3
North Star Elementary School, DE

Fox-ku

Fox lives in the woods
They run and catch their own food
They watch people too.

Olivia Guarino, Grade 2
Paine Primary School, AL

Rain

Rain
drizzles from the sky.
It smears
on windows.
It feels
so cold.
It makes your shirt wet
and puddles on the dirt.
You get your shoes
wet and muddy.
Rain

Savannah Betsill, Grade 3
Reidville Elementary School, SC

My Puppy

Fun, sweet, athletic
Barking, running, jumping, growling
Lovable, furry, fast
Pia

Becky Fernandez, Grade 2
St Mary's School, NJ

The Fake Ache

There once was a girl named Sue
Who had a cupcake or two
She got an ache, but it was fake
And now she really is feeling blue.

Cemone Toney, Grade 3
Perrywood Elementary School, MD

Rainbows

Rainbows are colorful.
They have colors of green and pink.
I love rainbows.
You can see rainbows in the sky.

Contessa Gonzalez-Mercado, Grade 3
Mendenhall Elementary School, FL

A Heart Is Red

A heart is red
It's in my head
It beats and beats like love.
It reminds me of my family above.

Nicole Suppa, Grade 1
Holland Township School, NJ

Fall

Red and yellow leaves
Leaves crunching
Apple pie baking

Ashley Canales, Grade 1
Northeast Elementary School, NY

A Rainy Day

The rain is falling down
I have to stay inside today
Now I wear a frown
The rain has spoiled my day
I only wanted to play
Please rain go away
So that I can play

Brenelle Dundas, Grade 2
Forest Street Elementary School, NJ

Scary

If you cry,
please do not try,
because when the candles go out,
you will shout.
When the ghosts are in sight,
you are in for a fright!

Kaden Culp, Grade 3
Ellicott Road Elementary School, NY

Fall/Cool

Fall
Cold, fun
Jumping, running, playing
Exciting, happy, breezy, fun
Cool

Sara Ramos, Grade 3
Wapping Elementary School, CT

Maria

M ad I am sometimes
A lways loving my mommy and daddy
R esting at 8:00 pm
I am a shy girl
A nd most of all I have the best brother: Alvaro

Maria Cercedo, Grade 1
Oliver Hoover Elementary School, FL

Summer

Summer camp is fun
The butterflies fly around
Swimming is fun too

Lilli Levinson, Grade 2
Virginia A Boone Highland Oaks Elementary School, FL

Me

J ustin likes running, wears a
U niform every day in school,
S tudies for the math tests,
T errific in reading,
I ncomplete homework
N ot bad in math.

Justin Steele, Grade 2
Public School 152 School of Science & Technology, NY

My Dad

One day my dad went to Iraq,
I miss him so much, I wish he'd come back.
Here are some things that I really miss:
like a goodbye hug and a hello kiss.
A roll in the park
and listening to larks.
I love the summer
but without daddy it's a bummer.
I play soccer in the fall,
but I want daddy to see me kick the ball.
In the winter I love the snow,
but without daddy I have to go slow.
In the spring I like baseball,
and dad needs to help me hit the ball over the wall.
Yeah hurray!! My daddy is coming home soon
I'm going to give him a big balloon!!

Jonathan Brooks, Grade 2
Prince William Academy, VA

Pokemon

P okeballs are nets.
O oze is a Pokemon.
K ilgar is my Pokemon's nickname.
E vee is a cute Pokemon.
M y Pokemon is on high levels.
O ctokus is very powerful.
N ew Pokemons are cool.

Trey Pruitt, Grade 3
Bensley Elementary School, VA

Art Work

Art work talks about your feelings,
Art work can be portraits,
Art work could be pretty pictures,
Art work can be different,
Art work has dark colors,
Art work has light colors,
Art work is easy to do.

Ciara Negron, Grade 2
Marie Curie Institute, NY

Dog

You can take away my TV.
You can take away my bed.
But PLEASE!
Don't take away my dog.

I can do without food.
I can do without a house.
But
I CAN'T
Do without my dog!

Peyton Falk, Grade 2
Annsville Elementary School, NY

Megan

M agnificent
E xcellent
G reat
A mazing
N eat

Megan Prendergast, Grade 2
Long Meadow Elementary School, CT

Dolphins

Dolphins all sleek and shiny,
catching fish to eat,
bobbing in the waves all day,
and playing games at sea!
Dolphins grab a little snack,
as they roam around at speed,
jumping with their friends,
in the coral reef!

Katarina Pfeifer, Grade 3
North Star Elementary School, DE

Nature

trees sway in the wind
while birds make noises in trees
and dogs bark happily

Colin Bauer, Grade 3
The Parke House Academy, FL

Brook the Book

Brook
Is a book
She holds so much information
She has no imagination

Lexie Kwak, Grade 3
The Parke House Academy, FL

Hibernating

When the winds get tough,
bears find warm places and sleep,
and they hibernate.

Ryan Hallaert, Grade 3
Coral Cove Elementary School, FL

Fearfest

F reddie Kreuger is a scary villain
E ndless scary fun
A dventures
R eally spooky at night
F ull of fear
E xcellent costumes all around
S carier than fiction
T here are screams everywhere!

Mauricio Acosta, Grade 3
Bensley Elementary School, VA

Strange Family

My family is strange
We need to rearrange
My sister has a dragon
My family rides in a wagon
We don't have a car
So we do not travel very far
When my brother tries to reach the basketball goal
He puts the ball in a hole
My family house
Looks like a mouse
One day in Huckleberry Town we had a blizzard
My cousin said it was a lizard
It is a good thing I am smart
Or my family may fall apart
My family is like a herd
Or a small bird
When my family was in City Hall
My aunt said that we were in a bouncy ball
It is a good thing my family has a heart
But they need to learn how to be smart

Mariana Glenn-Toland, Grade 3
Foster Park Elementary School, SC

My Fantasy Land

My fantasy land would be a world full of changes.
Like streams and forests and huge rearranges.
A farm and a forest with life in the air,
if this were my place, I would probably stay there.
From pastures and pig pens to chickens in coops,
I'd explore every path from loopedy loop,
in my fantasy land.

Savannah Brinker, Grade 3
Smethport Area Elementary School, PA

How I Love Kelly Clarkson

There was a girl named Kelly Clarkson.
Who loves to sing songs so fun.
And enjoys eating a sticky bun.
After so many calories she needed to take a run.
Oh, how I love Miss Kelly Clarkson.

Gianna Collins, Grade 2
St Mary of the Assumption Catholic School, PA

Veronica

V ery cute
E xciting
R eally good student
O n time
N ice
I love people
C lean
A wesome
Veronica Burkheart, Grade 2
Park Elementary School, AR

Zebra-Ku

Funny stripes silly.
Cuddly stripy likes to play.
Zebras play in zoos.
Ashley Cash, Grade 2
Paine Primary School, AL

What Is Black?

Black is the color
Of an unlucky cat
Black is a crow
That sits on a wire
Black is dark
Like an unlit candle
Black is the smoke
Of a factory at work
Black is cloud
From a thunder storm
Black is as sweet
As black licorice
Black is the color
Of a new night
Sina Analoui, Grade 3
Jeffrey Elementary School, CT

My Favorite Place

Disney World
the water parks
going on the rides
getting souvenirs
my favorite character is Pluto
Victoria Georgiou, Grade 1
Sundance School, NJ

I Am

I am a very smart boy who loves math
I wonder if I can be the best mathematician
I hear spheres falling from the sky
I feel the energy from $e=MC^2$
I want to be the best mathematician
I am a very smart boy who loves math

I pretend I know vector calculus
I feel a hexagon tumbling down
I touch a big octagon
I worry when I think I got something wrong
I cry when I can't do it
I am a very smart boy who loves math

I understand that I make mistakes
I say, "I love pi!"
I dream to know pi to one thousand digits
I try to get really good grades
I hope I finish my math course
I am a very smart boy who loves math
James Pickering, Grade 3
McKinley Elementary School, PA

Keep Christ in Christmas

Jesus is the reason
For the Christmas season.
The presents are so nice,
But it's about the birth of Christ.

Jesus was born on Christmas day,
His only bed was a manger of hay.
The wise men found him cute and warm.
Mary and Joseph helped keep him from harm.
Nicholas Stelly Jr., Grade 3
St Edward the Confessor School, LA

Fall

Fall
Cooler, colorful
Playing, raking, singing.
The leaves are falling.
Autumn
Toby Fox Jr., Grade 3
Chestnut Street Elementary School, PA

Brooke

B eautiful
R esponsible
O utstanding
O utgoing
K ind
E xcellent

Brooke Krantz, Grade 3
Virginia A Boone Highland Oaks Elementary School, FL

The Fall

In the fall, I see fat orange leaves falling off the tree in my yard.
In the fall, I hear plump brown squirrels storing nuts for the winter.
In the fall, I feel a smooth silky blanket warming me up on a cold fall night.
In the fall, I taste yellow crunchy corn at the dinner table.
In the fall, I smell the rushing wind going by me.
In the fall, I don't smell sweet strawberries.

Dakota Rogers, Grade 3
Watsontown Elementary School, PA

The Nightmare in the Chair

Once I had a nightmare
It was really a bad scare
I heard a ferocious noise which was loud
So I peeked out from my covers made out of a cloud
And there sitting in my comfy chair
Was a giant in his underwear
He was tall and tan
He was a scary man
Oh for the love of thee
He is going to eat little old me!
I woke up and my bed was wet
That dream really gave me a sweat!

Daniel Malizia, Grade 3
Infant Jesus School, NH

Skating

Skating is my favorite sport.
It makes me feel like I'm flying.
I jump and I spin
And I dash through the ice.
And when I compete
I'm a champion.

Arnae Molin, Grade 3
Noonan Elementary Academy of Fort Myers, FL

Fall Leaves

Red leaves
Orange leaves
Yellow leaves
Brown leaves
These are the colors of fall

Gracie Kon, Grade 3
Concord Elementary School, PA

Rabbit

A rabbit is as soft as a squishy pillow
it is as white as a cloud
it has big front teeth
his blue eyes
remind of the ocean
He is so furry
and cuddly
like
a Teddy bear.

Luz Valle Lopez, Grade 3
Public School 148 Ruby Allen, NY

The Park Is Fun

I like to play in the park
Swinging on the swings
I love to count to five
And hear the birds sing
Back and forth I go
In the swings
Jesus' name Amen

Beres Strachan, Kindergarten
J E S Memorial SDA School, FL

Colors

I like colors,
Any kind of colors.
Bright colors, dark colors,
Pretty colors, dull colors.
Colors in pictures,
Colors on a house,
Colors with mixes,
Any kind of color.
I like colors.

Grayson Windham, Grade 3
Landmark Christian School, GA

Autumn

Brown leaves are coming
Pumpkin and pecan pie comes
Yellow flowers bloom

Sofia Quartararo, Grade 2
Wellington School, FL

Things I Like About Nature

Birds tweet gratefully
The beautiful smell of flowers
Leaves sway in the wind

J.R. Kidd, Grade 3
The Parke House Academy, FL

Cookies

C ookies are good
O urs are chocolate
O urs are vanilla
K ind of burnt
I cky cookies are bad
E asy to bake some
S o I ate them

Terrian Graves, Grade 3
Bensley Elementary School, VA

Soccer

I like kicking the ball in the net.
I wear a yellow shirt, yellow socks
And black shorts.
We are the yellow team.
One time I was against Olivia.
I kicked the ball so far!
Everybody clapped!
Soccer makes me happy!

Nadav Griver, Kindergarten
United Hebrew Institute, PA

Snowmen

Snowmen are cute.
Snowmen are fun.
Snowmen are cool.
And snowmen are cold.

Mazana Boerboom, Grade 2
Atlantic Elementary School, FL

Sad or Happy

When you see my face you think I'm sad, but I know I'm really happy inside
When I see your face I think you're sad but I know you're also happy inside.
When I look at myself in the mirror I also think I'm sad but all I know is that
I'm really happy inside.

Caitlyn Stoltzfus, Grade 3
St Genevieve School, NJ

Victory

Bases loaded, 2 outs down,
Can't let him hit the ball.
I'm going to throw
Three strikes in a row,
I'm giving it my all!

Here we go — strike ONE, TWO, THREE!
I am happily grinning.
It's the bottom of the 9th —
They very last inning
And guess what? We are winning!

Anthony Robert DelNegro, Grade 3
Noonan Elementary Academy of Fort Myers, FL

The Backward World

I'm so confused and all messed up
I'm going to be down when I should be up.
The seams of my clothes are inside out
Something is wrong, without a doubt.
I walk through the windows and look through the doors.
I walk on the ceilings and look up to see the floor.
My world is backward and my mind is in a whirl.
Oh! This crazy backward world.

Josh Witt, Grade 3
Belfast-Elk Garden Elementary School, VA

Money

M y mom has money to support our family.
O ur school uses money to help students learn.
N o such thing as a four dollar bill.
E veryone should save for the future.
Y ou need a wallet to hold your money.

Sydney Greer, Grade 3
Bensley Elementary School, VA

Red

I am an apple.
I am a ladybug.
I am a rose.
I am red.

Cristina Guevara, Grade 1
Northeast Elementary School, NY

Chanler Green

My name is Chanler Jerome Green.
I like to keep my room clean.
My class assignment for today,
Is to write a poem in a creative way.
It's not easy for me,
But I have to hurry
So I can be free!

Chanler Jerome Green, Grade 3
Coral Cove Elementary School, FL

Police

Police are always on someone's tail
If they catch them they'll go to jail.
Police are rough
Police are tough
They have cuffs
They are buff
Police chase and chase
Until they're face to face.
If someone stole your wreath
It was probably a thief.
But do not worry
The police are coming in a hurry
Now you know
Police are with you as you grow!

Justin Heredia, Grade 3
Marie Durand Elementary School, NJ

Snow

S now is a frozen drop of rain
N ew snow is deep
O n Christmas you usually see snow.
W ind blows snow.

Joseph Pittman, Grade 1
Annie Belle Clark Primary School, GA

Cat

Cat
Fluffy, soft
Clawing, climbing, jump
Happy, proud, love, sad
Kitten

Justin Gilbar, Grade 2
Woodland Elementary School, KY

Merry Christmas

Christmas tree
It has a glowing star
At the top.
It has a lot of decorations.
It has presents under it.
When Santa comes
He eats our cookies
And says
Ohh ohh ohh
Merry Christmas.

Samantha Oughton, Grade 3
Evergreen Elementary School, PA

I Am From

I am from my beautiful bedroom
where my cozy bed is waiting
for me to go into it.
I am from my lovely living room
where my TV is waiting for me
and I am sitting on a couch.
I am from my grassy front yard
where my brown and green tree
is waiting for me to climb.

Kaylin Talley, Grade 1
Berkeley Lake Elementary School, GA

Dear Blaze

Dear Blaze,
You are a cat.
I wish you could go
trick or treating with me,
Then you could eat candy with me.
What would be your favorite kind?

Joseph McCollum, Grade 1
Cool Spring Elementary School, NC

The Night That Is Bright

Stars shine very bright,
Wolves howl very light.
The moon shines as bright as the sun until midnight.
I sleep through the night until daylight.

Kassie Kimble, Grade 2
Evangelical Christian School, TN

Fall

I see the earth changing
With lots of different things
Like houses with Halloween decorations
And leaves turning red, yellow, brown, and green
I smell new things like bonfires
I hear crunch, crunch, crunch
It's fall!! Hooray!

Tommy Billard, Grade 2
Wellington School, FL

Autumn

A pples are in the tree, and I picked them.
U p is where a bird flies in the air.
T hanksgiving is a good time.
U gh! I have to rake the leaves again.
M om gets me a pumpkin for halloween.
N ow the leaves are beautiful and colorful.

Jillian Padgett, Grade 3
Central Park Elementary School, FL

Horse

H orsing around and playing as the days go past.
O h all the stuff you and I can do!
R iding on and on like you just feel like flying!
S oaring round and round!
E ating apples, hay, grass, and oatmeal!!!

Anna Elizabeth Pitney, Grade 3
Stone Academy, SC

What Is a Hamster?

What is a Hamster? A Hamster is cuddly, furry and tiny, too.
What is a Hamster? A Hamster has colorful fur, brown, black, gold and honey, too!
What is a Hamster? A Hamster is a pet and a good one, too!
What is a Hamster? A Hamster has no bark or meow, but a hamster is a pet, my pet!

Veronica Connors, Grade 3
West Lake Elementary School, NC

Love to Cheer

I love to cheerlead
for Del Val.
But sometimes
I'm out of breath.
When we win
I'm proud.
But sometimes
we lose
and I'm not happy
but not mad.
My team
relies on me,
and I have to
rely on them.

Stephanie Coppola, Grade 3
Holland Township School, NJ

Pumpkin Pie/Dessert

Pumpkin pie
pumpkins, yummy
eating, baking, making
Smells great for Thanksgiving.
Dessert

Andrew Cadmus, Grade 2
Consolidated School, CT

Cupcakes

Cupcakes
Frosted, pretty
Saving, keeping, eating
They are the best.
Vanilla

Jordyn Gross, Grade 2
St Andrew School, NY

Beautiful Heart

This looks like a lip.
It's red.
It's a heart.
It's really beautiful.
It looks like an apple.
You can give it to your mom.

Kayla Sullivan, Grade 1
Holland Township School, NJ

What If

What if I could fly?
I might help people.

What if my dad died in the Army?
I might cry really hard.

What if I didn't see my brother ever again?
I would call mom and ask how he is doing.

What if I died?

Sheyenne Barnell, Grade 3
Byrns L Darden Elementary School, TN

A King Was Born

Jesus Christ was born on Christmas night
It was a great honor to see that sight.
The shepherds saw a great star.
That's why they traveled very far.

For in a manger Jesus lay,
There was no danger that whole day.
Angels flying in the sky,
Angels rejoicing for Jesus' cry.

Ashley Maykut, Grade 3
St Edward the Confessor School, LA

Halloween

I see Anna in her vampire costume.
I smell Grandma's tasty cookies.
I hear kids screaming "trick or treat."
I taste my yummy double chocolate candy.
I feel the wind rushing through my hair.

HALLOWEEN

Alexis Cummings, Grade 3
Wellington School, FL

Sea Sounds

It is peaceful at the seashore.
Because I like to hear the sea sounding.
I stand on the beach waiting
to hear the sea pounding.

Danial Ludwig, Grade 1
Four Seasons Elementary School, MD

Autumn

The sky is as blue as the sea.
The sun is as bright as light.
There is an ocean of leaves
and the acorns are hard like marbles.
The leaves crunch like popcorn
as the squirrels prance about.
Pine cones smell spicy and minty
and some leaves blow away with the wind.
Like chameleons, the time is changing.

Lillian Homann, Grade 2
Worthington Hooker School – K-2 Campus, CT

True Friend

My true friend cares about me both in and out,
If I'm in trouble they will give a little shout;
They will always listen, but never shout,
If you want to be my friend, know what friendship's about.

Molly Shacter, Grade 3
Virginia A Boone Highland Oaks Elementary School, FL

Thanksgiving

T hanksgiving is the best of all feasts!
H ow did I find myself in front of a big beast?
A best day turns into a worst day with my brother around.
N othing seems to be right, I'd rather get outta town!
K rabs, turkey, ham, stuffing, gravy, and cheese.
S o good it's easy to squeeze.
G inger cookies and ice cream were dessert, but made me throw up.
I ncluding refreshments, and iced tea in a cup.
V isiting me was Grandma!
I also saw someone else with her, Grandpa!
N ow to me this is a special occasion.
G uess next year I can make invitations!

Camara Wimbish, Grade 3
Dr Martin Luther King Jr School Complex, NJ

My Pets

Once I had two birds.
Their names were Jacko and Flint.
They were my best friends.

Gabrie Knoch, Grade 3
St Mary of the Assumption Catholic School, PA

Golf

The game of golf is fun.
You have to bend your knees.
Try to get a hole in one.
Don't hit it in the trees!

Aim the ball down the green.
Don't send it to the rough.
Swing it straight, try not to lean.
The game of golf is tough!
Christian Troemel, Grade 2
McKinley Elementary School, PA

Apple

Apple
Apple
Oh so bright
Apple
Apple
Nice and white and red
When you bite
It makes a crunch.
Andrew Salmon, Grade 2
Annsville Elementary School, NY

What Is He?

He's not a guppy.
His name's "Hush Puppy."

His eyes are black.
He doesn't quack.

His ears are floppy,
But he's not sloppy.

I can make him talk
Or even walk.

He's warm to hug;
He doesn't have a bug.

Hush Puppy fell on his head,
But he's a puppet, so he's not dead.
Felicity Miller, Kindergarten
The American Academy, PA

My Rabbit

My rabbit is
as fluffy as the clouds
My rabbit is
as white as a crystal
She is as cute
as an angel
She jumps as
high as a frog
She is as cute
as Mrs. Ricupero and
Mrs. Boyle
I love my rabbit
because she is so
sweet her name
is sweetie when
she eats she
crunches and crunches
she wiggles and
wiggles her nose
Sweetie, Sweetie
you are such a treat
Shantel Mena, Grade 3
Public School 148 Ruby Allen, NY

Young and Old

Boy
Young, hyper
Playing, studying, eating
Little kid, tall man
Work, drive, shop
Old, tired
Grandpa
Emmanuel Arias, Grade 1
Oliver Hoover Elementary School, FL

Fun Music

Music
Fun, loud
Singing, dancing, moving
You dance to music.
Awesome!
Jackson McMath, Grade 3
Landmark Christian School, GA

The Small Penguin

The small penguin loves to catch small fish
The small penguin has his own little dish

He cries when he's without his mommy
He cries when he's without his daddy

The small penguin likes to be so cool
The small penguin lives at the North Pole

When he's mad he goes squeak! squeak! squeak!
When he's scared he goes eek! eek! eek!

He loves to ski on his small belly
He loves to shout with lots of glee

He loves to play and play and play
He loves to do that on a snowy day!

Victoria Carcaise, Grade 3
St Alexis School, PA

Happy

G rass is growing
A nd I am at the park.
I sometimes go out for ice cream,
L ike waiting in line.

Gail Guay, Grade 2
Public School 152 School of Science & Technology, NY

I Am From

I am from my awesome bedroom
where my soft blanket is covering me with warmness.
I am from my pink makeup room
where my mirror shows me when I am glancing at it.
I am from my hard front yard
where my cool shiny scooter is sparkling at me.

Sally Sir, Grade 1
Berkeley Lake Elementary School, GA

Birds Flying with Their Friends

The birds are flying
And they went high with their friends
They land together

Vanessa Bahamondes, Grade 2
Virginia A Boone Highland Oaks Elementary School, FL

Teeth

Pain
Teeth tingling
Under the covers
Very sad
I have fewer teeth now!

Kobee Hunt, Grade 3
A L Burruss Elementary School, GA

Letter to Tree

Dear Tree,
I hope you aren't cold
when you lose your leaves.
I hope the snow will cover you
with a pretty white blanket.

Cullen Hensley, Grade 1
Cool Spring Elementary School, NC

School

S chool is fun for my brain
C lass is hard, like math and science
H ard, hard homework
O ur class is fun
O ur knowledge is good
L earning is fun to do

Keion Toler, Grade 3
Bensley Elementary School, VA

My Dad

My dad
is so
nice
we will never
be apart
I love him
from the
bottom of my heart
he plays
with me
we will always be together
Dad
you are always there for me

Jaldeep Singh, Grade 3
Public School 148 Ruby Allen, NY

Flying

I wish I could fly!
Watch the trees go whizzing by.
I don't want wings,
those silly things.
I'll use my arms,
I'll need some charms.
I'll fly like Peter Pan,
I really know I can.
I'll fly so very far,
I'll finally touch a star.
Oh my, oh my,
I'd love to fly!

Elizabeth Cleveland, Grade 3
Infant Jesus School, NH

Here Comes Halloween!

Halloween is here!
Creepy monsters all around.
Trick or treating rocks!

Erin Fullen, Grade 2
Wanamassa Elementary School, NJ

Talking About a Clock

My clock likes to
tick, tock a little
its numbers go up to 12
it comes in different
colors and sizes
it has a minute hand
and an hour hand
tick, tock, tick, tock
I must go!

Elijah Gonzalez, Grade 3
Public School 148 Ruby Allen, NY

The King Cobra

The cobra went hiss slither slather spit
The cobra chased the zebra
The cobra leaped at the zebra
The boy cobra hit the girl cobra
Swoosh swish swift
Soon the cobra raced through the mud

Christian Cheatham, Grade 3
Briarwood Christian School, AL

The Beach

The Frisbee zoomed by my head like a flying saucer
A volleyball flies like a punch
Seagulls singing like children hollering
Children playing like wild bulls
Wet dogs smell like trash
Suntan lotion smells like cooking butter
The sea water tastes like sour candy
The sand tastes brittle to my teeth
The water makes me feel three thousand pounds
The sand feels like lotion on my skin
It makes me feel like a child.

Christopher Morgan, Grade 3
Bailey Elementary School, NC

What Is Pink?

Pink is roses opening in the spring,
Pink is the sunset,
Pink is the taste of fresh squeezed pink lemonade
And fresh out-of-the-oven baked strawberry cake,
Pink is what you smell like when you put on perfume,
Pink feels happy,
Pink is the color of my soft pink blanket,
When I think of pink, I think of summer,
Pink sounds like a pig oinking.

Cynthia Reed, Grade 3
Scott Elementary School, MO

Armadillo

Armadillos roll into a ball
Armadillos are not very tall
This animal is a mammal
And is always nocturnal
Always traveling in small bands
They sometimes like digging in the sand
They have hard bony shells called the scutes
And also have canines but no incisor tooth
Armadillos live in trees and so are called terrestrial
Their skeleton is rigid and is axial
They feed on all kinds of invertebrates
Armadillos do not go to sleep when the sun sets

Pavan Savio, Grade 3
St Alexis School, PA

Skating on Ice

They drift gracefully
Day or nighttime they practice
Slide across the ice
Catherine Magos, Grade 3
Holland Township School, NJ

Priya

Priya
Funny, thin
Playing, tricking, climbing
I like tricking people
Priy Priy
Priya Bommaraju, Grade 2
St Stephen's School, NY

Stars

I like that
a star is yellow.

You see them
in the sky!

It reminds me
of
astronauts.
Nicholas Padovani, Grade 1
Holland Township School, NJ

Amazing Fall

Squirrels gathering nuts
People are leaving the beach
Plants change red and gold.
Alec M. Duquette, Grade 3
Ross Elementary School, PA

Hannah

H elpful
A wesome
N ice
N iece
A mazing
H opeful and helping
Hannah Freeman, Grade 2
Park Elementary School, AR

God's Mightiness

God He is all mighty
He is all powerful and He is my strength.
For now I have him in my heart
And He and He only will be with me.
He is with me when I am in bed.
He gives me courage in hard times.
So if you follow your God
You will then be saved.
Emma Johnson, Grade 2
Evangelical Christian School, TN

My Bike

My bike is fun to ride;
It calms me down when I'm upset.
When I ride my bike I'm relaxed and joyful.
I ride with speed, energy and great power.
Then when I'm done riding
I feel joyful that I have my bike.
Justin Francis, Grade 3
John Hus Moravian School, NY

Cats

I like cats in summer,
Cats can jump,
And scratch and play,
And eat fish and mice,
And cats can eat cat's food.
Cats can rollover,
And sit and bathe.
Mena Botros, Grade 3
St Joseph Catholic Grammar School, NJ

Pumpkins

I went to trick-or-treat.
I wanted something sweet.
Then I saw some pumpkins.
Some were painted green.
Some looked really mean.
Some looked happy. Some looked sad.
Some looked nervous. Some looked mad.
Pumpkins, pumpkins everywhere.
What if pumpkins are growing in my hair?
Zoë Aleksa, Grade 3
Nativity Catholic School, FL

My Fish

My fish is so colorful,
My fish is so wonderful,
My fish is a Betta
And it eats other fish.
That is something that I would not wish!
I think she is happy,
But she's not very nappy,
She sleeps in the dark
And at night it's very quiet.
I get her lots of food —
The people in the store make me buy it.
Everybody likes to see her swimming around;
She is like a queen…
She should be crowned!
She is a wonder, a good wish, a sight.
Wouldn't it be a real delight, to have a fish like that?
It would be much better
Than a mouse or a rat,
Critters we were going to buy at the store.
Those rodents, they would be such a bore!

Natalie Cotter, Grade 3
John Ward Elementary School, MA

The Amazing Beach

Birds are soaring in the blue sky
Mountains of sand piling on my brother
The sand is as hot as ashes coming out of a blazing fire
The waves are as cold as snow on a winter day
The aroma of hot dogs on a summer day
The scent of amazing trout
Waves crashing down like roaring lions
Pelicans screaming their lungs out
The nasty taste of salt water fills my mouth
The cool taste of fresh water revives me
I feel happy and content.

Kaitlyn Daniel, Grade 3
Bailey Elementary School, NC

Winter

Snow is in winter
Snow always turns to water
It will be freezing

Gabrielle Barnes, Grade 2
Virginia A Boone Highland Oaks Elementary School, FL

Costumes

Costumes are different in many ways,
Costumes are for dressing up in,
Costumes are for Halloween,
Costumes can be scary or funny,
Costumes make you look different,
Costumes can be fun to scare people.

Maria Bottisti, Grade 2
Marie Curie Institute, NY

What Do I See?

I see a chalkboard.
I see a flag.
I see paper.
I do not see a vampire.

Demitrius Wall, Grade 1
Northeast Elementary School, NY

Geckos

They are very fast
I saw them in Jamaica
They are cold blooded

Chance Chavies, Grade 3
Miami Country Day School, FL

An Alien from Mars

I once saw an alien from Mars.
It went in my brother's room
and broke all his cars.
She said, "See ya later"
When she saw my pet gator
I said to myself, "How bizarre."

Alexia Peralta, Grade 3
Coral Cove Elementary School, FL

Wrestle

W ild
R ough
E nergy
S trong
T ough
L imber
E ndurance

Bryce Tumberg, Grade 3
Reidville Elementary School, SC

Wampanoags/Indians

Wampanoags
Nice, helpful
Farming, fishing, canoeing
They would help others
Indians.

Pilar Betts, Grade 3
Wapping Elementary School, CT

Born Free

America is the place.
Freedom is the case.
We're born free
That's the way it should be.
Red, White and Blue
America is true.
It's who you are inside
It doesn't matter your size.
We're all strong in a way.
So today is the day that I say
We're all special and born Free!

Amanda Sickler, Grade 3
Vassar Road School, NY

My Favorite Color

I like blue.
The sky is blue.
Cookie Monster is blue.
My dad's car is blue.
I like blue.

Julius Lorenzi, Grade 1
Northeast Elementary School, NY

Heart

Loving, candy
cry, beating
courage, kindness
sweet, love,
joy, peace
faith, February,
red, veins
courage, move blood

Bethany Mullins, Grade 2
Hilton Head Christian Academy, SC

The King's Crown

I see crowns on many people.
But crowns should be on Jesus Christ.
Most people think crowns should be on kings.
Jesus is a king so he has a crown.
When you think of crowns
You should think of Jesus.

Emma Baltz, Grade 2
Evangelical Christian School, TN

A Swan's Song

Oh swan your song is bright and gay,
You often give a musical display.

You sound like a trumpet, loud and clear
For, of losing, your talent you never fear.

You sing in the morning, you sing in the night,
Your song is always very bright.

Emmylou Kidder, Grade 3
Mary Walter Elementary School, VA

Autumn Is Here

Some people like to play ball
when the leaves drop in the fall.
This is how I describe fall.
Leaves twirling, swirling, whirling, twisting;
magic in the air.
Great things happen when colored leaves appear everywhere.
Fall is beautiful. Autumn is here for me and you.

Corinne Walker, Grade 3
Vassar Road School, NY

Fall

In the fall, I see loud, chilly, messy, small children running down the road like road runners.
In the fall, I hear gray, fuzzy, plush, itty-bitty geese flying over me.
In the fall, I feel a comfortable, fuzzy, decorative sweater on my cold body.
In the fall, I smell warm, roasted, cinnamon, apple pie upon my plate.
In the fall, I taste roasted, big, incredible tasting crunchy turkey alongside the corn at the Thanksgiving table.
In the fall, I do not taste red juicy cold small strawberries in my mouth.

Erica Keim, Grade 3
Watsontown Elementary School, PA

October Again

Every October, I rake the leaves.
I wish I didn't hear that truck, please.
Oh no, a pumpkin fell out.
It makes me sad about that.
I'll push it in the street.
I hope it doesn't splat, for pete's sake.
I'll bake pies, treats, pudding and cake.
So I'll bake and bake and bake.
I'll sell them all I hope
Or, I'll eat them with some help.

David Nelson, Grade 3
Nativity Catholic School, FL

The Frog

There once was a frog
Who was a very ugly green.

His friends all laughed.
They were very, very mean.

Then on Halloween,
When the frog's friends came,

They never got their candy.
They got a big scary thing.

There was no candy.
There was a monster instead.

They all ran for their lives,
Leaving the frog monster behind.

Lindsey Stauber, Grade 3
St Alexis School, PA

Halloween

Halloween Halloween
Bats goblins witches
flying everywhere going boo
Boo. But when it's Halloween
I say I love
You.

Makiah Jackson, Grade 2
Southside Elementary School, KY

Pumpkins, Pumpkins

Pumpkin, pumpkin, pumpkin bread
Roasted seeds and chocolate leaves.
Pumpkins, pumpkins here and there
Pumpkins growing everywhere!
We have lots of pumpkins here
And way over there.
Their vines are not like lines
But they can be pretty fine.
They grow in the autumn time
And they do quite fine.
From looking at all of those pumpkins
I think it is time for a treat!

John Zielinski, Grade 3
Nativity Catholic School, FL

My Favorite Sport

Alex Rodriguez sleeps
And he plays third base,
Plus he bats on fourth,
And trips on his shoe lace.
When he hits a homerun
He has a smile on his face.

Shai Silverstein, Grade 2
Yeshiva Ketana of Long Island, NY

Michael

M agnificent
I nnocent
C lever
H eroic
A dventurous
E legant
L ovely

Michael Savoyski, Grade 2
Long Meadow Elementary School, CT

My Favorite Color

I like pink.
The gum is pink.
The balloon is pink.
The backpack is pink.
I like pink.

Gracie Eccleston, Grade 1
Northeast Elementary School, NY

Dance

Dance, dance, dance that's what I love to do.
From tap, ballet and even jazz too!
Every dance has a different step in a different shoe.
Dance, dance, dance that's what I love to do.

When I dance I twist and twirl,
It makes me such a happy girl.
It is so much fun to twist and twirl.
I like it so much because it makes me a free girl.

On the stage you see glitz and grace,
It becomes such a magical place.
All the dance moves put a smile on my face.
As they move along at a different pace.

Dance, dance, dance that's what I love to do.
It makes me feel so special too!
Dance, dance, dance that's what I love to do.
Try it sometimes — maybe you would love it too!

Anna Laura Cobb, Grade 3
Pike Liberal Arts School, AL

Princess Bauer

There was a girl name Princess Bauer.
Who lived in a tower.
It was the last hour.
While she was waiting for her prince she watered her flower.
Such a beautiful princess was Miss Bauer.

Cassie Cornelius, Grade 2
St Mary of the Assumption Catholic School, PA

Fall

In fall leaves look like a rainbow. It is beautiful.
But when leaves fall off the trees they look dead.
By being so cold fall lets us know winter is around the corner.
Fall is a time that warms my heart, I enjoy it so.
I love to play outside, but it's too cold — I freeze.
I am glad to come in, because mom makes me hot chocolate.
I always love to jump in leaf piles like a jackrabbit.
I do not enjoy raking leaves. It gives me blisters.
But when fall is over I am pleased
Because Christmas is not far away!

Maximilian Bossi, Grade 3
Marie Durand Elementary School, NJ

Witches/Scary

Witches
Big hat, big nose
Flying, stirring, scaring
Stir their bubbling brew.
Scary
Kaylyn Ferony, Grade 2
Consolidated School, CT

Pumpkins/Jack-o-lanterns

Pumpkins
Orange, round
Picking, growing, rolling
Usually round or flat.
Jack-o-lanterns
Sydney Collentine, Grade 2
Consolidated School, CT

Pizza

I like pizza pie.
I like the cheese piled high.
I save the crust for last.
Then I eat it really fast!
Frank Ross Cesare, Grade 3
Our Lady of Hope School, NY

Moon Shoes

The moon looks like cheese!
It's white.

You would see it in the night.
It reminds me of a cookie!

It glows too.
Charlotte Molter, Grade 1
Holland Township School, NJ

My Favorite Place

Italy
Sorrento
Capri
swimming in the ocean
happy
Kelly Lawrence, Grade 1
Sundance School, NJ

My Brother

My brother is funny
He really likes honey
My brother has a hat
His name is Zach
I love my brother
I wish I had another
Kailei Caggins, Grade 2
Herbert J Dexter Elementary School, GA

Night Time

I shut my eyes softly
The dark spooky night
The sound of owls howling in the smooth air
Do birds like the night?
A dark spooky feeling
Pops into my head
I shut my eyes again softly
Once again!
Shira Malka Mittel, Grade 2
Bais Yaakov Academy for Girls of Queens, NY

Basketball

basket, ball, court
what an awesome sport
throw, catch, run
playing basketball is lots of fun
dribble, coach, score
It's time to go but I want to play some more!
Caylla Bush, Grade 3
Broadway Elementary School, NC

What If

What if I get a puppy for being good?
I might dress it up in clothes.

What if my Mom was in the Army?
I could cry all night.

What if my brother got married?
I would visit him and his wife all the time.

What if I grow up and become famous?
Kira Kelly, Grade 3
Byrns L Darden Elementary School, TN

Leaves/Maple

Leaves
Red, big
Falling, blowing, raking
I like raking leaves
Maple

Lexi Walton, Grade 3
Chestnut Street Elementary School, PA

Reading

R eading is fun!
E arly in the morning…I read.
A t school… I read a lot.
D uring lunch… I read
I n the afternoon…I read a book,
N ot when I am sleeping, I do not read!
G o read a book sometime…it's fun!

Jalina Alosi, Grade 2
Dr Martin Luther King Jr School Complex, NJ

Grandpa

Grandpa ever since I can remember
You have taught me many important things
Like on hot summer nights
You can turn over your pillow
Find coolness on the other side

Daisha Hall, Grade 3
McKinley Elementary School, PA

My Mom*

My mom,
She is the bomb
When she was wed
The two beautiful words she said,
"I do!"
She stuck by our sides and loved us true,
But now she's gone
And it's past dawn
When we found out
She was without a doubt,
In her sweet dome
My loving mom was finally home.

Stephanie Palma, Grade 3
Marie Durand Elementary School, NJ
**Dedicated to Susan D. Panichelli*

Giraffe

My neck is very long
To hold me up it must be strong.

On my body I have spots
Shaped like big tater tots.

I eat leaves from a tree
I'm very tall as you can see.

I have a very long tongue
I hope it does not get stung!

You will see me at the zoo
And in Africa too.

I have a very short tail
But if you pull it I will wail!

I look funny, but do not laugh
Cause I am a *giraffe*!

Delaney Lisco, Grade 3
St Alexis School, PA

Autumn

Autumn has life, air
Autumn has sunlight, leaves fall
Autumn is breezy

Alyssa Stewart, Grade 2
Wellington School, FL

My Dog

My Dog
He is on the log
He is clean
He is mean

Milly Hernandez, Grade 1
Northeast Elementary School, NY

Fall Leaves

Leaves are on the tree.
Leaves are falling to the ground.
Leaves are on the ground.

Jose Jimenez, Grade 2
Weston Elementary School, NJ

Family Days

Even though some days are rough
And you've really had enough
Be happy because the best days
Are with your family
Good or bad.

Hunter Gutierrez, Grade 1
Cedar Creek Elementary School, NJ

Jasmine

J elly and peanut butter sandwiches
A llie, my best friend
S ocks and shoes I can put them on
M y friends
I can dress myself
N et for butterfly catching
E at apples

Jasmine Reynolds, Kindergarten
Eden Gardens Magnet School, LA

White Tip Sharks

They are fast and smart.
Live in the Caribbean.
Can eat piranhas.

Jesse Grosman, Grade 3
Miami Country Day School, FL

Penguins

Penguins pip.
Penguins hop.
Penguins hide, hide, hide!

Mathew Sabolenko, Grade 1
Northeast Elementary School, NY

Girls

Girls
pretty lovely
joyful playful restful
happy sad scared worried
running skipping playing
bright smart
kids

Ally Gresham, Grade 3
Blakeney Elementary School, GA

September

S eptember is one of my favorite months.
E veryone likes fall.
P icking apples is fun in the fall.
T ime to go back to school for me.
E verything is colorful in the fall.
M y mom does not want to go back to school.
B aseball is ending very soon.
E ating apples.
R aking leaves is fun.

Nicole Finn, Grade 2
St Stephen's School, NY

What Now?

What now? I don't have anything to do,
Except to tie and untie my shoe.
A rainy day does not help at all,
For then all I do is complain and bawl.
A sunny day might help a lot,
For then I can skateboard and make a stick cot.
You know, I'd wish it would rain all day,
So then I can be lazy and don't have to play.

Minh-Anh Dinh, Grade 3
Idlewild Elementary School, NC

Football

Muddy, brown field and a brown paper bag colored ball.
Passing, fumbling, touchdown!
I feel like a tiger running so fast that the other team can't even see me.
Some day I'll run as fast as lightning.
Passing, fumbling, touchdown!

Noah Washington, Grade 2
Worthington Hooker School – K-2 Campus, CT

These Are Fall Things to Me

In the fall, I feel my warm and soft coat on a cold day.
In the fall, I smell pine cones that are very pointy
and that are falling from a big tree.
In the fall, I hear the fireplace crackle and the smoke comes out like crazy.
In the fall, I taste the warm chocolaty cocoa and I put in sticky marshmallows.
In the fall, I see trees that are bare
because the wind blows really fast and winter is coming.
In the fall, I don't see buds that are blooming on trees.

Kaitlyn Bittenbender, Grade 3
Watsontown Elementary School, PA

Snowflakes

Snowflakes are pretty
Snowflakes glimmer all day long
Snowflakes are so bright.

Preetma Singh, Grade 2
Coral Cove Elementary School, FL

Dolphins

Dolphins live in the ocean,
Where there is lots of motion.

Dolphins like the salty spray,
Where they can have fun and play.

Dolphins eat squid and fish,
And catch them before they go swish.

Dolphins can jump up and down,
Splashing the water all through town.

Dolphins like chasing boats,
Swimming by them as they float.

I like dolphins very much,
They are very smooth to touch.

Vivian Chen, Grade 3
St Alexis School, PA

The Spaghetti Is Ready

My favorite food is spaghetti.
I can't wait for it to be ready.
I like it with sauce or soup.
Most of all, I like to twirl it in a loop.
Finally, it is in my dish.
Mom, thank you for granting my wish.

Michael Azzara, Grade 3
Our Lady of Hope School, NY

Fall

Leaves falling from trees.
Jumping into crunchy leaves,
Windy and cooler

Kiana Hernandez, Grade 3
Coral Cove Elementary School, FL

Equestrian

Look at that white pole,
your brown horse is super fast!
Good job with that jump!

Allison Moore, Grade 3
Holland Township School, NJ

School: My Favorite Place

School is fun.
There is lots to learn.
Reading is cool.
Teachers are fun.
Principals are nice.
Lunches are delicious.
Homework is the best.
Come with me to my school.

Brandon Nwokeji, Grade 1
Grahamwood Elementary School, TN

Sammy Snake

Sammy snake is a sassy snake
So small as can be
Slithers silently slowly sliding
Across the grass you see.

Baylee Gore, Grade 3
A L Burruss Elementary School, GA

Plants

Plants live in the dirt.
They have a stem, roots and leaves.
Roots take in water.

Taegan Charles, Grade 3
Miami Country Day School, FL

Autumn

All the leaves falling,
Autumn is calling.
Can we make a leaf pile, please?
Thanksgiving turkey, stuffing, and peas.
Off we go to trick or treat,
Look at the shimmer in the street.
Leaves catching in the breeze,
All those leaves make me sneeze!

Allison Gracie, Grade 3
Birches Elementary School, NJ

Scarecrows

Scarecrows
Short, tall
Standing, shivering, frightening
Scarecrows can be scary.
Field

Daphne Buzard, Grade 3
Chestnut Street Elementary School, PA

Nature

Nature is beautiful day and night.
Sunny, starry, dark, and bright.

Birds chirp, owls hoo
The crickets help them too

Warm wind, brisk breeze
Makes me want to catch some z's

Daydream, night dream, light blue, dark blue,
In nature all of your dreams come true.

Maya Suarez, Grade 2
Forest Street Elementary School, NJ

An Everlasting Light

The Sun is a pumpkin
floating way up high;
with a billion seeds
right by its side.

The Sun has a candle
that lights up the entire sky;
that probably won't burn out
until after we die.

Hugh Overman, Grade 3
Hunter GT Magnet Elementary School, NC

There Once Was a Boy from the Moon

There once was a boy from the moon.
He wanted to go home very soon.
But he tripped on his back,
And fell off track,
That is the end of this tune.

Caroline Cohen, Grade 3
John Ward Elementary School, MA

Leopards

Leopards. Dangerous.
Because they are very strong.
They run really fast!
Sara Seewald, Grade 1
United Hebrew Institute, PA

My Favorite Place

Costa Rica
surfin the waves
coconuts, water
crabby beaches
happy!
Jared Epstein, Grade 1
Sundance School, NJ

Jonathan

J ohn Cena fan
O atmeal eater
N ephew
A ctor
T ough
H unter
A rtist
N eat
Jonathan Halcomb, Grade 2
Park Elementary School, AR

Fish

It looks like a sword.
Fish are blue.
Fish live in the sea.
Some fish are little.
Some are big!
Fish are fast!
Andrew Buniowksi, Grade 1
Holland Township School, NJ

My Favorite Place

Maine
swimming, lobster claw
fishing and boating
fun with my family
Jeremy Enslin, Grade 1
Sundance School, NJ

Bull Master

I like bulls.
They look buff and tough.
They are so soft and furry.
I like bulls because I feel
Big and strong like a bull.
Sometimes when I play football
I run over people and they fly up in the air.
When someone makes me mad,
I can attack them.
Harrison Johnson, Grade 3
Lee A Tolbert Community Academy, MO

Nishey, the Dog

I gave him his bone.
When I was a little baby, he jumped on me.
He felt fuzzy, and he was white.
He jumped in the pool.
He licked me.
He stuck his head out the car window.
He had accidents in the house.
Coby Kornfeld, Kindergarten
United Hebrew Institute, PA

Anthony

Funny, helpful, nice
likes to play with my daddy
I play lots of sports
Anthony Morreale, Grade 3
Thelma L Sandmeier Elementary School, NJ

My Car

I have a car that looks like my bed.
It is shiny and it is red.

My car goes very fast.
In a race it is never last.

My car is just a toy.
That I have since I was a boy.

That's why my car is special to me.
Because I got it for free.
Julian Aguirre, Grade 3
Mother Seton Inter Parochial School, NJ

Fall

It's the first day of fall.
The leaves are falling.
The wind is breezing
and the hot air is dazzling.
The cold air is coming,
but the sun is shining.
Goodbye summer
Whoo, whoo, Halloween is coming.

Casey Solomon, Grade 2
Robert E Lee Expressive Arts Elementary School, MO

Clouds Above Me

The clouds above me look like ice cream.
The clouds above me move like wind.
The clouds above me might smell like perfume.
The clouds above me might feel like silk.
The clouds above me might sound like the wind.
The clouds above me might taste like whipped cream.
The clouds above me make me feel soft.
Aren't clouds fluffy?

Anasia Jones, Grade 2
Clover Street School, CT

Izzy

There once was a rocker named Izzy,
Whose music made everyone dizzy.
And when he stopped playing,
The trees stopped swaying,
So Izzy was swaying no more.

Sarina Caskill, Grade 3
Virginia A Boone Highland Oaks Elementary School, FL

I Like Summer

I like summer.
Do you know why?
You get to have ice cream.
Don't be shy.
Do you know when summer starts?
I just like summer when it starts.
So shed your sweaters
And put some short sleeves and shorts on
Before you get out of your house.

Brianna Chachoute, Grade 2
Philadelphia Performing Arts Charter School, PA

Thanksgiving

Thanksgiving is sweet
Lots of food to eat!
Turkey, mashed potatoes, and stuffing
And lots of activities to do!
I like to watch the big parade
Hope those memories won't fade!
Wherever you go, whatever you do,
Happy Thanksgiving from me to you!

Nikolas Gavin, Grade 3
Birches Elementary School, NJ

Lions

L ike to eat meat
I nteresting
O nly cats
N ot tamed
S een in Africa

Manuela Arroyave, Grade 2
Broadway Elementary School, NC

Fall Is Fun

Fall is fun! Fall is fun!
It is a good time to run.
I hear squirrels chatter.
The leaves are all scattered.
Fall is fun. Do you like fall too?
We jump up and down.
It's the right season for you.

Grayson Roberts, Grade 2
Eagle's View Academy, FL

Lion-ku

Roar, roar, hear me roar,
sneaking, sneaking, roar, roar, roar,
Bite, biting, roar, run!

Abigail Inman, Grade 2
Paine Primary School, AL

Leaves

Red, orange, yellow;
leaves are changing colors now.
Jumping into leaves

Lucia Farina, Grade 3
Coral Cove Elementary School, FL

The Jelly Fish

I am a jelly fish
I bite fingers and bzzzz hand
and be with jelly fish friends.

Jennyfer Chavez, Grade 1
Forest Street Elementary School, NJ

A Girl Named Sue

There once was a girl named Sue.
Who wore a size fifteen shoe.
She tripped and she fell.
You could hear her yell.
All the way to Timbuktu.

Nick Cannone, Grade 3
Memorial School, NH

Powder

Powder, oh Powder,
I hate you so.
I scowl at you
And I stare at you,
You evil foe.
The reason I hate you is
because of this,
My allowance is high
It's a thousand!!!
But the only amount I
Can buy with my ounce
of money is powder!!!
A mountain of powder!!!
All I eat is powder!!!
Now I am a coward
and that's it.
Oh powder oh powder
I hate you!

Sunil Rajan, Grade 3
Herndon Elementary School, VA

Penguins

Penguins flop.
Penguins hide.
Penguins waddle, waddle, waddle!

Evesha Harry, Grade 1
Northeast Elementary School, NY

Playing Basketball

I see defense!
I see dribbling!
I see shooting!
I see offense!
I see Ben doing a hook shot!
They beat the hardest team!
Basketball is the best sport I ever played!
I love basketball because I play it!

Dovid Seewald, Kindergarten
United Hebrew Institute, PA

My Name Is Kyle

My name is Kyle,
I like to smile,
as I jump into a pile of toys!

My name is Kyle,
I have a cat who likes
rats and is fat!

My name is Kyle,
I want to be a clone trooper
because I think they are super duper!

My name is Kyle,
I like cartoons,
they put me in a good mood!
What about you?

Kyle Joslin, Grade 1
Thomas Jefferson Elementary School, VA

Karate

We follow the instructors every command
Which includes forward horse stand.
If we do what we are told, he compliments us,
If we do not he throws a fuss.
When we leave him we bow
This he taught us how.
We learn many ways to kick
So many it makes me sick.
It teaches us self defense
Doesn't that make a lot of sense.

Kayla Newton, Grade 3
Marie Durand Elementary School, NJ

Penguins

Penguins hop.
Penguins pip.
Penguins dive, dive, dive!

Marya Penaranda, Grade 1
Northeast Elementary School, NY

Music Room

In the music room…
The drums go
Boom! Boom!
The cymbals go
Crash! Crash!
The trumpets go
Bum badadadada
Bum dadadadadumdumdum
That is why…
I love the music room!

Alicia Hardison, Grade 2
Annsville Elementary School, NY

My Fish

She wiggles her tail
it goes splish, splash
She is as orange
as the sunset
She is as soft
as a cloud
When she
hears music
she begins
to dance
around
and around
in her bowl
She goes
up and down
until she gets
tired
her name
is
Flower

Dayana Panora, Grade 3
Public School 148 Ruby Allen, NY

The Lucky Little Leprechaun

Lucky Leprechaun
Under the rainbow
Little Lucky Leprechaun
With a Pot of Gold.

He's so lucky
Nothing happens to him
Except —
Good luck!

You better catch Lucky
Before time's up.
If you don't catch Lucky
Bad luck comes.

He takes his Pot of Gold
And runs, runs, runs
And all you've got to say is —
That was fun!

Isaiah Bowman, Grade 3
Ocean Academy, NJ

A Fall Day

A fall day, A fall day,
I want to go out and play today.
The leaves are falling,
The sky is blue.
Now all that I need is you.
Let's go to the park,
And take a slide.
Maybe even 100 times.
Good-bye! Good-bye!
I'll see you soon.
I have to go now.
Bye-Bye to you!

Adriana Simiriglio, Grade 3
Birches Elementary School, NJ

Race Track

Cars are cool and fast.
They race on concrete and dirt.
Past the checkered flag.

Jordan Balcom, Grade 2
St Peter the Apostle School, GA

I Am From

I am from my cozy bedroom
where my cute cat is in
my lovely blanket.
I am from my loud TV room where
my cool games are played.
I am from my clean backyard where I push my truck.

Elijah Kernahan, Grade 1
Berkeley Lake Elementary School, GA

Football

Football is my second favorite sport
but if you play with the pros
you might get injured.
You run, you pass, you kick, you punt,
you catch, you drop it, you kick a field goal,
you fumble, you intercept a pass, and you score.
It is fun to play and fun to watch.
Terrel Owens is my favorite player in football.
I have a lot of fun playing the game
and watching the game.

Bryan Camuso, Grade 3
Evergreen Elementary School, PA

The Magical Feathers

Outside my house was a very bad weather.
Which made the birds lose each and every feather.
The feathers few around.
And made a circle that was round.
So I went out with my coat.
But saw an angry goat.
Then the goat started to chase me.
The goat was so clean he didn't have one flea.
I started to shout "help, help, help!"
But the goat just said "yelp, yelp, yelp!"
Suddenly, a feather landed on the goat's head.
Then, the goat turned into a dirty but soft bed.
Just than another feather fell on the bed which turned into a boss.
The boss caught a feather and turned into a person who plays lacrosse.
I caught a feather and turned into a bird.
"I'd better go home," I preferred
I wanted to go home to get some wash.
But instead, I just said "Oh my gosh!"

Aryton Hoi, Grade 3
Infant Jesus School, NH

Red Heart
Love
It reminds me of X's and O's.
They stand for hugs and kisses.
It looks like a diamond.
Carly McCormick, Grade 1
Holland Township School, NJ

The Bee
Buzz buzz
Sting sting
Oh no!
I have to go!
Jessica Ashmore, Grade 2
Trinity North Elementary School, PA

Snuggles
Snuggles
Adorable, nice
Running, eating, growing
Snuggles is cute!
Pet
Emily O'Brien, Grade 3
Evergreen Elementary School, PA

Green
I am like my eyes.
I am grass.
I am leaves.
I am green.
Jeffrey Godoy, Grade 1
Northeast Elementary School, NY

Flowers
Flowers are red
and blue,
and purple,
and yellow,
and white.
So many good colors!
Flowers give nectar and pollen to bees.
Little flowers are good.
Flowers so pretty.
George Loughrin, Grade 1
Alvaton Elementary School, KY

To the Beach
The water was hot and cold
The sand was very hot
There were many rocks
The water
was dirty
full of seaweed
There were
so many waves
big ones and small ones
My feet were burning and
My hair felt like fire
My sandals
felt as hot as the sun
my goggles
felt like toast
so,
I jumped back
in the water
oooh, sooo
cold!!
Jayleen Miranda Reyes, Grade 3
Public School 148 Ruby Allen, NY

Love
When I'm sitting oh so sad
You come up and make me glad
Your smile is oh so sweet
My love for you is now complete
Rachael Cross, Grade 3
Evergreen Elementary School, PA

Baseball
We play in the spring,
If we win, we get a ring.
My favorite player is David Wright,
He plays hard day and night.
When it comes to stealing a base,
I always win the race.
When I swing hard,
The ball leaves the yard.
There are nine men on the field.
Their gloves act like a shield.
Ryan Neuweiler, Grade 3
Our Lady of Hope School, NY

Spring Turns to Summer

Spring is here,
Bees, birds, butterflies are here too,
The sun brings sunlight,
Bees get honey and nectar from the flowers,

Now it is summer,
Summer is very very hot,
I swim and I splish-splash in the water,
We go on vacation in the summer,
Ahhhhhhhh a shark is coming,
Crunch, crunch.

Barron Wei, Grade 2
Public School 229 Dyker, NY

Fall

All day long jumping in leaves.
Silly me,
Falling on my knees.
Pumpkin picking in the patch.
I thought my pumpkin looked
Cool like that.
Kids dressed up for Halloween,
Some looking scary it made me scream.
Leaves falling down.
One boy dressed up as a clown.
Too scary for me.
I had to look down.

Nina Orsimarsi, Grade 3
Birches Elementary School, NJ

Ice Dog Gets Sick

Ruff, puff, ice dog what?
It can't be true.
Could I be catching the flu for real?
No, no, I have a show, oh no!
I've got to get better soon.
I should go to my room.
Ruff, yeah, I got a doctor's appointment.
Wow, nothing bad, will feel better soon.
Cool, I get to go to my ice show!
It's amazing, you know it's true.
Oh doctor, I love you!

Caroline Jones, Grade 3
Briarwood Christian School, AL

School

School is
fun to me.
I like to learn.
I like to go to school.
School is
special.
School is
reading books.
School rules.

Taylor Whitfield, Grade 1
Broadway Elementary School, NC

The Cloud

The giant black cloud
in the dark stormy sky
galloped like a knight on a horse
charging at another knight in the forest

Dalton Shettle, Grade 3
Wellington School, FL

My Dog Bruno

M y Buddy
Y ou will like him

D oesn't play when biting
O nly dog in the house
G oes to the bathroom outside

B runo is funny when he flips
R ides in the car
U sually bites everybody
N ot nice about biting
O ften bites

Preston Whiten, Grade 3
Reidville Elementary School, SC

Baseball

Getting the ball, clapping
Announcer speaking, sliding on base.
Red Sox win! Yeah!
I love the Red Sox!

Michael Fenlason, Grade 2
Clover Street School, CT

Penguins

Penguins pip.
Penguins hop.
Penguins flop, flop, flop!

Katelyn Vasquez, Grade 1
Northeast Elementary School, NY

Friends

Friends are caring and they are fun.
Friends are great, they help you too.

They never say to go away,
They're helpful, they are sharing.

The only thing better is love and family,
but to me friendship is the answer.

Danielle DeVito, Grade 1
Alpena Elementary School, AR

Seasons Are

Winter is
white
freezing
cozy inside
flaky.

Spring is
blooming
growing
time for baby animals
pretty bursting flowers.

Summer is
playful
freedom from school
hang out time
rejoiceful.

Fall is
leaves crunching
changing color
time to go back to school
lovely.

Shaunell Holcombe, Grade 3
Reidville Elementary School, SC

Halloween

Halloween is fun.
You can go trick or treating.
You can put up spooky decorations.
You can carve a pumpkin.
You can dress up in a costume.
Halloween is fun because you can roast pumpkin seeds.

Joseph Scherreik, Grade 3
St Mary's School, NJ

Ode to My Stuffed Dog

I have had you forever.
You remind me of my dog Titus,
that died when I was a baby.
Your eyes look like brownies.
That is why I named you Brownie.
Your cotton is as soft as a pillow.
Your fur is as shiny as glass.
You keep me warm at night,
when I am cold.
When your nose is wet it,
actually feels like a real dog's nose.
I always play with you.
I hope I will always have you.

Mackenzie Ewing, Grade 2
Worthington Hooker School – K-2 Campus, CT

Twilight's Gift

A cerise and peach sky awakens the day by erasing the stars off the blackboard.
The wind carries the birds to the trees.
I walk down the streets, the street lights flicker.
I can see the autumn leaves dancing in the rocky road.
I pass by the bakery; the smell of doughnuts makes my stomach rumble and growl.
It is so hard to tell what time it is.
A crack opens between night and day.
I hear the soft sound of the hummingbirds drawing nectar in the dawn light.
The moment the town clock strikes 6:00 am,
the mosquitoes disperse through the air.
Cars begin to fill the road into the town square.
As I walk down the road I see dew sparkled spider webs
between branches on the tree.
I'm home now. I shut the wooden door with excitement.
I tell my parents the adventure of twilight's gift.

Erica Lynn Capobianco, Grade 3
Jeffrey Elementary School, CT

Captain Mickey

Michael
Fast, twin
Running, playing, jumping
I play ice hockey
Mickey

Michael Pappano, Grade 2
St Stephen's School, NY

Football

People yelling touchdown!
They cheer for football.
people are tackling,
We win!
A great football game.

Myles Kitchens, Grade 2
Clover Street School, CT

Deer/Fawn

Deer
Swift, spotted
Playing, jumping, staring
Running and jumping around.
Fawn

Amanda Marsh, Grade 2
Consolidated School, CT

Halloween

Haunted hay rides
Freddy Krueger really scary
Ghosts saying booooo
Witches with brooms
Mummies in toilet paper
Haunted Manors oh my
Skeletons in funny dances
G why?
Spiders in webs
You should see the costumes
Really scary
Now you know
What Halloween's like
Next time you will be
Scared

Ramon Ruiz, Grade 3
St Mary's School, NJ

Running

Running is fast,
legs making air as you go.
As your body
produces
sweat all
over you.
When you
run away from fears,
you feel
like
you are
running to graceful joy!
Running after a soccer ball
to score the winning goal.
Running with a football
to make a wonderful touchdown.
Everything you need to do,
a little voice inside you says:
"Run, run run!"

Paige Masten, Grade 3
Hunter GT Magnet Elementary School, NC

My What If

What if my mom had a baby girl?
I might cry my eyes out.

What if I had to change the diapers?
I could play with her all day.

What if the baby loved me.
I would love my mom and my baby sister.

What would you do if your mom had a baby?

Jazmyn Bennett, Grade 3
Byrns L Darden Elementary School, TN

Witch

Witch
Ugly, magical
Flying, brewing, cooking
Witches are the meanest.
Wizard

Austin Kelly, Grade 3
Chestnut Street Elementary School, PA

A Day at Camp

Some warm cuddly sleeping bags
Some cold snowballs hitting the window
Lots of cooked meat
A fun hard game
Some good tasty crunchy salty chips

Justin Bell, Grade 3
Bradford Township Elementary School, PA

The Moon, a Trustworthy Guard

The moon is a trustworthy guard
Watching all of us
In the black night
The dark will crawl upon us
But he protects
Dark
Light
Fighting in the night
As I sleep
With the moon guarding
Watching
Protecting
When the sun comes up, the moon rests
He has had a long battle
Now the sun has a turn
To watch over us.

Ian Tisdale, Grade 3
Hunter GT Magnet Elementary School, NC

Colors in the Sky

Fireworks shooting in the sky,
like balloons popping boom, boom, boom.
It's a rainbow spraying pretty colors
In the dark, lonely sky.

Madison Miller, Grade 3
Munsey Park Elementary School, NY

Bouncing Basketball in the Olympics

She sweats and runs as
fast as she can, just like
an aggressive tiger, a brave
bear, bouncing a ball up
and down like a roller coaster.

Jordan Reina, Grade 3
Holland Township School, NJ

Seasons

I love the seasons
That's summer, spring, fall, and winter
Spring is the nicest
Zvi Goldstein, Grade 3
Yeshiva Ketana of Long Island, NY

School

School is
a place where
we do everything
to learn.
we read
we write
we draw
we play
we color
we eat lunch
Greeley Hibbard, Grade 1
Broadway Elementary School, NC

Nature's Life

The breeze blows slowly.
The trees flow back and forth fast.
Grass is everywhere.
Zoe Miller, Grade 3
The Parke House Academy, FL

My Dogs

My dogs are at home.
They drink milk and chase their tails.
My dogs play at home.
Eric Berley, Grade 1
United Hebrew Institute, PA

This Is Me

This is me
I am 9 years old
I have 13 cousins
I love to play baseball
and basketball.
I love to draw.
This is me
Elias Candelario, Grade 3
Public School 148 Ruby Allen, NY

American Flag

American flag,
Don't you ever get tired
of listening to people?
I do.
Do you ever get tired?
When I look at you,
you look tired.
Ashbur Gibbs, Grade 3
Cool Spring Elementary School, NC

Best Friends

We are best friends
Sometimes friendship ends
but
we will always
be together
And friendship begins again
Our friendship is
lovely, and fun
Friendship is fun
for everyone
We laugh,
we sing,
we play,
and dance.
La, La, La, La
all day long
We will spin around
in circles
until we get all dizzy
Then we can start
all over again.
Alaces Sarmiento, Grade 3
Public School 148 Ruby Allen, NY

Turkey

Turkey
Good and juicy
Eating, tasting stuffing
Do not eat the wish bone
Happy holidays
Matthew Russo Jemmott, Grade 3
Marie Curie Institute, NY

Roller Coasters

Up, up, up
The end of you is here.
You are frozen in terror.
You have never experienced real fear,
Until now.
You notice blue skies turn gray.
Finally when you think you will never go down,
Woosh!
Sheer and absolute terror.
The monster throws you around.
There is a tunnel.
You are scared.
Until
Woosh
It is all over.
You have finally conquered,
Your first,
And last,
Roller coaster,
Ever.

Liam Kelley, Grade 3
Oak Ridge Elementary School, PA

Sun

The sun is very hot.
People never go there,
because they would get
burned very badly,
burned to ashes.
Now I told you about the sun.

Kira Garvin, Grade 2
Robert E Lee Expressive Arts Elementary School, MO

Mom Mountain

As Mom Mountain stands tall and proud she is the
greatest mountain of all.

She tumbles snow off the animal's feet and that means
it's the morning to rise up sweet.

Mom Mountain is the strongest mountain and she yells
through the wind in a very soft voice.

Jasmine McMorran, Grade 3
Sundance School, NJ

Snow

I like snow.
Any kind of snow.
Muddy snow, sparkling snow,
White snow, brown snow.
Snow in winter,
Snow on the ground,
Snow with hot chocolate,
Any kind of snow.
I like snow.

Gabrielle Cerasoli, Grade 3
Landmark Christian School, GA

My Friend

Ashly
pretty, nice
helping me put the books back
playing with me outside.
Ashly

Asia Hilliard, Grade 2
Bensley Elementary School, VA

Irish Dancer

Lass on stage,
Beginning to dance.
A pretty blue dress,
At last, her chance.
The change, the cut,
The point and back,
Irish Dancing at its best.
At the end — a rest.

Addie Bradley, Grade 2
St Peter the Apostle School, GA

My Pet

Dog
Black and brown
Runs in the woods
Barks at night
Howls at the moon
Wags tail when happy
I love dogs

Rider Abercrombie, Kindergarten
Broadway Elementary School, NC

Pizza

Pizza
Great, soft
Tasty, eating, cooking
Happy, good, excited, full
Hungry

Tyresha Holt, Grade 3
Woodland Elementary School, KY

Pink

I am a flower.
I am a heart.
I am a pretty color.
I am pink.

Patricia Peña, Grade 1
Northeast Elementary School, NY

Sky

Sky so blue
like the ocean in the summer.

Sky so windy
in the fall.

Sky, a show
at night
a spotlight
on you!

Shelby Praytor, Grade 3
Reidville Elementary School, SC

Orange

Round soft happy orange
Growing on the big orange tree
Let's make orange juice sweet!

Caroline Bailey, Grade 2
Roseland Park Elementary School, MS

Madison and Mom

Daughter, mother, friend
Scrapbook, caring, sewing, baking
Games, stickers, books,
Madison and Mom

Madison Tarlo, Grade 2
St Mary's School, NJ

Wild Tune

Flowing,
Ready to pounce on a new note,
Feeding on the keys,
Up and down,
Left to right,
Retracing his notes,
Sneaking,
Waiting for notes and prey,
The Piano is a Cheetah,
Waiting for notes to play.

Kate H. Kushner, Grade 3
Hunter GT Magnet Elementary School, NC

I Am

I am a girl who goes to McKinley School.
I wonder about school.
I hear the bell ring.
I feel happy at school.
I want to go to the library.
I am a girl who loves school.

I pretend I am reading a book
I feel happy
I touch the book
I worry school will be over
I cry when I get hurt at school.
I am a girl who loves McKinley

I understand school
I say, "I want to watch a movie."
I dream about going to the library
I try to touch a ball
I hope I read the book
I am a girl who loves reading.

Jada Wilson, Grade 3
McKinley Elementary School, PA

Christmas Shopping

I didn't have much fun
Because all we did was run, run, run!
We went to malls and stores to shop.
We didn't stop, until we dropped!

Lily Parker, Grade 1
St Vincent De Paul Elementary School, MO

My Friend

My friend likes me.
I like my friend.
She likes me.
She plays with me
And I play with her.

Fannie He, Grade 1
Children's Village, PA

Thanksgiving

Thanksgiving
Good yummy
Biting chewing eating
Cook the turkey
Dinner

Hope Adair, Grade 3
Marie Curie Institute, NY

Fall

In fall the color is red.
The squirrels chatter.
Leaves fall.
I rake leaves.
I jump in the leaves.
Fall is fun!

Rebecca Stull, Grade 2
Eagle's View Academy, FL

Pup-Ku

They are really cute.
I have a two year old pup.
I play with my pup.

Grace Cole, Grade 2
Paine Primary School, AL

Elvis Presley

Elvis loved to sing,
Elvis sang songs,
Elvis made a lot of movies,
Elvis had sparkly clothes,
Elvis made CDs,
Elvis was famous,
Elvis has left the building.

Daniel Gentile, Grade 2
Marie Curie Institute, NY

Hunting

I like to hunt with my Dad,
We have a good time because we are not sad.
I missed a doe and a coyote,
Hunting is fun to me.
It's fun to hunt and go up a tall tree
with Mom and Dad.
Its fun to feed deer in the wild.
When I kill a deer it makes me smile.

Seth Arrington, Grade 3
Pike Liberal Arts School, AL

Math

I like math
Just because all
Kinds of problems
Like addition, subtraction, and multiplication
Make me happy

Meredith Duncan, Grade 3
A L Burruss Elementary School, GA

Jesus Was Born at Night

Jesus was born at night.
The Kings then saw a light.
The three kings saw a star.
But they saw it far.

Jesus and his family were singing.
Then the three kings heard a bell ringing.
The manger was Jesus' bed.
He laid down his little head.

Katie McKenzie, Grade 3
St Edward the Confessor School, LA

I Hate Red Lights

Blinkey winkey stupid red lights
They're *so* boring and much too bright
Driving, driving you come to a stop
You wait so long you want the bulb to pop
Why is it always me? I get stuck every time
So over the light I will put green slime
The slime will be the color of lime
So I will make the light every time

Noah Merenbloom, Grade 3
Hunter GT Magnet Elementary School, NC

My Best Brother

My best brother is so nice to me.
When he needs help with his homework
he asks me to help him with it.
I guess that is what an older sister is supposed to do!

Jasmine Veliz, Grade 2
Mother Seton Inter Parochial School, NJ

How to Decorate a Pumpkin

There are different ways to decorate pumpkins:
Paint, markers, even knives too.
You can make them spooky
Or silly, and into jack-o'-lanterns too!
They can even be weird or cute.
Or wear a shoe or a boot.

Cynthia Almodovar, Grade 3
Coral Springs Elementary School, FL

Pets

Pets are fast.
Pets are fun.
Pets are faster than me when they run.
Sometimes they are bad.
Even when I'm sad, they cheer me up and make me glad.
Some people don't like pets, but I do.
I love pets.

Cameron Jones, Grade 3
Contentnea Elementary School, NC

School

School is where you go for seven hours, five days a week.
First there's reading, then there's language, after that recess and lunch,
and then science or social studies, and finally the last subject of the day…MATH!
My favorite part of the day is specials because there is P.E., library, art, and music.
How cool is that?
This is how I spend my school day.

Darian Hawkins, Grade 3
William Southern Elementary School, MO

Our Class Garden

In our class garden
We have lots of yummy food
That fill my tummy

Jared Ratner, Grade 2
Virginia A Boone Highland Oaks Elementary School, FL

Swimming

Splash!
Boom, loud smack
Dive into the water.
That was so much fun!
Zaviana Desarmes, Grade 2
Clover Street School, CT

Fish

I like when fish swim
because they are
good at swimming.

Fun in the ocean!

Dad surfing
in the

ocean.
Gino Colucci, Grade 1
Holland Township School, NJ

Gymnastics

Pow!
Wshh, pop!
Flipping, flips handstands,
Oh I love gymnastics!
Samantha Scott, Grade 2
Clover Street School, CT

My Favorite Place

Puerto Rico
fancy beach
very comfortable bed
yummy foods
good place
Andrew Cen, Grade 1
Sundance School, NJ

Parakeets-Ku

Parakeets are fun.
Parakeets like to play some.
They are very cute.
Hayley Mikell, Grade 2
Paine Primary School, AL

Halloween

I like Halloween
Because you get candy
Also, Halloween is fun
Because it's my birthday!
Trick-or-treating is more fun
Because you get to dress yourself up!
Angel Kaufman, Grade 3
St Joseph Catholic Grammar School, NJ

Different Kinds of Roses

Roses are sweet
And sometimes smell like feet
With my love on display
I will smell them all day
Pink, yellow, white, red, orange and peach
Different colors but they are pretty
And smell great.
Alana Demmings, Grade 3
Melwood Elementary School, MD

Fall

Amazing! It's fall!
Red leaves fall to the green grass
and twirl all around!
Alec Faber, Grade 3
Catherine A Dwyer Elementary School, NJ

What Do You See?

What do you see inside of me?
What do you see?
Oh, please tell me!
Don't say yes and don't say no.
Just say maybe that is all I need to know.
But if you say yes, don't tell.
And I'll make a guess.
Kaylee Gaia, Grade 3
Evangelical Christian School, TN

Steel Crushers

The steel crushers are driven to the ball
Focused on the ball, they never give up
The parents cheer as we score a goal
Grant Barrett, Grade 3
Holland Township School, NJ

Rocky and Rex

My dogs play a lot together.
My dogs play tug-of-war together.
My dogs fight each other.
I have two dogs.
My dogs are named Rocky and Rex.
My dogs are smart.
My dogs love to have their bellies rubbed.
My dogs snore.
I love my dogs.

Megan Monroe, Grade 2
Contentnea Elementary School, NC

The Hockey Player in Me

I was born to play hockey.
There is a hockey player in me.
I play roller and ice.
It's cold inside it is really nice.
My family comes to watch my game.
I hear them cheer and call my name.
It doesn't matter if we lost or won,
Only that we played our best and had fun.

Joshua Pezzulo, Grade 3
Coral Cove Elementary School, FL

The First

It was the first day of school
I was shaking like a mouse
I was in class 3-303
My teacher was as nice as a rose
because her voice was as soft as silk
I felt calm and was not nervous anymore

Stephanie Garrido, Grade 3
Public School 148 Ruby Allen, NY

I Love Cats

My cat smells like cat food
most of the time.
She looks kind of scary because
in the dark her eyes turn green
and in the morning they are brown.
She is silly because she plays with
crochet needles and hay.

Tyrah Childress, Grade 3
Lee A Tolbert Community Academy, MO

My Two Cats

I have two cats,
They act like brats.
They sleep all day,
At night they want to play.
They want to catch my fish,
To eat them is their wish.
I have a toy mouse,
They chase it around the house.
My cats keep me busy,
Watching them play gets me dizzy.
Sometimes my cats are so curious,
They make me furious.
Even though my cats act crazy,
After playing they get lazy.
They curl up and sleep together,
I will love my cats forever.

Olivia Molinari, Grade 3
St Anselm School, PA

Football

foot, ball, touchdown
all through town
stadium, goals, field
in a huddle kneeled
coach, players, timeout
now cheerleaders shout
cheer, spirit, win
fun for women and men

Corey Lee Maddaloni, Grade 3
Broadway Elementary School, NC

Blue

Blue is my favorite color.
Blue is a part of the flag.
Blue is a bright color or dark.
Blue is like a blue whale.
Blue smells like blueberries.
Blue tastes like joy.
Blue sounds like the birds in the sky.
Blue looks like the sky.
Blue feels like a soft pillow
Blue makes me happy.

Jake Coppola, Grade 3
Evergreen Elementary School, PA

Raccoons

Raccoons can climb trees.
Raccoons will come out at night.
Raccoons are so cool.

Benjamin Griffey, Grade 3
Clinton Christian Academy, MO

My Dog

Beautiful, small,
Brown hair, smart and cute,
Makes me feel happy,
That's my dog.
Two big black circles
On his funny face,
And a very wet nose
That I love to touch.
Long ears, strong chest,
Always on the lookout,
He barks so loud,
Trying to be the best dog.
With his long tail
And his short feet,
He jumps and jumps,
I really love my dog.
Some people
Call him a hot dog,
Others a mini dog,
But for me he is my big love.
Because he is my dog.

Lauren Ginoris, Grade 1
James H Bright Elementary School, FL

Lightning

L ightning is bright
I saw lightning
G et inside
H ow is God making lightning?
T he lights go off
N ice for light
I like lightning
N ice for reading light
G ood for light

Wil Brown, Grade 1
Annie Belle Clark Primary School, GA

The Moon

The moon is a clock telling the time at night.
Lightning is a yellow fish swimming in the ocean.
Day is a big yellow apple ready to be eaten.
Night is a big scary crow looking for its dinner.

Gabriella Resnick, Grade 3
Virginia A Boone Highland Oaks Elementary School, FL

Fall

Fall is a ball that rolls around in and out of Halloween.
And then you have Thanksgiving full of food and family.
On comes December, you can't wait for Christmas fun but that's another season.

Grant McGrew, Grade 3
West Lake Elementary School, NC

Fall

In the fall, I see red leaves falling off the tree in the park.
In the fall, I hear the fireplace crackling in my living room.
In the fall, I taste the cool cider that is sweet.
In the fall, I feel plush, soft, fuzzy mittens.
In the fall, I smell crunchy, tasty, juicy apples.
In the fall, I don't smell flowers in the flower bed.

Abbie Reed, Grade 3
Watsontown Elementary School, PA

A Little White Puppy

A little white puppy with spots so black
Runs through the house and tail goes whack whack

When he sees me he jumps up for joy
Because he knows I have a new toy

Out the door we go to play and run
Oh how my puppy and I have fun

He likes to walk and bark all day
Sometimes he doesn't listen to what I say

We run up and down and all around
Passing time until the sun goes down

Soon it is time to come in for a treat
Nothing is sweeter than seeing him eat!

Megan Carcaise, Grade 3
St Alexis School, PA

The Rug

I am soft.
I am furry.
I am flat.
I am dirty.
People walk on me.
I don't like that!

Edrich Collin, Grade 1
Forest Street Elementary School, NJ

Fall

I love Halloween.
Dressing up is fun for me.
Spooky bats are cool.

Evan Scarpino, Grade 2
Wanamassa Elementary School, NJ

Rain

Rain brings water to
Oceans, lakes, and ponds.
Rain falls soft and hard.
Everybody needs water
To live and grow.

Anthony Doucet, Grade 2
Roseland Park Elementary School, MS

The Zoo

We all went to the zoo.
There was a really big kangaroo.
Then my crew and I went by the bats,
Then we saw some really big cats.
We then went by the scary lions,
And then we played with the sea lions.
We all laughed and had a great day.
We really, really wanted to stay.

Kelly Byrnes, Grade 3
Our Lady of Hope School, NY

Fall

Squirrels eating nuts
Geese honking and fire burning
Crunchy leaves

Alondra Calderon, Grade 1
Northeast Elementary School, NY

Candy Stealer

Slowly
the candy stealer
creeps in
Tap! Tap! Tap!
Then…
Woph!
Candy
dropping like
rain drops
all over the floor
and it keeps on
dropping
candy
falling
from
the sky
Clap! Clap! Clap!
the sound was like people
clapping for me
Candy stealer
who could you be?

Richard Romero, Grade 3
Public School 148 Ruby Allen, NY

Halloween

Halloween is coming near.
Soon it will be finally here.
I will get candy on that day.
I wish that we could do it again in May.
There will be decorations everywhere.
Sometimes I just look and stare.
I can't believe it's coming now.
Soon I will be saying wow!
It is my favorite holiday.
I do not want it to go away.

Tia Waterhouse, Grade 3
Ellicott Road Elementary School, NY

Snakes

Snakes are in the leaves.
Snakes bite people in the leaves.
Be careful of snakes!

Dakoda Richman, Grade 3
Clinton Christian Academy, MO

Turkeys

Turkeys, turkeys fat as a pig.
Turkeys, turkeys, as colorful as a rainbow.

Turkeys, turkeys juicy as steak.
Turkeys, turkeys as loud as crows.
Turkeys, turkeys as big as you!

Grayson McAlister, Grade 3
Reidville Elementary School, SC

Halloween

Halloween is fun and spooky,
My favorite is the candy and the costumes,
My costume is a runaway diva,
My sister is a fairy.
My mom has a costume too
She is an M&M
I like the decorations, they are cool

Alexandra Capobianco, Grade 3
St Mary's School, NJ

Zorse

Black and white and has four legs
For breakfast the Zorse likes his eggs

Some days he feels like a big old horse
Trotting down the lane of a green golf course

Other days like a zebra, black and white
He is coated like a striped kite

During the course of the day
He eats apples, alfalfa, and hay

He likes to trot, he likes to run
He likes to play in the sun

His mom is a zebra
His dad is a horse

He is both of these things
He is a *zorse*!

Nick Baldasare, Grade 3
St Alexis School, PA

Rufus

First Hamster
Black stripe
Eats nuts
Rufus plays
So cute.

Haley Madej, Grade 2
Marie Curie Institute, NY

Apples/Snack

Apples
juicy, crisp
baking, eating, picking
can be different colors
Snack

Kayla Seftner, Grade 2
Consolidated School, CT

Luke

L ovable
U nderstanding
K ind
E veryone's friend

Luke Rogers, Grade 2
Park Elementary School, AR

Jesus' Birthday

I like Christmas.
I sing and play in the snow.
I get a Christmas tree.
I listen to Santa say, "Ho! Ho!"
We have a Christmas dinner.
We set up the tree.
We play games at night.
Jesus' birthday is fun for me.

Jake Schick, Grade 1
Westlake Christian School, FL

Buzzy Bees

Flying, buzzing, stinging
Building hives
Bees do it
All day long

Lori Mangone, Grade 3
Our Lady of Hope School, NY

The Banana Talking and the Pear Walking

Little girl, little girl what do you see?
I see a banana talking to me.
I see a pear walking to me.
I will not eat you!
What will happen if I do eat you?
You will have a party in my tummy.
Why will I have to eat you?

Shayla Carter, Kindergarten
Thomas Jefferson Elementary School, VA

The Olympic Sport of Snowboarding

He is
SOARING
in the air,

is
GLIDING
like a bird,

is
BRAVE
like a cliff diver,

and
is practicing
DAY and NIGHT.

Julia Lieto, Grade 3
Holland Township School, NJ

Thanksgiving

T is for yummy turkey.
H is for very happy people.
A is for anything to help my mom-mom.
N is for napkins on the table.
K is for kittens in their beds.
S is for sharing good food.
G is for giving thanks to God
I is for "Is the pudding done?"
V is for very loving.
I is for I love Thanksgiving.
N is for napping — babies in their cribs.
G is for giving, giving, giving.

Lauren Potter, Grade 3
Birches Elementary School, NJ

Lightning Flashing

When the weather man says "lightning" "beware"…
my beating heart beats like the earth is about to "explode,"
in a big "rumbling" "bumbling" sound.
The lightning went "flicker flicker."
When the rain "drip dropped" the puddles were as deep as a pool.
I was inspired when I saw the hail that was as big as trucks.
The clouds were as gray as a gray cat.
The lightning sounded ferocious!

Alec George, Grade 3
Bridge Valley Elementary School, PA

As I Walk Through the Park

As I walk through the park
I see cardinals darting
Through the trees.
Squirrels are chewing at nuts
And the leaves swirl around.
I smell a strong scent of pine.
And I hear a crow shrieking
As I walk through the park.

Emma Bromage, Grade 2
Worthington Hooker School – K-2 Campus, CT

Soccer

Hi, my name is Shocker.
I love to play soccer,
At my school,
Where I have a locker.
When I kick the ball, people run away.
They trip and they fall, and then they just lay.
I usually play my games at night.
That is when the stars shine bright.
I do my best to help my team.
When I score a goal, the crowd starts to scream.

Drew McDonald, Grade 3
St Mary's School, NJ

Thanksgiving to Share

On Thanksgiving we eat turkey that tickles our tongues.
Everybody takes tomatoes that are juicy.
And shiny soda soaks our food.
Prickly peach pie makes everyone happy.

Danielle Sudol, Grade 3
Our Lady of Hope School, NY

I Miss You
I miss you
I miss you
especially
your beautiful
smile it is
like a bright sun
in the sky
When I think
of you
I feel
my heart beating
like a drum
boom, boom, boom.
When I think again
it is like you are
here I know you
are in a better place
I wish I could see your smiling face
Valeria Erazo, Grade 3
Public School 148 Ruby Allen, NY

Leaves
Blushing red.
Glazed with purple blue.
Sprinkled with cheddar yellow.
That dark shade of light baby green
scuttering up the vines.
The wind brushing against the leaves
as they dance to the ground.
Sweet as sugar brown walnuts,
shaded like coffee beans.
Colored leaves surround me
wherever I go!
Nelmarie Roman, Grade 3
Wolcott School, CT

Sarah
Sarah
Tall, sweet
Play with animals, pool, soccer
Always plays with others
Sarah bear
Elizabeth Campbell, Grade 3
Briarwood Christian School, AL

My Cousin
She is nine years old
we play together all day long
she's as nice as a cat
with soft white fur
Stefany is my pal
that I love very much!
Cory Sierra, Grade 3
Public School 148 Ruby Allen, NY

Ryan
R eliable
Y ankees
A mazing
N ice
Ryan Coccaro, Grade 2
Long Meadow Elementary School, CT

The Washing Machine
Charlene my green
Washing machine
Is keen.

Swish, swish — ding.
It's done!
My clothes are clean.

Oh Charlene
My green washing machine.
Karen Moore, Grade 1
Antonia Elementary School, MO

Me
I am a girl
I am 8
My eye's are black as a circle
My nose is skinny as a finger
My nails are the size of teeth
I am the color tan
I like to play baseball
Baseball is my favorite sport
My name is Muniyath
Muniyath Chowdhury, Grade 3
Public School 148 Ruby Allen, NY

Love

Love is pink
It sounds like two butterflies' wings flapping
It smells like wine being poured
It tastes like cupcakes
It looks like hearts being sewn together
Love feels like a cat brushing against you

Kyle Hilsee, Grade 3
Anne Frank School, PA

Keep Christ in Christmas

You can have fun at Christmas
But don't forget about Jesus.
You can have fun and play
But you can still pray.

Christmas is an important time of the year
Because Jesus' birthday is near.
Christmas brings lots of joy
To every girl and every boy.

Jenna Pepiton, Grade 3
St Edward the Confessor School, LA

What If

What if I didn't pass the 3rd grade?
I might get grounded.
What if I lost my best friend?
I might call to see if he is at home.
What if my dog ran away?
I might run after him.
What if Ravon moved?
I would have to find a new friend.

Bokeem Love, Grade 3
Byrns L Darden Elementary School, TN

Santa's Workshop

Toys that are made for fun
Machines working hard
At Santa's workshop
Greasy oil
A control panel in the middle of the workshop
Rich milk and warm sweet cookies

Benjamon Fye, Grade 3
Bradford Township Elementary School, PA

The Winter Cloud

In the fluffy puff ball
is a globe
a winter wonderland
telling the future sparkling divine
shimmering snowflakes
snow forts and snowballs
not a sound, not a noise
but the yells and kicks of kids.

Rebecca Maher, Grade 3
Wolcott School, CT

Eagles Are Our Friends

They fly high in the sky.
Chase the sun all around.
Lay their eggs in their nests,
And watch their baby eagles come out.
Now the sun is fading away,
And the eagles follow.
Good night eagles.

Tniyah Kitt, Grade 3
Oak Ridge Elementary School, PA

My Pig

I have a pig
he is big
he likes to dig

William Moncrief, Kindergarten
Taylor Road Academy, AL

Red

I am a stripe in the flag.
I am an apple.
I am fire.
I am red.

Joseph Vigil, Grade 1
Northeast Elementary School, NY

Gold Fish

They are colored gold
They are very small and light
They are really fast

Riley Leoni, Grade 3
Miami Country Day School, FL

My Sister

I love my sister
Because she plays with me.
The game we play is tag.
We play lots of games together.
I love my sister.

Raymond Aday, Grade 1
James H Bright Elementary School, FL

Grass

The grass is so tall,
A home for a grasshopper,
Ladybugs live there

Julius Tuberman-Solon, Grade 3
Miami Country Day School, FL

Sunshine

The sunshine is shiny and bright,
Shooting down light,
With all its might.
We like the sunshine,
It gives us day,
Only today,
It's gray.

Madison Surmacz, Grade 3
Rossmoyne Elementary School, PA

Birthdays

People sing to you
You eat delicious cake — yum!
You have lots of fun.

Hunter Merchant, Grade 3
Ross Elementary School, PA

I Am From

I am from my soft bedroom
where my big television is on
when I watch cartoons.
I am from my playroom
where my big television is on
when I watch movies.
I am from my long backyard
where my swing set and I go fast.

Bryan Alberto, Grade 1
Berkeley Lake Elementary School, GA

Veteran's Day

V eterans go fight for us.
E very day one of the veterans die
T rue that veterans get hurt
E verything was for freedom
R un away from a bullet
A ccording to the Army 200 and up soldiers stay alive
N o post office is open on Veteran's Day
S aved The United States

D onna Cries
A ll veterans are heroes
Y oung children see Veterans

Alexandria Warring, Grade 3
Susquehanna Community Elementary School, PA

Fall

In the fall, I see bubbling, liquid brown hot chocolate in a cup.
In the fall, I hear crunching, red, sharp leaves in my yard.
In the fall, I taste steaming, hot chicken noodle soup in a bowl.
In the fall, I feel orange, growing, bumpy pumpkins in my yard.
In the fall, I smell steaming, delicious pumpkin pie on my plate.
In the fall, I don't see growing, red, juicy strawberries in a garden.

Myles Derr, Grade 3
Watsontown Elementary School, PA

My Apple

I see pretty shining stars on my pretty apple.
I smell pretty flowers. They are so so so happy.
I hear ponies running and with their feet making a "tick-tick-tickee-tack" sound.
I taste yummy lemonade juice. Yum! Yum! It tastes so good!
I feel pretty ponies licking me on my hands.

Patricia Inirio, Grade 2
Arlington Elementary School, MA

Fall

In the fall, I smell tasty, delicious apple pie
with my family and friends at the Thanksgiving table.
In the fall, I taste fruity apples from a tree, and then I share them with my friends.
In the fall, I see red leaves falling off the trees and onto the ground.
In the fall, I feel wet, cold rain dripping from the waterspout.
In the fall, I hear children laughing from having fun jumping in the leaves.
In the fall, I don't hear children jumping in the pool.

Hunter Confair, Grade 3
Watsontown Elementary School, PA

A Circle

It is bouncy!
I play catch with Liana.
It's special,
looks like a swimming pool.
It is a circle.
It looks like a tennis ball.
It is round!

Victoria Verdi, Grade 1
Holland Township School, NJ

Madeline Mountain

Madeline's hair drops down
her back like snow
It used to be like summer.

She is my best friend
She is kind and helpful
and always there for me.

I love to be near her.

Kendall Jacobs, Grade 2
Sundance School, NJ

Apple Pie/Dessert

Apple pie
Yummy, sweet
Making, tasting, baking
Air smells delicious too!
Dessert

Isabella Scofield, Grade 2
Consolidated School, CT

Landforms

Landforms are big
Landforms are tall
Landforms are short
Landforms are small
One of shapes
Of Earth's surfaces
Some are capped
Some are flat
Landforms!!

Alexis Millett, Grade 3
Public School 235 Lenox, NY

Flowers

Flowers grow all year long.
They come in different colors and shapes.
They are pretty in the Spring, Winter, and Fall.
Some are short and others are tall.
My favorite are Sun Flowers.
There're yellow with a brownish center.
They follow the Sun and stand in TALL fields.
They disappear when the first frost comes.
SUNFLOWERS are the BEST.

Patrianne Stevenson, Grade 3
New Orleans Free School, LA

Animals and Love

Animals are creatures
like us.
We live together.
Some are mighty,
like bears.
Some are gentle,
like cats.
Some are real,
like my hamster.
Some are not.
There is one
I love
very much,
NuNu…my cat.
I've had him
since I was one
day old.
He is by my side
exactly
when I need him.

Geordy Noppe-Brandon, Grade 2
Public School 41 Greenwich Village, NY

Apple

Apple
Round, red
Growing, picking, eating
I like eating apples.
Fruit

Austin Labesky, Grade 3
Chestnut Street Elementary School, PA

Trick-or-Treat

People going door to door
People wanting candy more and more!
If they don't get some
They will walk through a corridor
They will go home and look in a drawer
Do you know what they will find?
One piece of candy, never more!

Nathan Sanders, Grade 2
Wellington School, FL

Mikaela

Smart
Loving
Active
Sweet
Wishes to have a happy life.
Dreams of being a pop star.
Wants to be a multiplication master.
Who wonders where yaks live.
Who fears thunder and lightning.
Who is afraid of strangers.
Who likes apple pie with whipped cream.
Who believes in God.
Who loves their family.
Who loves God.
Who loves cats.
Who loves beautiful days.
Who plans to help the homeless.
Who plans to live in peace.
Who plans to have fun.
Whose final destination is to be with Jesus.

Mikaela Forrey, Grade 3
Central Park Elementary School, FL

Horseback Riding

Horseback riding is so much fun
I think I'm number one
My favorite horse's name is Big Boy
I wish I could take him home like a toy,
When we ride the wind goes through our hair
I love riding in the fresh air

Parker Ray, Grade 3
Reidville Elementary School, SC

Mala Koala

Mala Koala is my dog
she is cute and cuddly
but most of all
she is sweet
she likes to lick my face
but
she is the most
lovable dog
in the world
we are like two bones
glued together
and
we
will
never
break
apart

Tatyana Natalia Sierra, Grade 3
Public School 148 Ruby Allen, NY

What Is Green?

An alligator in a swamp,
A nice, sour green apple,
A pine tree waving in the wind,
A patch of soft, wet grass,
A frog croaking gently in the grass.

David Jarvis, Grade 3
Scott Elementary School, MO

House at the Beach

The house at the beach
Is the place for grasshoppers
And caterpillars.

Mackenzie White, Grade 2
St Peter the Apostle School, GA

Irish Dancers

We're the Irish dancers
That look like little prancers.
Our shoes of little laces
And blue in all the spaces
Fill the people with happy faces.

Genevieve Dowd, Grade 2
St Peter the Apostle School, GA

Green

Blue as the water
Yellow as honey
Green is a dollar
The color of money
Red is a fire truck
Brown leaves fall in autumn
Green is the grass
That's cool on the bottom
Orange is a fruit
White is soft and bright
Green is the color
That I really like

Kamron Bruton, Grade 2
Contentnea Elementary School, NC

Golf

Golf balls, drivers, tees,
look out for those trees!
Irons, putters, shoes,
give some clues.
Golf carts, keys, gloves,
no one shoves.
Air, sun, cold,
playing is so bold.

Dalton Mauldin, Grade 3
Broadway Elementary School, NC

Blue Shark

Shark
Toothy blue
Chasing chewing zooming
Fins eyes
Blue Shark

Andrew Economos, Grade 1
Guardian Angels Catholic School, FL

Will

W ater for swimming
I ce cream
L ikes the number one
L ogan, my best friend

Will Wright, Kindergarten
Eden Gardens Magnet School, LA

Flippy

He is playful
He is cute
He is white
He loves to play with socks,
His eyes are so cute when he looks at me
He is as white as a sheet of paper
He loves to run around the yard chasing rabbits.

Paulina Diaz, Grade 3
Public School 148 Ruby Allen, NY

Thanksgiving at Home

I get out of school in a rush to get home.
My mom is cooking turkey and can't get the phone.
Dad is busy and in a rush too.
He tells me get the phone, it's all up to you.
I pick up the phone and no one is there.
This is so much fun I don't really care.
Mom and Dad stop to grin.
Our Thanksgiving is about to begin.

Luke Renda, Grade 3
Our Lady of Hope School, NY

Getting a Cold

I hate getting a cold,
Because I have to lie down like I am dead.
All day long,
Drinking soup in bed!

Lara Soysal, Grade 2
Virginia A Boone Highland Oaks Elementary School, FL

Shelter

I climbed up the mountain
Then I fell down
So I went to the fountain
I heard a thunder sound
I drank a lot of water
Then it started to rain
I ran for the station, but I missed the train
I ran for the hills, but I got the chills
I drank so much water, it made me ill
I used my brain from beginning to end
Then I knocked on the door of my very best friend.

Tsahai Corbie, Grade 3
Public School 235 Lenox, NY

My Journey
Spring
Dizzy
Rain
Splish, splash
Wet
Feeling wet and soggy
Following my journey
On my way to school

After school we sing and play
On our way to the park
We see the sun
Hot and big
We see the ice cream man
Later, later it got dark
It started to rain
Where's my umbrella?
Now I am wet.
Kayla McGrane, Grade 3
Coram Elementary School, NY

Grandparents
Grandpa
Funny, playful
Fishing, camping, hunting
Gene, Bill, Gail, Carol
Smoking, playing, laughing
Funny, careful
Grandma
Jessica Owens, Grade 3
Pottsville Elementary School, AR

Halloween Day
Pumpkins, Pumpkins!
Come out to play.
Pumpkins, Pumpkins,
On Halloween Day!
The sky is dark.
The clouds are gone.
Halloween Night has just begun!
Pumpkins are bright orange and big!
Marcus Exceus, Grade 3
Coral Springs Elementary School, FL

I Love the Candy
At Christmas I wake up,
I go to the Christmas tree.
I open my presents,
I love the candy!
Santa feeds the reindeer,
They fly to everyone.
They magically go through the roof,
Playing with Christmas toys is fun!
Alexander Graden, Grade 1
Westlake Christian School, FL

My Brother
My brother is kind.
My brother is sweet.
I love my brother as he sleeps.
Vincent Colavita, Grade 3
McKinley Elementary School, PA

My Friend
Ashly
nice, funny
helping friends in my class
playing jump rope with me
Ashly
Kayla Harris, Grade 2
Bensley Elementary School, VA

Thanksgiving
I ate too much on Thanksgiving.
The turkey's gone,
The stuffing stuffed me,
The cranberries gone,
My brother's laughing,
Off his head.
Knew I should of stayed in bed.
Gobble, Gobble,
What was that,
Seemed to be coming from my back.
Oh my stars,
Is it true,
I ate a real turkey,
But now it's through.
Maggie Kishbaugh, Grade 2
Fishing Creek Elementary School, PA

The Best Present Ever!

Christmas is a very good time.
There is a mountain of presents to climb!
I hope that I receive a doll.
That would be the best present of all!

Carly Pujol, Grade 1
St Vincent De Paul Elementary School, MO

Around My Yard

Around my yard,
in my house,
on top of the first floor,
between my brother and my dad's room
through my door,
across my room,
during my sleep,
instead of doing my homework.

Will Durbin, Grade 3
McKinley Elementary School, PA

Christmas Fun

On Christmas we had fun.
At my house there is more than one!
I think Christmas is great,
Because we don't have to wait!

Hannah Dodson, Grade 1
St Vincent De Paul Elementary School, MO

Like a Lion

Smart and Strong like a lion
ripping open anyone in my way
King of the jungle
never backs down
Smart as a lion
I can growl and the whole jungle hears me
pouncing with a growl in my heart
Unstoppable with a squint in my eye
no one can stop me
I know poison from five miles away
like a lion knowing his prey
People run when they see me
I am like a lion

Brandon Lee, Grade 3
Hunter GT Magnet Elementary School, NC

Fall

Leaves are falling off trees
Humans rake them as they fall
Fall is full of colors.
Amaan Chaudhry, Grade 3
Tuxedo Park School, NY

What Is Red?

An apple on a teacher's desk,
A juicy cherry,
As scented gingerbread house,
As lumpy as a red couch,
A robin in early spring.
Joshua Coots, Grade 3
Scott Elementary School, MO

The Bells Are Ringing

I love Christmas,
Christmas is so neat.
I wake in the morning,
And the presents are sweet.
Christmas is coming,
The bells are ringing.
The children wake up,
And Santa is singing.
Sophia Lee, Grade 1
Westlake Christian School, FL

Haunted House/Halloween

Haunted house
Scary, creepy
Scaring, haunting, spooking
People get really spooked.
Halloween
Allison Johansson, Grade 2
Consolidated School, CT

Thanksgiving

Turkey
Juicy sweet
Eating chewing swallowing
Thanksgiving is cool
Snacks
Anthony Nimmo, Grade 3
Marie Curie Institute, NY

Spring

Springtime is a happy time,
All the flowers look very fine.
They stand up straight, all in a line.
They smell pretty, I wish they were mine.
Tulips, roses and daisies so colorful.
It's a beautiful sight, oh how wonderful!
Melissa Rebecca, Grade 3
Our Lady of Hope School, NY

Thanksgiving Feast

Thanksgiving morning is a wonderful sight.
When you wake up, the sun shines bright!
I get ready to feast with family and friends.
And dance till the night ends.
Brianna Camille Lombardi, Grade 3
Our Lady of Hope School, NY

Caterpillar Changing

Stripes, stripes,
I saw you,
eating up the grass
like caterpillars do.

I put you in a cage
and took you inside.
I brought you fresh grass
where caterpillars hide.

You made a cocoon
on a stick so thin,
and you hibernated
when it was winter again.

You emerged from the chrysalis
with your wings so new,
you had to have a name
that was really brand new.

You flew on your wings
of white with black dots,
right there I knew
that your name should be Spots.
Clarissa Dyson, Grade 2
Jonathan Valley Elementary School, NC

My Happy Place

Excited, curious, powerful, like sugar surging through my body…
Mrs. Chenualt is taking us to the nature preserve to be explorers.

I could feel Mother Nature softly patting my back
I was so excited as I approached the nature preserve.
I noticed a sign
It read: Welcome to the nature preserve
Please don't touch anything
Thank you.

I heard birds chirping "Step in time"
It was amazing: it was an eagle
Oh how much I wish I had a camera but I didn't
Wait I found something more exciting…
A cocoon, I was as fascinated as a leprechaun who struck gold.

Shattered discouraged was the words that described me
once Mrs. Chenault hollered
"It's time to leave." That meant no more birds chirping "Step in time"
No more eagle sights no more anything.
We have to say bye-bye to the Nature Preserve
I will see you again ole beauty.

Cameron McGar, Grade 3
Woodland Elementary School, KY

Fall

In the fall, I see different shaped leaves on the ground.
In the fall, we hear the strong, heavy wind flowing through the sky at the park.
In the fall, I love to feel my soft knit scarf that my gram made for me.
In the fall, I love to smell sweet pumpkin pie that we eat at Thanksgiving.
In the fall, I can taste the chocolaty, warm hot chocolate after playing in the park.
In the fall, I don't taste any mint ice cream at my house.

Kiera Goss, Grade 3
Watsontown Elementary School, PA

Fall

The colorful leaves dancing to the ground.
Landing on the ground with a soft plop.
Kids run over the leaves. CRUNCH.
The kids wreck the golden red, orange masterpieces.
Then a gust of strong wind carries away the wonderful remains of the leaves.
I wish fall would never end.

John Whalen, Grade 3
Wolcott School, CT

Life Is Weird

Life is weird
because you have to take care of items
that aren't even yours.
You need to clean something up
even if you didn't make the mess.
You get in trouble by something
that you didn't even do.
You get called on
even if you didn't even raise your hand.
They guess you can't do it,
but you can.
They make you do something
even if you didn't offer.
You do it right
but they don't pick you.
Life is weird.

Michael Lee, Grade 3
Wolcott School, CT

Sneaky Little Cat

Sneaky little cat
As sneaky as a bat,
As sneaky as a log,
As sneaky as a mat,
As sneaky as fog,
As sneaky as a dog,
As sneaky as a sister,
As sneaky as a cloud,
As sneaky as a kid,
As sneaky as a bog,
As sneaky as a hog,
As sneaky as a gnat,
That fat little cat.

Timmy Hannah, Grade 3
Cool Spring Elementary School, NC

Pumpkin/Yummy

Pumpkin
Smooth, orange
Growing, picking, eating
Delicious, excited, strong
Yummy!

Aishwarya Mammayil, Grade 3
Wapping Elementary School, CT

My Friend

Arnesha
nice, cool
playing with me
helping me every day.
Arnesha

Zyaisa Archer, Grade 2
Bensley Elementary School, VA

Sharks

Big, rough, heavy
Biting, swimming, eating, hunting
Fins, tough, teeth
Sharks

Seamus Cogshall, Grade 2
St Mary's School, NJ

Christmas Tree

Gleaming and bright,
A tree full of bulbs,
Shining all night.

Benjamin Artuso, Grade 3
Trinity East Elementary School, PA

What Bugs Me?

My brother and his saxophone,
Bedtime,
Reading in front of the class,
Lunchtimes full of pokes,
Cleaning my room,
A noisy class,
Chatting people,
And people begging for my dessert.
That's what really bugs me!

Kelly Shaw, Grade 3
Mary Matula Elementary School, MD

My Dream of the Ocean

Over the ocean, where seagulls fly
Soaring high, up towards the sky
So deep, so blue, and salty too
I wish I could be, just like you

Alanya Haile, Grade 3
Concord Elementary School, PA

Leaves/Fall

Leaves
Yellow, red
Falling, raking, jumping
We play in leaves
Fall

Terri Schneider, Grade 3
Chestnut Street Elementary School, PA

Cry

Once I went through a glass door.
We had to go somewhere,
I was watching TV,
And my mom called my name.
I got a cut on my arm
And we went to the doctor.
I was little,
probably four years old.

I was crying.
I was bleeding
So mom put alcohol on me.
B U R N
Then she wrapped
A big towel around it.
I had to have stitches.

I still cry,
Sometimes during movies
When people get eaten by crocodiles.
Sometimes I keep
Being inside of my head
And cry at my nightmares.

James William Smith, Grade 3
Lee A Tolbert Community Academy, MO

Ghosts

Ghosts
White, creepy
Floating, flying, scaring
Ghosts like scaring kids.
Spirit

Shyanne Blankenship, Grade 3
Chestnut Street Elementary School, PA

Toy Cars

Toy cars can be raced with,
Toy cars can be built,
Toy cars can be traded,
Toy cars can be models,
Toy cars can break easy,
Toy cars can be shown to people,
Toy cars rule the world.

Jacob Preville, Grade 2
Marie Curie Institute, NY

Shelley

S uperb
H elpful
E xcellent
L ovely
L ively
E legant
Y oung

Shelley Rose, Grade 2
Long Meadow Elementary School, CT

I Am

I am a boy who likes chocolate.
I wonder if there are aliens in space.
I hear the wind.
I see millions of animals.
I want to go to France.
I am a boy who likes chocolate.

Yusef Robinson, Grade 3
Stone Academy, SC

Thankful

I am thankful for my family
They are always there for me
I am thankful for my friends too
We always have fun things to do
I am thankful for my food
It puts me in a happy mood
I am thankful for my house
Because I have never seen a mouse!

Daniel Martini, Grade 3
Our Lady of Hope School, NY

Butterflies

Ten million butterflies,
fluttering in my face.
Making air go past me,
what a beautiful smell.
They are all scattering,
making me say ohhhh.
Butterflies soar through the air.
When you spot them,
In the air,
making shapes.

Erin Mathews, Grade 3
Oak Ridge Elementary School, PA

The Hope We Share

God is great
He makes a way
He sends blessing from above
God is love
He gives us love and care
That's the hope we share

Lauren Caldwell, Grade 3
Western Hills Elementary School, AR

Spring

Spring is the very first season.
And oh! how the flowers grow.
The busy bees fly from one flower
to the other.
Birds are singing their pretty song
as they soar in the blue sky!
The colors of the rainbow show
as they light up the sky.
Oh! the joy of spring!

Haley Montalvo, Grade 1
Oliver Hoover Elementary School, FL

Farm Horse

I can blink
I can drink
I can jump
But I cannot bump.
I am Farm Horse.

Jessica Alvarado, Grade 1
Northeast Elementary School, NY

Stinky Homework

Stinky, stinky homework over ten feet tall.
Piles and piles every day and I sure do hate it all!
They give us way too much…I don't know where to start,
because now it's a sky scraper and I could never reach the top.
I may as well leave it till my dying day
cause my teacher's going to scream at me forever anyway!

Sadie Wheeler, Grade 3
Reidville Elementary School, SC

Autumn

A ll the leaves change.
U nder the leaves is grass.
T hanksgiving.
U nderstand that chemicals change the leaves.
M emories that I have about autumn are great.
N othing says jump in me like a pile of leaves.

Chava Kornblatt, Grade 2
United Hebrew Institute, PA

Autumn

A pples are good for you and they are good to eat.
U p in the tree, there are birds.
T urkey is good for me, and I like it.
U p there is an apple, a good apple.
M ashed potatoes are good to eat.
N ow I like the leaves because they change colors.

Julia Flores, Grade 3
Central Park Elementary School, FL

The Weird Day

As I walked into the sun
I was eating such a lovely bun
All of a sudden it started to rain
And then I was tied to a chain
After that the clouds turned all black
And I was pushed on to my back
So I turned around and a cloud fell to the ground
I closed my eyes and counted to three
But when I opened my eyes there was a ghost beside me
So I closed my eyes again
And when I opened them it was just a dream
So I took a bath and I was all clean.

Molly Hackley, Grade 3
Oakdale Elementary School, MD

Christmas

C hristmas
H appy
R udolph
I gloo
S anta
T insel
M erry
A ntlers
S led

Grace DePhillips, Grade 3
St Mary's School, NJ

Autumn

A utumn is here again
U mbrellas are used for rain
T hanksgiving is coming soon
U nder the rocks are leaves
M ushrooms are growing
N ew leaves are falling

Haley Rudofker, Grade 2
United Hebrew Institute, PA

Christmas/Holiday

Christmas
red, green, sparkling
wrapping, tying, sleighing
Santa visits on Christmas eve
holiday

Kevin Stone, Grade 2
Wells Central School, NY

Love to Do Gymnastics

Flexible
Strong
like a professional star.
My colors are
red, white and blue.
Doing my back walkover
is fun,
always
will do
gymnastics.

Clare Dougherty, Grade 3
Holland Township School, NJ

Snow

Snow falls from the sky.
Snow melts on the ground.
Snow is clean and white.
Snow comes in the winter night.
Snow is as cold as ice cream.
With snow you can play!
You don't see it every day,
The snow doesn't come in May
Nobody has a say if there is gonna be snow.
Snow is the prettiest thing I've seen in my way!

Camila Aro, Grade 3
John Ward Elementary School, MA

I Am

I am a person who loves soccer
I wonder if I will make a goal
I hear the referee blow his whistle
I feel the ball at my feet
I want to be forward
I am a person who loves soccer

I pretend that I am flying
I feel the wind blowing in my face
I touch the ball when I throw the ball in
I worry that I will kick it the wrong way
I cry when I get hit with the ball
I am a person who loves soccer

I understand that I can't be the best player
I say "kick the ball to me"
I dream that I am the best player in the world
I try to run fast and score a goal
I hope that I win a game
I am a person who loves soccer

Eileen Burner, Grade 3
McKinley Elementary School, PA

At a Camp

A big scary hairy spider
A buzzing loud bee
The grass swamp water
A huge tree with a lot of bark

Hunter Shaw, Grade 3
Bradford Township Elementary School, PA

I Love My Dog

I would like a dog in my house.
I know that they stink,
And sometimes have confusion
In their brains because they don't think well.
Some of them roll in the mud and get dirty.
But some puppies are smart and polite
And I would name my dog Reedy
Because that is my nickname.
I would still like a dog in my house.

Orban Reed, Grade 2
Lee A Tolbert Community Academy, MO

North Pole

A very mad polar bear
A white iceberg crack
Slimy fish
A huge icicle
Cold snow

Isaac Mulhollan, Grade 3
Bradford Township Elementary School, PA

Frog Who Would Croak

There once was a frog who would croak,
He always would like to joke.
He had a friend named Ted,
He liked the color red.
He died from a sudden stroke!

Brianna Acosta, Grade 3
John H Winslow Elementary School, NJ

What if Something Happened?

What if I had a million dollars?
I might have a big family.

What if my grandma died?
I would be sad for two years.

What if I bought a pet for my mom?
I could buy a dog for my mom.

What if I died?

Anthony Sledge, Grade 3
Byrns L Darden Elementary School, TN

Bryant

Bryant
tall, skinny
video games, neighbors, Legos
very friendly to others
Bry Bry

Anna Fay Frost, Grade 3
Briarwood Christian School, AL

Fall

Red, blue, violet, purple, scarlet.
I like you.
You make me nice and cool.
Squirrels, squirrels
Can you scatter
When you chatter?
Come on let's make a bonfire
I'll get the marshmallows
You get the sticks.

Toby Heimbach, Grade 2
Eagle's View Academy, FL

Sweet and Juicy

Candy is Yummy,
I know that for sure,
I feel it in my tummy,
Can I have some of yours?
My favorite is gum,
It's juicy and sweet,
It makes me say "yum,"
What a wonderful treat!
As I lay in bed,
I think about my day,
Candy is in my head,
My story is done, Okay!

Keyshan Patel, Grade 3
North Star Elementary School, DE

Baseball

Stomping, clapping
Thuds, shhhh, cracking peanut shells,
You're out!
My turn now!

Steven Richardson, Grade 2
Clover Street School, CT

Eating

I like to eat!
Chicken and fish are my treat!
My favorite ice cream is bubble gum.
Do you want some?

Jacob Wilfred, Grade 2
McKinley Elementary School, PA

Baseball

Baseball is fun,
but you have to know how,
so grab a ball,
a glove,
and a bat.
Hit the ball,
over the wall,
and there it is,
a home-run.

Jake McCormick, Grade 3
North Star Elementary School, DE

Rainbow Colors

White is for a cloud.
Pink is for paint.
Red is for roses.
Orange is for a carrot.
Yellow is for the sun.
Green is for grass.
Blue is for the sky.
Purple is for violets.
Brown is for wood.
Black is for the night,
When we all go to sleep.

Rohan Gupta, Grade 2
Frankstown Elementary School, PA

Love

L ove is really great.
O thers that I love, love me too.
V ery amazing love is.
E very day love could be this good.

LesLee Powell, Grade 3
Blakeney Elementary School, GA

Ode to My Talking Parrot

Oh talking parrot I have had you for six years.
You are so special to me because my grandmother gave you to me.
Your feathers are as soft as a cat's fur.
Your eyes are as green as spring leaves.
Your nose is as orange as a pumpkin.
You are my talking parrot.
Your colors remind me of a colorful dress.
Your cage is as bumpy as a potato.
You're my only parrot.
I will always love you.
I will always keep you.

Maya Geradi, Grade 2
Worthington Hooker School – K-2 Campus, CT

Baseball

Baseball is a sport.
It can be played anytime of the year.
The fans are what I like to hear.
I like to hear the crack of the bat, so does Coach Matt.
I am a catcher.
My glove is leather.
When I hit the ball, I am glad.
When we lose, I am sad.

Zachary Turner, Grade 3
Contentnea Elementary School, NC

A Day at the Beach

I like to play games in the sand
feed the seagulls with my hands
I splash in the ocean and crash with the waves,
surf with my board and never get bored

I search for seashells by the shore
there are never enough so I fill up some more
white, black, beige, and gray
those are the colors I like best

Then my mom calls me, it's time to eat
I like the sandwiches and all the treats
finally it's time to go
I had a good time can't wait
to come back and do it again

Katelyn Suastegui, Grade 3
Coral Cove Elementary School, FL

For My Family*

Every kernel loves a pop.
Every floor loves a mop.
Every kick loves a chop.
And I love you.

Keegan Coon, Kindergarten
Eden Gardens Magnet School, LA
**Inspired by Jean Marzollo's*
"I Love You: A Rebus Poem"

Who Has Seen?

Who has seen the sunset?
Not me, not you.
But when the clouds turn pink,
The wind is passing through.

Who has seen the sunset?
Not you, not me.
But when the sun goes down,
The wind is passing through.

Emily Kiernan, Grade 3
Sundance School, NJ

The Lights Are Glowing

The lights are glowing,
The ornaments are shaking!
Santa is landing on the roof,
And the kids are waking!
The kids are running down the steps,
To the Christmas tree.
They're opening the presents,
The kids play with glee.

Jacob Stamas, Grade 1
Westlake Christian School, FL

Beach

B ig waves
E verything washes away
A piece of seaweed washes up
C ame to the top of a
H ill of sand

Kevin Harvey, Grade 3
Bensley Elementary School, VA

Sculpture

Still, hard
Standing, modeling, breathtaking
Made of stone
Mannequin

Veronica Talbert, Grade 3
Mary Walter Elementary School, VA

The Olympic Sport of Badminton

My red shirt is wet.
Moving fast like a cheetah.
My black hair flowing.

Rebecca Karcher, Grade 3
Holland Township School, NJ

About My House

I live in a house.
I saw a mouse.
It is fun.
I like to run.
I eat pizza.
It is good.

Avi Herskowitz, Grade 2
Yeshiva Ketana of Long Island, NY

The Beta Fish

The beta fish swims in water,
It has a bright red color.

The fish will die inside the water,
If his tank get hotter and hotter.

It swims with a big swish,
It eats without a dish.

It swims in the ocean,
It doesn't need suntan lotion.

The beta fish swims high and low,
Sometimes fast or slow.

It makes a nice and quiet pet,
Even though it's always wet.

Matthew Olon, Grade 3
St Alexis School, PA

My Dog Chloe

C hloe is so cute.
H er head lies in her arms.
L ove her so much.
O h, so black!
E veryone likes her.

Meagan Perro, Grade 3
Leicester Memorial Elementary School, MA

Rudolph Is Lead'n the Way

Santa will soon be coming.
Rudolph is lead'n the way.
He leads the way on Christmas Day.
I wish I could see Rudolph's nose.
I know it has to look like a bright light.
It was a white night.
The moon wasn't very bright.
It was a very, very foggy night.
Santa will eat his muffins
He'll put the presents under the tree
Then he'll go to his sleigh.
Now once again Rudolph's lead'n the way.

Faith Newton, Grade 3
Fort Dale Academy, AL

Fall Love

Football is my favorite sport,
I play it every day,
When my work is done.
I have lots of fun,
Playing my favorite game.
My favorite play is the fake handoff,
I fake them out all the time,
I make a touchdown
I kick, I run, really fast
To beat little brother,
To throw a pass,
My team is the Redskins,
We never lose.
That's why I love my team.
Football is my favorite sport,
I play it every day!

Jayden Perry, Grade 2
Narvie J Harris Traditional Theme School, GA

Angel Way Up High

Christmas is fun,
Beginning with the lights.
The presents are waiting,
Santa comes in the night.
My Christmas tree is so tall,
I put an angel way up high.
It looks beautiful,
Santa's reindeer fly.

Tristan Lopez, Grade 1
Westlake Christian School, FL

My Favorite Place

Hershey Park
afraid of rides, no more
Ben's first Hershey Kiss
roller coaster, I'm too short
I wanna go back

William Goldmark, Grade 1
Sundance School, NJ

My Favorite Place

Tennessee
mini golf
fun zone
UT games
'tis fun

Carson Stacy, Kindergarten
Sundance School, NJ

Snake-Ku

Slimy, nasty, gross
They sleep down in their hole
Sleeping silently

Kyree Blackburn, Grade 2
Paine Primary School, AL

My Favorite Place

Maine
fancy ships
Diver Ed and Mini Ed
Jasper Beach
a perfect place

Theo Won, Grade 1
Sundance School, NJ

Christmas Time Is Here!

Home! Home! Home for the holidays!
Christmas time is here,
Jingle bells and silver shells,
Gold'n green holly and mistletoe,
Holly jolly oh by golly,
Christmas time is here.
Have some chocolate from your stocking,
and have a great big cheer!
Ho! Ho! Ho! There he goes,
out with his great big pack!
And now it's Christmas Eve,
so you'd better hit the sack!

Emily Wood, Grade 3
North Star Elementary School, DE

That's What I Can Do

I do lots of flips.
I can even do some kicks.
These are special tricks.
That's what I can do.
Cartwheels are lots of fun.
They're so easy to do in the sun.
It's better than a run.
That's what I can do.

Ankhtra Maa´ Battle, Grade 3
Thelma L Sandmeier Elementary School, NJ

Oh How I Love Shoes

Oh shoes, oh shoes Oh how I love shoes.
With so many styles, I just can't choose.
Some are flats and some have heels.
There are some that even have wheels.
Some have sparkle, some have shine
all I want is for them to be mine.
Some are suede and some are leather.
They could be heavy or light as a feather.
Boots for the cold, flip flops for the heat.
I need them both to protect my feet.
When I shop for shoes I have so much fun.
I can't just leave with only one.
Stripes, polka dots, red, green or blue
Oh shoes, oh shoes I will always love you!!!

Gabriella Gonzalez, Grade 3
Coral Cove Elementary School, FL

That Is Who I Love

There she is, the love of my life.
I may be in the third grade
I don't care I'm falling in love with her.
She is the love of my life and she has the initials of C.E.M.T.
I will never tell you who has those initials.

Adam Laslo, Grade 3
Concord Elementary School, PA

Pathways

P a is challenging!
A ttitude should always be positive!
T o try to do something!
H ow do you brainstorm?
W ays to stretch your brain.
A lways do your best!
Y ears don't matter, it's only about one thing…
S tudents working well!

Owen Ivan, Grade 3
Madison Station Elementary School, MS

Autumn

Fall is coming soon.
The Earth will be so chilly.
The birds' songs are gone.

Caelan Hinterlang, Grade 3
St Mary of the Assumption Catholic School, PA

Cheerful Leaf

I'm as colorful as a fish
Swimming in the sea.
I'm as smooth as a river
Rushing down by a waterfall.
I'm floating in the wind
Like a dancer.
I'm a cheerful leaf.

William Suzuki, Grade 2
Worthington Hooker School – K-2 Campus, CT

The Sport of Olympic Skating

The skaters are PROUD because they are skating for the crowd
Wearing pretty clothes as they dance.
Lots of people in the audience watching them.

Helena Habib, Grade 3
Holland Township School, NJ

My Mother

She gives me cookies
because she's nice.

I ask for cookies
sometimes twicc.

Sometimes she's happy
Sometimes she's glad
She's never never mad or sad.

She sometimes goes to the wood shop.
I miss her so I'll never stop.

Mary Davis, Grade 1
Lula Elementary School, GA

Friends

My friends are rather nice.
They have trusting hearts.
They are very, very helpful.
I help them, they help me.
I like my friends.
I trust my friends.
They are nice, they are mean.
I do not care.
My friends light me up
When I am down.
That is friends.

Jessica Smith, Grade 3
Oak Ridge Elementary School, PA

Summer Time

I like summer time
I like riding my scooter
Fun playing in camp

Simi Flegmann, Grade 3
Yeshiva Ketana of Long Island, NY

My Friend

Spirit, happy, smiles
Running, jumping, swimming, playing
Great, nice, writer
Ana

Deisy Almazan, Grade 2
St Mary's School, NJ

Cardinal

A cardinal flies in the snow
With a bright red glow

A cardinal sits in its nest
Where it likes to take a rest

Cardinals pick and preen their feathers
This they do to deal with weather

He looks all around
To look for food under the ground

A cardinal sings a cheery song
That takes all day long

As winter does come near
The cardinal shows no fear

Loren Suttmiller, Grade 3
St Alexis School, PA

Holiday

From walls to halls,
Decorations everywhere on holidays.
From cookies to cakes
Ummm, so good!
From lights to blow ups
Oh, so beautiful!
Jack-o'-lanterns to Christmas trees,
I love Holidays!

Peter Franceschi, Grade 3
St Mary's School, NJ

Guess Where I Am?

I see people swinging on the swings.
I hear children laughing and playing.
I smell hotdogs roasting.
I touch sand, grass, and trees.
Guess where I am?

I am at the park.

Alexxis Travis, Grade 2
Roseland Park Elementary School, MS

What's in My Basement?
Big, black, slobbery dogs,
Red, green, blue bikes,
Basketball games and scary videos,
A big, blue, deflated pool
Brown and white ponies and
Lots of cousins, aunts and uncles.
Zane Harrison, Grade 3
Mary Matula Elementary School, MD

Penguins
Penguins hop.
Penguins pip.
Penguins dive, dive, dive!
Luke Doherty, Grade 1
Northeast Elementary School, NY

Penguins
Penguins pip.
Penguins hop.
Penguins slip, slip, slip!
Diana Lopez, Grade 1
Northeast Elementary School, NY

Fall
Fall looks like colorful leaves
Fall looks like beautiful clouds
Fall sounds like crunching leaves
Fall sounds like windy weather
Fall smells like yummy pie
Fall smells like outside
Fall tastes like summer sausage
Fall tastes like candy apples
Fall is a season!
Olivia Provance, Grade 1
Alvaton Elementary School, KY

Soccer/Goalie
Soccer
Exciting and fun
Kicking, passing, scoring
Happy to score,
Goalie.
Carli Johnson, Grade 3
Wapping Elementary School, CT

Football
balls, helmets, pads
people and their fads
touchdowns, games, cheers
this is the best of years
cleats, shirts, pants
hear the cheerleader chants
Amber Johnson, Grade 3
Broadway Elementary School, NC

Where Is My Cat?
Maybe she is in the kitchen,
Maybe she is in the living room,
Maybe she is in the closet
Maybe she's on my bed

I'm looking for a long time
I'm looking everywhere
I can't find her anywhere
I've gotten pretty tired
So, I sit in the couch
I felt something soft.
Oh! There she was.
Sylwia Wisniewska, Grade 3
Public School 131, NY

Who Am I
She liked to sing
She lost her shoe
She married a prince

Cinderella
Marlon Castaneda, Grade 1
Northeast Elementary School, NY

William
William
Eight, funny
Baseball, football, art
Always helping hurt people
Willie
Katlyn Gandy, Grade 3
Briarwood Christian School, AL

Dobbit

It lives in Brazil
Eats grass and not big
Very rare and smart
Prescott Ho, Grade 3
Miami Country Day School, FL

Snowy, Snowy, Frosty

Frosty nice
pretty quiet
cold loving
good fluffy
snowy
Grey Anne Cummings, Grade 1
Hilton Head Christian Academy, SC

Rivers

Rivers, rivers, rivers
So beautiful
As they roll in the sun.
Clark Thomas, Grade 3
Tri-County Christian School, MO

Hail

H ail is hard
A big golf ball
I ce
L oud
Jazlyn Slade, Grade 1
Annie Belle Clark Primary School, GA

The Dance of the Ballerina

In ballet you wear a tutu.
In ballet you're graceful.
Your feet dance.
And you prance.

You're beautiful as you pirouette.
You *are* a ballerina.
And as you leap,
You don't make a peep.
Alexis Pickering, Grade 2
McKinley Elementary School, PA

Penguins

Penguins pip.
Penguins dive.
Penguins flop, flop, flop!
Thomas Buckhannon, Grade 1
Northeast Elementary School, NY

A Parrot

A parrot can be a pet
It's not like any bird you've met.

It is better than the rest,
It's colorful on its chest.

You can even teach them to speak.
But they have a very hard beak.

Some have green feathers on them,
Like the color of a rose stem.

A parrot can be light blue,
And some other colors too.

A parrot likes to mock you.
But I don't care. I want two.
Kailee Koryak, Grade 3
St Alexis School, PA

Katlyn

Katlyn
Short, funny
Soccer, reading, art
Always helping other people
Ka Ka
William Salchert, Grade 3
Briarwood Christian School, AL

Orange

R ound, good, eat it, sweet.
O range, good, eat it, sweet.
U nder a tree, good, eat it, sweet.
N ever bad, always good.
D one! Have another one!
Rhys Kawaguchi, Grade 3
West Lake Elementary School, NC

Dog Makes Dough

There once was a dog
Who made pizza dough
He rolled it, and rolled it
Before a good throw
Up in the air, as light as light can be
So everyone watching had something to see
Mouths were watering, and tummies growled
But that crazy dog just giggled and howled
Go away you people, leave me be
This pizza is for no one except
I, myself, and me!

Andrew Gardner, Grade 3
Mary Walter Elementary School, VA

Rusty the Fat Cat

Rusty eats a lot
he has such a cute chubby face
When he sleeps he looks so
adorable he loves when I pet him
Rusty is as fluffy as a cloud
"Meow, meow" says my big furry friend.

Bethany Katehis, Grade 3
Public School 148 Ruby Allen, NY

Princesses

I like Belle.
I like Sleeping Beauty.
I like Snow White, Jasmine and Cinderella.
They are always smiling and look happy.
I think being a princess would be great.

Anya Laxton, Kindergarten
Our Savior New American School, NY

A Halloween Night

On Halloween night, I went trick or treating
I spotted a house of ghosts and goblins
A man was outside giving out candy
He gave me a piece hoping I would join him
I went inside and thought it was frightening
Mummies jumping and skeletons hanging
I ran back home happy it was over

Andrew Bendezu, Grade 3
St Mary's School, NJ

Early Morning

What does early morning sound like?
Like this, trit trot and don't forget.
Deer are running in the woods.
The birds go peep, peep.
If they could stop,
So I could go to sleep.

Hunter Whatley, Grade 3
Briarwood Christian School, AL

My Early Morning

The wind was blowing in my face.
swish, swoosh
swish, swoosh
I see a bee flying out of a tree.
swish, swoosh
swish, swoosh
I see a funny bunny isn't he clumsy.

Lindsay Dick, Grade 3
Briarwood Christian School, AL

My Cookie

I had a cookie
I dropped it on the floor mat
I still ate it up

Isaiah Bowden, Grade 3
John Ward Elementary School, MA

On Thanksgiving

My mom and her sisters
cook chicken on a grill
in the front yard
on Thanksgiving
because it's delicious.

Logan Pathman, Grade 3
Miami Country Day School, FL

Slow Horse

I like to have fun.
I like to run.
I like to be fast.
But I do not mind being last.
I am Slow Horse.

Nicole Pon, Grade 1
Northeast Elementary School, NY

My Brother

His name is Rodolfo
He is mean
He is 13 years old
He likes school
He likes to watch TV
He likes to play soccer
I love him and he loves me!

Kevin Beckford, Grade 3
Public School 148 Ruby Allen, NY

My Pool

I'm getting a pool.
That is cool.
I have swimming gear.
Under the water you cannot hear.
The water is cold.
I am so bold.
There are drains.
I cannot use it when it rains.

Kenny Kruszka, Grade 3
Ellicott Road Elementary School, NY

My Pig

My pig is fat,
My pig is huge,
I do not know what to do.
I just scream, "Ahhh!"
My pig is muddy,
And his skin looks ruddy.
I do not know what happened to him,
I think I'll tell him to hit the gym.

Maggie Adcock, Grade 3
Briarwood Christian School, AL

Sparkling Light

My family and I
ski Mammoth, a hard run
on Thanksgiving eve
in Park City Utah
to see the torch light sparkle.

Alec Rosen, Grade 3
Miami Country Day School, FL

I Am

I am a smart girl who loves skateboarding.
I wonder if I could be as good as Tony Hawk.
I hear the wheels rolling under my feet.
I feel the wind rushing through my hair.
I want to learn more tricks on my skateboard.
I am a smart girl who loves skateboarding.

I pretend to be a professional skateboarder.
I feel great when I master a new trick.
I touch my skateboard when I flip it up.
I worry that if I fall people will laugh.
I cry when I can't do a new trick.
I am a smart girl who loves skateboarding.

I understand why I can't do some tricks.
I say I can do more than I can.
I dream I am a pro skateboarder.
I try to be the best I can be.
I hope I will not lose my balance.
I am a smart girl who loves skateboarding.

Rachel Levin, Grade 3
McKinley Elementary School, PA

The Flower

I know how the flower grows.
You have to put some water in the flower.
I know why we have to put water in it.

Ailin Li, Grade 1
Children's Village, PA

City Sidewalks

City sidewalks, city sidewalks
Dressed in holiday style.
People laughing and playing
All over the place.
Eating chocolate and pops
Birds singing la, la, la
La, la, la, la, la, la, la.
Playing with their friends.
Having so much fun.
Only with each other.

Meghan McNamara, Grade 3
Leicester Memorial Elementary School, MA

I Am

I am a girl who loves soccer
I wonder how many goals I will make
I hear the crowd cheering
I feel excited to score a goal
I want to win every game
I am a girl who loves soccer

I pretend to be a professional
I feel important to my team
I touch a soccer ball
I worry when I upset the team
I cry when I lose
I am a girl who loves soccer

I understand how to play
I say try my hardest
I dream to be the best
I try to be awesome at it
I hope I win next time
I am a girl who loves soccer

Nicole Gerhardt, Grade 3
McKinley Elementary School, PA

The Margay

Secretly prowls in the night,
Giving his prey, the Macaw, a fright.
Color and glory in his coat,
He has a reason to gloat.

The Margay

Elise Emory, Grade 2
Home School, TN

Autumn

A pples are good to taste.
U p the birds go.
T hanksgiving is for giving thanks.
U p I jump in the air.
M om makes me turkey.
N uts are for squirrels.

Ashley Dandashi, Grade 3
Central Park Elementary School, FL

My Doggy

I have a doggy.
She is a puppy.
Her name is Muffy.
Her body is fluffy.
Sure she's a toughy,
Because she's my puppy.

She likes to play
On a rainy day.
But I'm not happy,
Because it's gray.
And I cannot play
When it's rainy.

When I call her Muffy
Her tail gets waggy.
She runs in a hurry.
Then wants me to carry.
She is a little tricky,
But I love my puppy.

Thisal Yatiyawela, Grade 3
Duncan Elementary School, SC

Pizza

I like pizza.
Any kind of pizza.
Pepperoni pizza, sausage pizza.
Barbecue pizza, bacon pizza.
Pizza in my stomach.
Pizza on my plate.
Pizza with more pizza.
Any kind of pizza.
I like pizza.

Austin Humphrey, Grade 3
Landmark Christian School, GA

Yellow Cat

I like to lick.
But I don't like to be sick.
I like milk.
And I feel like silk.
I am Yellow Cat.

Sabrina Ventura, Grade 1
Northeast Elementary School, NY

Monkeys

M onkeys swing vine to vine
O n a hot sunny day in the rainforest.
N ight falls and the howling stops.
K ingly nightingales coo in the morning when the sun rises.
E ating termites is their normal breakfast.
Y elling and screaming continues all day until
S unset and the day starts all over again.

Will Sands, Grade 3
Pride Elementary School, FL

I Am

I am a smart boy who loves computers
I wonder who invented the computers
I hear the computer keys typing
I see a computer screen
I want to have a computer of my own
I am a smart boy who loves computers.

I pretend I am a spy
I feel like an astronaut in the sky
I touch the moon
I worry about silly things
I cry when I get hurt
I am a smart boy who loves computers.

I understand I have to work hard
I say there is life on other planets
I dream about being a rich man
I hope someday I will live in India with my family
I am a smart boy who loves computers.

Raunak Sethi, Grade 2
Clark Elementary School, FL

Candle Light

Candle light shining in the dark,
Like two squiggly lines meeting together at the top,
lighting up the dark night.
Like a candle in a pumpkin on Halloween.
Like a candle glowing in a room at night,
lighting up the whole house,
flickering on and off the whole night.
Whoosh, the candle is out.

Catrina Hidalgo Schick, Grade 3
Lincoln Elementary School, PA

Halloween

I love Halloween
Halloween at night
Is good for a fright
At night
When the pumpkins are out
Haunted houses glaring
At night
Spiders crawling all around
It's when we Trick or Treat
It's when the bats come out
And the ghosts fright

Danielle Pickard, Grade 2
Annsville Elementary School, NY

Dog

Dog
Black, brown
Digs, catches, runs
Happy, like, mad, sad
Puppy

Donovan Swiger, Grade 2
Woodland Elementary School, KY

I Love You More

Roses are red;
Violets are blue.
I love you more
Than a silly old shoe.
I love you more
Then all the seas.
I almost love you more than me.
I love you…
You love me.
It is a possibility
I love you more
Than the water.
I love you more
Than the houses.
I love you almost more
Than anything I know.
I love you
'Cause you are mine.

Jillian Cooper, Grade 2
Memorial School, NH

In My Room

In my room,
on my bed,
by my curtains
underneath my blanket
with my stuffed animal,
I lie in my bed dreaming about art.

Olivia O'Brien, Grade 3
McKinley Elementary School, PA

My Brother Is a Devil

My brother is a devil.
He bites me.
He kicks me.
He punches me.
He smacks me across my face.
He tackles me,
And he pulls my clothes
And never leaves me alone.
And he always watches his baby shows
When I'm there.
And he takes my food and eats it.
Told ya, my brother is a devil.

Catherine Pileggi, Grade 3
Oak Ridge Elementary School, PA

Jack-o'-lantern/Pumpkin Pie

Jack-o'-lantern
Strong, small
Carving, eating, baking
You can carve pumpkins.
Pumpkin pie

Jonathan Carlucci, Grade 2
Consolidated School, CT

Thanksgiving Fun

Thanksgiving is a lot of fun.
We give thanks for what we have.
The food is never done.
We eat until we're full,
And then everyone goes home.

Daniella Leggio, Grade 3
Our Lady of Hope School, NY

The Color Black
The color black

Black is the color of the night sky
which makes a cool fresh breeze.
Black makes creatures show their true colors
in the dark night sky.

The color black

Thomas Nucatola, Grade 3
Sundance School, NJ

Ten Little Dogs
Ten little dogs came out of the fog.
Three little dogs sat on a log.

Seven little dogs got on a cot.
Three little dogs got real hot.

Four little dogs went to the mall.
Two little dogs went through a hall.

One little dog hit her head.
The other little dog is ready for bed.

Lauren Hurt, Grade 3
Belfast-Elk Garden Elementary School, VA

My Mare in the Forest
One day I went out with my mare.
The wind was blowing in my hair.
Swish, swoosh.
Then I heard the leaves fall off the trees,
Crunch, crunch, crunch.
My mare said "Neigh!"
And I heard her galloping away.
I wanted this to last all day, all night,
Then suddenly I looked, oh no, oh dear!
There was a bear!
My mare and I went home
As fast as a rabbit
And now we know
Never go riding in the woods.

Cynclaire Jones, Grade 3
Briarwood Christian School, AL

My Teachers
My teachers are great
Because they help us to learn.
Teachers — great for me!
Oriel Bruce, Grade 1
United Hebrew Institute, PA

Squirrels/Animals
Squirrels
Brown, fuzzy
Running, eating, hiding
Gather acorns for winter.
Animals
Bridget Kenny, Grade 2
Consolidated School, CT

Jacob
J oyful
A wesome
C lean
O ffspring
B obcats
Jacob Price, Grade 2
Park Elementary School, AR

Dogs
Dogs are nice.
Dogs will do whatever you say.

Dogs like to play.
They will show respect to you.

They also will never get tired
Because they are so fast.

They have a cold wet nose,
That are cute as a button.

They have happy little tails
That wag all the time.

Dogs are very loyal
They love their human family.
Kyle Shaffer, Grade 3
St Alexis School, PA

Candy
Candy
Sour, yummy
Finding, opening, eating
It is hard candy.
Lollipop
Thomas McGuire, Grade 3
Chestnut Street Elementary School, PA

Halloween/Holiday
Halloween
Spooky, scary
Trick-or-treating, going, visiting
I am a pumpkin
Holiday
Trey Wennerstrom, Grade 3
Chestnut Street Elementary School, PA

I Am From
I am from my cozy bedroom where
my pretty lamp is lit for me and
my fluffy pillow is waiting for me.
I am from my neat basement
where my cool computer is waiting for me
and my excellent books are ready for my Dad.
I am from my playful backyard where
my colorful leaves are in a stacks for me
and I slide down my hill.
Sasha Zuberi, Grade 1
Berkeley Lake Elementary School, GA

My Dog Spike
Spike is fun
He likes to run
He is soft and cuddly
When he sleeps on my bed
He licks me when I am sad
He protects me from harm
He plays catch and Frisbee with me
I love him so much
That is why I feed him lots of food
And walk him every day after school
Spike is not only my pet, he is my friend.
Dante George, Grade 3
John Hus Moravian School, NY

The Green Waterfalls of Heaven

In the light over the clouds,
Higher than the trees that flutter in the breeze.
Over the hills that gleam in the sun,
Past all those is a gift.
It is called Heaven.
Close by there are waterfalls that shimmer in the light.
Fish with fins, snouts and bulgy eyes,
Seaweed reaches high off the dirt.
You can say it is a sight.
And down we go to Earth again…

Tristen Koerber, Grade 3
Birch Hill Elementary School, NH

The Three Shepherds

The three shepherds saw a bright light.
They followed it and traveled with all their might.
Then they considered it was a star.
They followed the star and traveled so far.

Mary and Joseph went door to door.
Some said they had no room, others said no more.
They found a stable and had a baby with no danger.
They held him while he cried and put him in a manger.

Mallory Maza, Grade 3
St Edward the Confessor School, LA

The Color Green

Green is the color of the leaves before they turn red.
Green is the color of grass before it turns yellow.
Green is the color of plants before they have snow on them.

Jordan Gasson, Grade 3
Sundance School, NJ

My Landform

Small landform, big landform,
large landform, tall landform,
and short landform.
The landform is the shape of the earth's surface.
So, I live on a landform.
But, wait!
There's more landforms like,
mountains, plains, islands, countries, and cliffs.

Taylor McKenzie, Grade 3
Public School 235 Lenox, NY

Winter

In the cold winter,
When the wind starts to blow,
My favorite thing to do,
Is play in the snow!

Andrew Eaton, Grade 3
Christ at Home Lutheran School, MO

Up at the Shore

Water is whizzing toward the sand
A wave splashes in my face.
Sea animals swimming in tiny pools.
I lean for a star from the sea.
Hard on top
Soft on bottom.
Red as blood from my body.

It crawls out.
My eyes glow
At a sea anemone
Like an octopus.
Then I look down at a hermit crab.
Chomping on solid seaweed.
Time to go home
Till next time
Sea shore.

Maisie Bernstein, Grade 3
Zervas Elementary School, MA

Jack

J oyful
A wesome
C olorful
K ind

Jack Rafferty, Grade 2
Long Meadow Elementary School, CT

Winter

You leave cookies out
Tomorrow they are gone
And presents nice as gold

Haroun Ihsan Haque, Grade 3
Tuxedo Park School, NY

Bee

Bee
Fast, pretty
Stings, morphs, mimics
I really like the bee!
Bug!

Sarena Hunt, Grade 3
Clinton Christian Academy, MO

My Cat

I like to hug my cat.
He is fun.
Ashes is funny.
If it is raining,
He is fun.

Joseph Frye, Grade 3
McKinley Elementary School, PA

Jessica

J aguar
E agle
S nake
S eth, my brother
I ce cream
C locks when they tick
A pples, I eat them

Jessica Guerra, Kindergarten
Eden Gardens Magnet School, LA

Red

I am an apple.
I am a heart.
I am a throne.
I am red.

Pamela Guardado, Grade 1
Northeast Elementary School, NY

Big Chicken

I can eat
Grains but not meat
I can run
And eat buns
I am Big Chicken.

Jonny Perla, Grade 1
Northeast Elementary School, NY

The Sport of Football

Players running like the wind.
Watching my favorite team score touchdowns.
They use teamwork to win.

Allison Beljan, Grade 3
Holland Township School, NJ

Natural Resources

Big, tall trees
Dark brown soil
Hard heavy rocks
1 yellow star
Tasty juicy fruits
See through water
Real black oil
Cold and hot air
Natural
Resources!
Soon they might all be gone because of…
Pollution

Fabiana Netus, Grade 3
Public School 235 Lenox, NY

Making a Difference

Everyone can make a difference.
You can make a difference too.
Now let us start at the beginning,
you can even start it too!
You can make a difference by not polluting.
I can make that difference too.
If you pick up trash on your hiking trail,
you will make a big difference too.
We are almost to the end!
But I have a lot more to say.
Making a difference in your community
gets you a lot of hoorays!
Now in your community,
you will even say good day!
Now we are almost at the end.
Just five more words to go.
Making a difference in the world,
is the right way to go!

Karan Jacob, Grade 3
Springfield Park Elementary School, VA

Blue Jay
I love the blue jay.
The blue jay is white and blue.
The colored blue jay!
Skyler Bruck, Grade 3
Clinton Christian Academy, MO

Time
Time can go slow or fast.
It can be fast if you waste it.
It can be slow if you use it wisely.
Don't waste time.
Rosa-Maria Diez, Grade 3
Wolcott School, CT

The Titanic
TITANIC, TITANIC
Long and fast.
The TITANIC so beautifully made
With its black coat of paint
Unsinkable…
No, no, no…On April 12, 1912
It sunk in the Atlantic.
It hit an Iceberg and sank
Many lives were lost.
This is a calamity
The world will never forget.
Robert E. Butler, Grade 3
Evangelical Christian School, TN

My Favorite Color
I like blue.
The blueberry is blue.
The gum is blue.
The coat is blue.
I like blue.
Genny Eccleston, Grade 1
Northeast Elementary School, NY

Lizards
They run really fast
Their tails break off easily
They are hard to catch
Jordan Lips, Grade 3
Miami Country Day School, FL

Let the Noises Begin
P andemonium
A junction of noise
N oisy
D estructive
E nergetic
M any yells
O n the stands nothing but sound
N oises untamable
I n zone nothing is heard
U nstoppable
M ore noises the better
Sarah Henderson, Grade 3
Pottsville Elementary School, AR

Grant
Grant
Funny, tall
Football, baseball, soccer
He is always nice
Tiger
Mary Elise Nolen, Grade 3
Briarwood Christian School, AL

Friends
Friends
Kind, helpful
Working together, playing
Happy, loving, friendly, caring
Friends
Divya Rathinavel, Grade 3
Wapping Elementary School, CT

Animals
Bird
colorful, cute
flying, sitting, singing
Rainforest, sky, Wilbur, barn
oinking, wallowing, rolling
fat, pink
pig
Jalein Jenkins-Johnson, Grade 2
Bensley Elementary School, VA

Sun

S un is a big star.
U mbrellas shade us from the sun.
N ight the sun goes down and the moon comes up

Jessica Brown, Grade 1
Annie Belle Clark Primary School, GA

Selena

Nice
Pretty
Smart
Funny
Wishes to have a loyal husband.
Dreams of cotton candy clouds and milk as raindrops.
Wants to have my house in the snow.
Who fears to be severely injured.
Who is afraid of heights.
Who likes cherries.
Who believes there's magic beyond the stars.
Who loves to be artistic.
Who loves all my friends and family.
Who loves my pets.
Who loves Christmas.
Who plans to be a 1st grade teacher.
Who plans to go to Las Vegas.
Who plans to go to North Carolina.
Whose last steps are in heaven.

Selena Ramos, Grade 3
Central Park Elementary School, FL

Horses

Neigh, neigh, neigh that horse wants some hay.
Swish, swish, swish that horse tail is going swish.
Stomp, stomp, stomp can you hear that horse stomp?
Sit on the saddle and kick it's side. That's how you ride.

Taylor Baldwin, Grade 3
Briarwood Christian School, AL

Tali

T oys
A crobatics
L ovable
I ntelligent

Tali Benzaken, Grade 3
Virginia A Boone Highland Oaks Elementary School, FL

Christmas Is Fun

Christmas is fun.
We get a lot of toys.
We make cookies for Santa.
He likes girls and boys.
We have hot chocolate.
Snow falls from the sky.
We get a lot of presents.
The tree has a star up high.

Billy Bennett, Grade 1
Westlake Christian School, FL

Autumn

Fall trees and grass grow
Squirrels bury their acorns
Pumpkins are growing

Nic Daniels, Grade 2
Wellington School, FL

Thanksgiving

Family and turkey
Playing eating singing
Try not to choke!!
Tasty

Khiara Feliciano, Grade 3
Marie Curie Institute, NY

Baseball

Cheer, whistle
Peanut shells breaking,
Homerun.
We won!

Thomas Nieman, Grade 2
Clover Street School, CT

Volleyball

She moves so fast,
its amazing, as she
dives and
jumps, and serves
the ball when it comes
to her

Julianna Ferraro, Grade 3
Holland Township School, NJ

Christmas

Christmas is here!
Christmas is there!
Christmas is everywhere!
It is fun! Christmas is one day not two!
But it is fun every day!
We get presents! Toys are inside!
Toys that we love!
Ho! Ho! Ho! Merry Christmas!
Christmas is my favorite holiday!

Nicholas Jones, Grade 2
Narvie J Harris Traditional Theme School, GA

Halloween

Halloween
Spooky, fun
Frightening, tricking, treating
Halloween is great fun.
Holiday

Madison Selan, Grade 3
Chestnut Street Elementary School, PA

I Can

I can see the cat sleeping sh sh sh.
I can see the dog eating.
I can see the sun moving.
I can see the apple falling thump thump.
I can see the people walking.
I can see the dog barking woof woof.
I can see the owl saying whoo whoo.

If you look you can see it too!

Chelsea Aviles, Grade 2
Public School 148 Ruby Allen, NY

Deserts and Mazes

Deserts are mazes
Difficult to survive
Impossible life
Never ending on all sides
Wandering, but never going anywhere
Wishing, hoping to escape
This trap of doom.

Nate Priebe, Grade 3
Hunter GT Magnet Elementary School, NC

Clock Business

A clock is a business man,
rushing through time,
working,
tuned to wake up and go to sleep,
ticking away for payday to come,
joyfully showing their work with hands.

Jared Goldman, Grade 3
Hunter GT Magnet Elementary School, NC

A Trip to Japan

Japan is a country that's far away.
My dad is going over there today.
He says good-bye to all of us.
And my little sister starts to fuss.
Dad says Japan is very clean;
They have robot toys I have never seen.
My dad has been there many-a-time.
He knows many Japanese words that rhyme.
Some day I'd like to go with him,
But I'd rather fly than try to swim.

Tad Lyon, Grade 3
The American Academy, PA

Summer

S wimming parties
U nder the sun
M aking new friends
M aking fun
E arly morning to enjoy
R elay races to enjoy
and so much more

Taylor Foster, Grade 3
Madison Station Elementary School, MS

Halloween

Halloween
Scary cats
Scary ghosts too
Vampire bats swoop around
Floating ghosts haunt the night
You see frightening skeletons on Halloween.

Nicholas Blanton, Grade 3
Mary Matula Elementary School, MD

At the Grand Canyon
I went to the Grand Canyon.
There were lots of rocks
I wish I did not wear my socks.
There were trees some
had leaves some had none.
Some dirt
flew on my shirt.
The blurry sky was light and bright!
Morgan Steele, Grade 3
Western Hills Elementary School, AR

My Pet
Cat
Bites her tail
Runs around
Inside house
Sits on floor
Flips around
Doing fun tricks
Kitty cat
Makayla Chapman, Kindergarten
Broadway Elementary School, NC

On My Way to School
Plot, plot
Here comes the rain
On my way to school

All I feel is rain
I feel wet bushes
Touching my legs
On my way to school

I am walking
Beside my friends
On my way to school

I see buildings
On a rainy day
On my way to school
Isaiah Taveras, Grade 3
Coram Elementary School, NY

Art Class
Glitter has sparkles.
Painting pictures of sunsets.
Sketching animals.
Emily Shapard, Grade 2
St Peter the Apostle School, GA

Listen
Listen to the birds.
Listen to the bees.
Listen to the wind.
Listen to the trees.

Listen to the sky.
Listen to the ground.
Listen to the water.
Listen all around.
Cecilia Esterman, Grade 3
Webster Montessori School, NY

My Brother
Nice, happy, funny
Reading, sleeping, playing, writing
Friends, sports, listener
Luke
John Campomenosi, Grade 2
St Mary's School, NJ

My Cat
Cat
Nice, lazy
Purring, meowing, sleeping
Always sleeps with me
Carrot
Connor Presley, Grade 3
Landmark Christian School, GA

Who Is It?
He wanted to be a star
He told lies
His nose grew

Pinocchio
Donovan Moore, Grade 1
Northeast Elementary School, NY

I Am

I am a girl who is good at soccer
I wonder if I will get the winning goal
I feel my heart beat after I run
I hear the coach call me in to trade places with another girl
I want to win all the games
I am a girl who is good at soccer

I pretend I am playing against older girls
I feel wind on my face when I am running towards the goal
I touch the ball when I am goalie
I worry when the other team has the ball and are ready to score
I cry when we lose
I am a girl who is good at soccer

I understand when other people get hurt and I have to stop
I say, "Are you okay?"
I dream I win every game
I try my best
I hope we win
I am a girl who is good at soccer

Kyrsten Bick, Grade 3
McKinley Elementary School, PA

Water Falls

I can hear the waterfall
rumbling and grumbling.
I can see the rainbow
As bright as the sun,
through the smoke like foggy clouds.
I can smell the coldness in the air as
the cool breeze rushes past my face.

Evan Chen, Grade 2
Worthington Hooker School – K-2 Campus, CT

Listen to the Sounds

I can see the wind blowing.
I can see the bee making honey.
I can see the rat in the house.
I can see the dog bouncing boom boom boom.
I can see an owl whoo whoo whoo.
I can see a cat saying meow meow meow.
I can see a baby crying waa waa waa.

Jennifer Gracia, Grade 2
Public School 148 Ruby Allen, NY

A Woman Called Pam

There once was a women called Pam
She liked doing magic with Sam
One day they messed up
Made volcanoes erupt
And then the whole world went kabam!

Jack Readman, Grade 3
Memorial School, NH

My Favorite Color

I like blue.
The sky is blue.
The balloon is blue.
The Care Bear is blue.
I like blue.

Bethzayda Guzman, Grade 1
Northeast Elementary School, NY

Horses

They are warm blooded
They come in lots of colors
They need to be brushed

Veronica Ortiz, Grade 3
Miami Country Day School, FL

Snowman/Frosty

snowman
large, white, frozen
building, standing, freezing
people made of snow in the winter
Frosty

Robby Zemken, Grade 2
Wells Central School, NY

Playland

Playland is big
and noisy
because you hear
the people screaming
on a fast scary ride
I go
again, again and again
I never get tired of it.

Naomi H. Isles, Grade 3
Public School 148 Ruby Allen, NY

Reading

Reading is fun.
Read a book every day.
In fact read a book today.
Reading helps you learn.
Read books about anything you like.
Read whenever you get a turn.
Remember to read a book every day.
And remember what I say
Read, read, reading is terrific.
Take a look
In a good book
And read, read
Every day!

Veronica Ochoa, Grade 3
Marie Durand Elementary School, NJ

Football

I like football.
It is fun to tackle people.
I like the sport football.
You can make new friends
And have a lot of fun.
It is a rough sport.

Benjamin Lane, Grade 3
McKinley Elementary School, PA

Peace

Peace is so friendly and
Makes everyone happy.
Just like moss on a tree
It is everywhere that life is, like
Where the trees hang around
And the hazel nuts fall,
Nut
By nut.
As the rain falls
so peacefully
and so beautifully
While
Falling.

Theo Spisak, Grade 3
Oak Ridge Elementary School, PA

Flowers

Flowers are happy.
Flowers are cool.
Appear in my garden.
Shoot out from the ground.
Bunches and bunches gliding around me,
Spinning around the fields.
Stems as green as a moth
On a tree.
When I lay down
In the bunches of flowers
It tickles my heart.
The fun does not begin or end
Anytime.
The flowers fade across my face.
My heart feels like it is powerful.

Nicole Secchiari, Grade 3
Oak Ridge Elementary School, PA

What If?

What if my grandpa didn't get in a crash?
I might play with him.

What if I got to see him before that happened?
I could ask him to teach me German.

What if he hadn't died?
I would love and play with him every day.

I would ask my mom where he is?

Sara Huggins, Grade 3
Byrns L. Darden Elementary School, TN

Football

Football is my favorite sport.
I love to play it.
Football is fun.
I watch football.
I play football.
I even play football outside.
Some say it is not cool.
But, I think it is just fine.

Logan Williams, Grade 2
Narvie J Harris Traditional Theme School, GA

Playful Girl

Gracie
Graceful, funny
Dancing, skating, playing
I like my dog
Gracie
Gracie Tompkins, Grade 2
St Stephen's School, NY

Emma

E mma likes clean
M om likes me
M y cat's name is Elvis
A lex is my best friend
Emma Gandolfi, Grade 1
St Stephen's School, NY

My Flag

The flag looks like a box.
They are usually red and
white and blue.
Flags are colorful.
Some have stars and some
have stripes.

I like flags.
Kristen Soden, Grade 1
Holland Township School, NJ

Moon

I am the moon
I wait for the sun to say
it's my turn
to shine in the sky
people go to sleep
while I watch over them
I play hide and go seek
sometimes showing half of me
sometimes showing all of me
I say hi to the planets
and they say hi to me
I am the moon
Shelby Brenton, Grade 3
Memorial School, NH

My Pet Turtle

My pet was a turtle.
He smelled like flowers.
He knew how to spin on his back.
He looked lovely.
My sister and I used to check on him
Every morning and every night.
His name was BD and he was handsome.
His favorite food was cookies.
I love him still.
Tyler Johnson, Grade 2
Lee A Tolbert Community Academy, MO

Kristen

Crazy pretty girl
funny loving caring friend
golden hair blue eyes
Kristen Rodriguez, Grade 3
NJ

The Sport of Soccer

Kicking is what I like to do
Running is what it is mostly about
Sweating is what I always do
Goals are what I try to make all the time
Michael Machiesky, Grade 3
Holland Township School, NJ

Candy

Candy
Sour, sweet
Eating, tasting, smelling
I like Halloween time.
Gum
Ashley Postlewait, Grade 3
Chestnut Street Elementary School, PA

Flowers

Flowers are colorful, beautiful.
Some differ from each other.
Some are small, some are big.
Not all of them are the same.
But they are all beautiful.
Jericho Elijah Pigon, Grade 3
St Joseph Catholic Grammar School, NJ

Trees Are Falling

Trees are falling down.
Why are the trees falling down?
The beavers are hungry.

Caileigh Marshall, Grade 2
Virginia A Boone Highland Oaks Elementary School, FL

Fall

In the fall, I see a big brown, roasting turkey in the oven.
In the fall, I hear a noisy leaf blower in the afternoon.
In the fall, I taste warm chocolaty hot chocolate by the fireplace.
In the fall, I feel dry, crunchy leaves on the hay ride.
In the fall, I smell hot, cinnamony spicy pumpkin pie at my Aunt Joyce's house.
In the fall, I don't see swimming pools that are full of happy kids.

Teha Reaser, Grade 3
Watsontown Elementary School, PA

Music Instruments

The violin, the viola, and the cello are stringed instruments.
The drums and horns are not.
The trumpet and the tuba are brass,
But the piano and the bass are not.
There are lots of different sections of the instruments.
They each make a different sound.
Which section do you fit in best?
I would prefer the strings.
Each has to prayerfully find his own section.
God will help you find your own special things.

Andrew James Crowell, Grade 3
Evangelical Christian School, TN

Dad Mountain

Dad Mountain is strong and powerful.
He is also very sweet.
He is like a rock.
He is very nice.
He talks to me…I talk to him.
When you see him he shows you his white soft suit.
It is really nice.
His green tie sways like a tree.
It is a beautiful sight.
He is my favorite mountain.
I love Dad Mountain!

Robert Anthony Catania, Grade 3
Sundance School, NJ

Big Pig

I watch the moon.
I eat at noon.
I drink milk.
I look like pink silk.
I am Big Pig.

Kevin Prudencio, Grade 1
Northeast Elementary School, NY

I Am From

I am from my cool bedroom
where my blue Ferrari poster
is staring at me.
I am from my clean office
where the music is loud.
I am from my trail path
where I hear the lake go sshhh.

Nick Zaslavsky, Grade 1
Berkeley Lake Elementary School, GA

Math

Math is good
Math is great
I just cannot wait
Math is my favorite subject
I am good at it
Math is good
Math is great
Yay math

Karlee Ruth, Grade 3
Evergreen Elementary School, PA

Water

Water
Wet, moist, hot or cold
All over the big world.
Held in so many places.
The life of many nations.
Water
Cleanser of dirt, sins and the earth.
The best of all natural resources.

Adrian Nesbitt, Grade 3
Public School 235 Lenox, NY

Books

I like books.
Any kind of books.
Happy books, sad books,
Chapter books, creative books.
Books in my room,
Books on my shelf,
Books with my bedtime,
Any kind of books.
I like books.

Mary Grace Bridges, Grade 3
Landmark Christian School, GA

Fall Is When...

the air is as cold as snow.
the trees are as colorful as a rainbow.
the birds sound like music.
the animal's coat is as soft as a pillow.

Monica Perez, Grade 3
Coral Cove Elementary School, FL

Rascal

My dog Rascal is so crazy
He lies around all day being so lazy.

If a stranger he does see
He barks and bristles to protect me.

We like to play in the yard
He lets us tackle him so very hard.

He's a jumper and a prancer
As if he was a famous dancer.

He licks my face and wags his tail
Watch his claws they're sharp as a nail.

Evan Rose, Grade 3
Pike Liberal Arts School, AL

Penguins

Penguins swim.
Penguins hop.
Penguins pip, pip, pip!

Daniela Ardila, Grade 1
Northeast Elementary School, NY

Baseball/Red Sox

Baseball
Running, happy
Sweating, hitting, catching
Winner, World Series, cheering, excited
Red Sox

Shayan Farooq, Grade 3
Wapping Elementary School, CT

Halloween Candy

H alloween is so neat
A ll my friends would like a treat
L ove your costume
L ike your mask
O h always scared with fright
W hen you go trick or treating
E ven with a friend
E ven with a neighbor
N ever ever go alone

C andy is for Halloween
A nd for fun
N ever steal any from trick-or-treaters
D o your best and
Y our candy will always be sweet

Danny Williams, Grade 3
Madison Station Elementary School, MS

Toy Department

A very tall green prickly tree
Loud choo-choo trains
Golden ornaments
Salty pretzels
Tasty green sour apple lollipop

Tyler Mullen, Grade 3
Bradford Township Elementary School, PA

The Tennis Ball

At the tennis match, a ball flew through the air
Like a lightning bolt zooming fast.
A flash of green made my eyes glare
And the final outcome of the players was cast.

Nicholas Ilgandi, Grade 3
Hunter GT Magnet Elementary School, NC

Fire Warning

Grill, stove, fireplace
Cigarettes, gasoline
Light matches
Be safe
Don't play with fire!

Danny Camacho, Grade 2
Weston Elementary School, NJ

Arielle

A greeable
R emarkable
I nteresting
E xcellent
L oving
L ovely
E xciting

Arielle Francis, Grade 2
Long Meadow Elementary School, CT

Stuck in a Tree

Chimpanzee
Stuck in a banana tree.
What will you do once you are free?
Tell me.

Bryan Carter, Grade 3
Reidville Elementary School, SC

A White Blanket

As snow is falling
Like the fleece blanket on my bed
It covers the ground.

Kate Frimet, Grade 3
Tuxedo Park School, NY

Spring

spring, nature,
happy, pretty,
grow, seeds,
stem, buds,
roots, smells,
sneeze, pollen,
bloom.

Hannah "Noni" Patrick, Grade 2
Hilton Head Christian Academy, SC

Thanksgiving

T ender turkey
H appy harvest
A pple pie
N apkins needed
K ind people
S ome family members
G iving thanks
I ndians are good friends.
V ery good food
I ndians are part of Thanksgiving.
N ot a bad holiday
G randparents come

Sidney Hager, Grade 3
Clinton Christian Academy, MO

Go Sabres

The Sabres are my favorite team,
they make the fans want to scream.
But the Sabres lost the game,
now I feel really tame.
And the Sabres had no luck,
now the Sabres are in a muck.
But the next time we win,
my family will have a celebration.
The Sabres are experts,
but sometimes they still get hurt.

Tyler Wright, Grade 3
Ellicott Road Elementary School, NY

All Things

God made all things
Isn't it obvious?
God made all things
Isn't it glorious?
God made all things
Like birds and trees.
God made all things
From the skies to the seas.
God made *all* things!
God made *everything!*

Mary Beth Lothrop, Grade 3
Evangelical Christian School, TN

School

School is very fun.
If you are very good in class you may get to play in the sun.
Television is not good for school.
But you need your brain as a tool.
School comes first.
But don't make your teacher burst.
Computers are for you to take some tests.
Please try to do your best.

Madison Brown, Grade 3
Pike Liberal Arts School, AL

Reading

R eading is fun!
E ach time you read, you might learn more.
A re you a good reader?
D o you like to read?
I n an atlas, you can discover the world!
N ever stop reading.
G et off your feet and read!

Olivia LeSure, Grade 3
Bensley Elementary School, VA

Winter

Winter is fun because last year
The snow was 15 inches high!
It was very fun
And I made snow tunnels
And when I opened my door
There would be a huge pile of snow.
Winter is fun.

Ellen Schmidt, Grade 2
Robert E Lee Expressive Arts Elementary School, MO

Painting

P retty
A rtsy
I nteresting
N ature
T ouching
I nnovative
N ew
G reat

Adam Gelman, Grade 3
Virginia A Boone Highland Oaks Elementary School, FL

The Cloud

The scary black cloud
in the dark dusk sky
drove like a car
on the highway

Jensen Gross, Grade 3
Wellington School, FL

School

School is hard work
And also fun
Because we do
A lot of work!

We use pencils and paper
And books to learn
We go to the gym
And play volleyball.

We learn the times tables
We learn about history
We learn to read stories
Like *Green Eggs and Ham!*

The teachers all help us
To do our work
They help us to learn
And become smart as we can!

Shawn Scott, Grade 3
Ocean Academy, NJ

Polly the Parrot

I am a parrot.
Polly would like a cracker!
Repeat everything.

Zachary Kornfeld, Grade 1
United Hebrew Institute, PA

Deer

Deer gallop in the woods
Fast as a scared cheetah
Disappear in the woods

Mark Coiro, Grade 3
Tuxedo Park School, NY

School Morning at My House

Beep…beep…beep…Paige, get out of bed!
Owww! I tripped over my broom,
I didn't even know it was in my room!
…Beep, bang I hit my head.
My sister is brushing her teeth,
Her toothpaste looks like it is blue,
Hurry, hurry I need to get to school.

Paige Marovich, Grade 3
Briarwood Christian School, AL

Gymnastics

Flipping, Flopping
Cartwheels and round offs
Front rolls and back rolls
Oh how I love them all
Balance beam is hard
I fall off a lot
I try my very best
To land on the spot
Vault is not just about jumping
You do handstand blocks
Act like the spring board is a pool of lava
Get your hands off quick
Bars oh bars oh bars
My favorite one
Get some chalk to do your skills
Pull over and up you go
Cast almost horizontal
And under the bar
Put your toes up on the bar
And fly off
Oh how I love gymnastics!

Kinsley Blakeway, Grade 3
Anacoco Elementary School, LA

Rainy Night

On a rainy night it will be slightly slippery.
You will hear, "Pitter-patter! Drip, drop!"
There will be loud lightning.
You can't tame rain.
Rain might be at a game.
With rain it is super stormy.

Katie Green, Grade 3
Briarwood Christian School, AL

Christmas Is the Best!

Christmas is here!
It is the Best time of year!
I like to see my family and friends!
I hope the day will never end!

Zane Thomas, Grade 1
St Vincent De Paul Elementary School, MO

The Holiday Season

The holiday season is here.
I've been waiting for this all year.
The month of December is one I remember.
Cookies, decorations and cheer,
The holiday season is here.
Jingle bells and mistletoe,
Ribbon candy, HO, HO, HO!!
A roaring fire, is what I desire.
I see Christmas cartoons before bed,
While thoughts of gifts dance in my head.
Stockings are hung, Christmas carols sung.
I close my eyes, boom, big surprise!!!!!!

Hope Abbott, Grade 3
North Star Elementary School, DE

Penguin Party

Penguins party on the ice
Swaying to music, oh so nice.

They look at the sky
As they waddle by.

They dance to the beat
With their happy feet.

Penguins play on the ice
With a fish, that is nice.

They make their way
On a very cold day.

My favorite animal is a penguin
Every time I see one, I can't help but grin!

Samantha Alioto, Grade 3
St Alexis School, PA

The War

People fighting for our country
Mud and dirt no fun at all
Tents, no sleep

Trumpets, get up in the morning
Weapons lots I can say
Bullets flying every which way

People fighting for our country
Michaela Porter, Grade 3
Tri-County Christian School, MO

Flowers

Flowers are red
Roses are blue
Cats are cute and kitties are cute too.
They are pretty
and cats and kitties are beautiful too.
Michelle Wu, Grade 1
Children's Village, PA

Spring

There was a breeze in the air
Blowing the leaves in directions.
Beautiful flowers shining bright.
Special seasons, delighted smile.
Glowing grass on the ground.
Pretty flowers blooming.
Spring is warm and sparkling.
It makes myself light up.
Spring is my favorite season.
I love spring!
Alexa Dluzneski, Grade 3
Oak Ridge Elementary School, PA

Cranky Mr. Hanky

Mr. Hanky
is cranky
So he started to cry
after that he said good-bye.
Anjana Srikumar, Grade 3
The Parke House Academy, FL

Nothing

A secret place within
Deep forests, waiting
To be discovered.
Paper airplanes, yearning
To be flown, gliding every
Which way in a mass of paper.
Birds dodging quick-flying
Airplanes in a flurry of wings.
Doing something on a day
When nothing has to be done
Is much better than doing
Nothing.
Jacob Adler, Grade 3
Somers Intermediate School, NY

Soccer

I love soccer.
I have a gym locker.
I have to wear pads.
In soccer, there are some lads.
You have to play in the sun,
Along with the ball you must run.
I wrote this poem for you.
I hope your friends read it too!
Sydney Slaughter, Grade 3
Briarwood Christian School, AL

My Pet

Fish
Eat a lot of food
Likes worms
Orange
In the pond
Swim their tails around
Fun to watch
Kenneth Ciechowski, Kindergarten
Broadway Elementary School, NC

Rabit-ku

Fluffy, soft, cozy,
Eats carrots, jumps high, higher
Looks for food to eat.
Brandon Dumas, Grade 2
Paine Primary School, AL

Who to Blame?

If I knocked the lamp over and it broke on the floor, who will I blame?
My sister Brianna.
She runs around the house a lot to look for her homework.

If I accidentally pressed a button on the oven,
and it caught on fire, who will I blame?
My mom.
She is always cooking and working around the house.

If I was sneaky and put extra powder in the washing machine,
and it actually blew up, who will I blame?
My dad.
He "sometimes" does jobs that he doesn't know how to do,
and they always come out wrong.

Blame! Blame! Blame!
I always get out of trouble.
He! He! He!

Samantha Grande, Grade 3
Wolcott School, CT

My Friend

My friend is kind, she is the best.
She never lies, she never cheats.
She is such a friend.
She helps me with my work.
All I can think about is her.
She is friendly, always pretty.
A friend I can trust.
She is the best.

Nienke Abarbanel, Grade 3
Noonan Elementary Academy of Fort Myers, FL

Have You Noticed the Autumn Day?

Have you noticed the bright sun
Feeling like a campfire on your face?
Have you noticed pine cones
Swaying with the wind?
Have you seen some leaves
As green as frogs
And others as red as ladybugs?
Have you noticed the autumn day?

Alexandra Cooper Ghee, Grade 2
Worthington Hooker School – K-2 Campus, CT

Family

F ather cares for my family.
A unt Siera loves me.
M y mother feeds us every night.
I treat my family nicely.
L ove surrounds my family.
Y ou should respect your family.
Treasure Brooks, Grade 3
Bensley Elementary School, VA

Nature

Nature is awesome
You can see deer and turkeys
Our nature is nice
Shelby French, Grade 3
Clinton Christian Academy, MO

Today on Christmas Day

The bells are ringing,
The children are singing.
Hooray Hooray,
It's Christmas day.
You can't even say how much I'll play,
Today on Christmas day.
And when Christmas is done,
You'll be sure to have fun.
But I won't say hooray,
Until the next Christmas day.
Laura Jans, Grade 3
Our Lady of Hope School, NY

My Sweet, Sweet, Sister

Her name is Genessee
she is smart as a genius
she smells as cotton candy
mmm, mmmm —
She helps people a lot of times
Sometimes she's mad
and sometimes she's happy
She is the best
from loud
to peace
she is my sister
James Rodriguez, Grade 3
Public School 148 Ruby Allen, NY

Monkeys

I like monkeys.
Any kind of monkey.
Funky monkeys, spider monkeys,
Howler monkeys, baby monkeys.
Monkeys in the jungle,
Monkeys on a tree,
Monkeys with tails,
Any kind of monkey.
I like monkeys.
Griffin Tillman, Grade 3
Landmark Christian School, GA

The Sport of Baseball

The player swung hard
The athlete missed the ball STRIKE!
It was a fast ball
Matthew Cunningham, Grade 3
Holland Township School, NJ

Fairy Tale

Evil
Tricky
Bad
Scared of alligators
Captain Hook
Tyrone Jahiem Vaughan, Grade 1
Northeast Elementary School, NY

Cats

Cats have fur,
They like to purr,
Cats have fun,
They sleep in the sun,
Cats like yarn,
Some live in a barn.

If you need to get rid of a mouse,
You should have a cat in your house,
I have three,
Lucky, Jules and Baby.
Shannon Hynes, Grade 2
St Anselm School, PA

Changing Seasons

Cold winds blow you off your feet
As they make a leafy seat
Leaves of different colors blow
Better dress warm from head to toe

Trees turn bare
As winter blows in
They stand and stare
For spring to bloom in

They'll have new green leafy hair
And no longer be cold and bare
The flowers on trees are works of art
It's time now for a bright new start

Savarni Sanka, Grade 3
Hunter GT Magnet Elementary School, NC

My Eyes

Very pretty eyes
Shiny glowing long lashes
As blue as the sky

Gracie Miskewitz, Grade 3
Thelma L Sandmeier Elementary School, NJ

My Pet Dog

My pet dog is nice to me.
She loves me and I love my dog too.
She is so cute and a friend to me.
I wish everyone had a dog like me!!!

Eliana Merced, Grade 2
Mother Seton Inter Parochial School, NJ

In the Dark

I'm afraid of the dark.
What shall I do?
Should I hide under the covers?
No.
Should I go snuggle with mom and dad?
No.
Should I close my eyes and go to sleep?
Yes.

Eden Teska, Grade 1
Eagle Elementary School, NY

I Love My Daddy
Makes me feel happy
at Valentine's Day.

Cheers me up
when I am feeling sad.
Emily Fleming, Grade 1
Holland Township School, NJ

Snow
Snow
Cozy, cold
Falling, covering, frosting
My snowman is melting
Winter
Chris Washington, Grade 2
St Andrew School, NY

Giraffes
Giraffes have very long necks
I wish I had one too
So it wouldn't be so hard
Just to get my food.

Giraffes live in Africa
Where it is warm with sun,
I'd like to live in Africa
It would be so much fun.

Giraffes are brown and yellow
Some have many spots.
All day on the Savannah,
Do you think they get too hot?
Hannah Schneider, Grade 3
St Alexis School, PA

What Is Pink?
Strawberry-kiwi Kool-aid,
Sweet strawberry Laffy Taffy,
Strawberry yogurt,
A soft scarf,
Opening a can of Cherry 7-Up.
Harley Willems, Grade 3
Scott Elementary School, MO

My Christmas Tree
My Christmas tree, it stands so tall.
My father put it in the hall.
I hope to God it doesn't fall.
Lamaan Qureshi, Grade 1
Childrens House Montessori School, MS

The Sport of Equestrian
I hold two reins tight
I go trotting up and down past the crowd
I sit up on my saddle
Emily Del Greco, Grade 3
Holland Township School, NJ

At the Beach
B uy some hot dogs,
E at some snow cones,
A re you in the water?
C ome get your floaties,
H ave on sunglasses.
Rachel Staehling, Grade 3
Madison Station Elementary School, MS

Jacob
Loves to play football
Not sensitive
Loves blue
Funny
Wishes to be a football player on the Cowboys
Dreams of being rich
Wants to have a Bentley
Who wonders what's in space
Who fears bugs
Who is afraid of heights
Who likes playing football
Who believes in God
Who loves pizza with no cheese
Who loves football
Who loves math
Who loves Bentleys
Who plans to be a football player
Who plans to go to the Super bowl
Whose final destination is heaven
Jacob Martin, Grade 3
Central Park Elementary School, FL

Summer

Summer is lots of fun,
Summer is days of hot sun.
Summer is going to the beach,
Summer is eating a juicy peach.
Summer is sleeping under the stars,
Summer is riding in convertible cars.
Summer is chasing lightning bugs,
Summer is smiles and hugs.
Summer is colorful flowers,
Summer is longer days and hours.
Summer is *no school!*
Summer is swimming in the pool.
Summer is going on vacation,
Summer is visiting different parts of our nation.
Summer is going to camp,
Summer is riding your bike up a ramp.
Summer is green grass and trees,
Summer is ladybugs and buzzing bees.
Summer is my favorite season.
Summer is *all* these reasons.

Khalil Goodman, Grade 3
Duncan Elementary School, SC

Fall Fun

FALL IS FUN, FALL IS FUN!
The plants grow, it's football season,
I wonder what I can do at home
Play around or play a game.
Play Madden 08, or watch the
St. Louis Rams versus the New Orleans Saints.
I went to bed, then I got up and went to school.
I went to school and I had some more FALL FUN!
FALL IS FUN, FALL IS FUN!

Brendan Reed, Grade 2
Narvie J Harris Traditional Theme School, GA

My Sister

I have a sister, her name is monkey.
Sometimes, she makes me dress funky!
Once she did not take a bath for a week.
So, she did not smell very sweet.
I was so embarrassed, I wish I could fly to Paris!

McKenna Quinn, Grade 3
Boiling Springs Elementary School, SC

Sun

S un is a star
U p in the sky
N ice for flowers

Tomyia Blackshear, Grade 1
Annie Belle Clark Primary School, GA

Periwinkle

Periwinkle
Sky, water, flowers
Cloudless skies high up in the air
Flowers blooming everywhere
Around me.
Periwinkle.

Eric Senior, Grade 3
John T Waugh Elementary School, NY

Lions

They are strong and fast
They are furry and have claws
They eat with their teeth

Luca Alves, Grade 3
Miami Country Day School, FL

Halloween

Halloween
Very spooky
Skeletons rattle people
Ghosts scaring humans everywhere
Witches flying in the air
Spiders all over your costumed hair!

Mayah Jenkins, Grade 3
Mary Matula Elementary School, MD

My Scooters

I love scooters
Riding them is fun.
My favorites are purple and white.
I ride them day and night
It's so much fun.
That's why I love my scooters.

Sheila Martinez, Grade 1
James H Bright Elementary School, FL

Friends

F un
R ecess
I rresistible
E verlasting friendship
N ice and kind
D ancing
S itting in the shade, laughing

Taityana St. Hilaire, Grade 3
Bensley Elementary School, VA

Christmas

I heard the bell jingle,
I could not wait for Kris Kringle.
I opened my eyes,
Then saw a surprise.
The presents were wrapped all in red,
I couldn't wait to get out of bed.

Amanda Hardardt, Grade 3
Our Lady of Hope School, NY

A Short Nap

I napped in sap
under the old oak tree.
It didn't last long
'cause I got stung by a bee.
I screamed so loud
it drew a crowd.
Poor bee and poor me.

Brooks Burgess, Grade 2
Briarwood Christian School, AL

I Am From

I am from my cozy bedroom
where my smooth blanket
is waiting for me to
bundle up in and sleep.
I am from my yummy kitchen
where my warm pot is
baking some pumpkin pie.
I am from my flat backyard
where my hard gate is
waiting for me to play in.

Lilas Verrill, Grade 1
Berkeley Lake Elementary School, GA

The Day Before Christmas

The day before Christmas is really neat!
We clean and cook things that are sweet.
There are presents to wrap
And of course take a nap!
Because I'm hoping to catch a peek
At Santa as he sneaks.

Noah James, Grade 1
St Vincent De Paul Elementary School, MO

Nicolette

Loving
Nice
Funny
Smart
Dream of being a teacher.
Wishes to swim with the dolphins.
Wants to save kids in need.
Who wonders which day my birthday is on.
Who fears dying.
Who is afraid of being blind.
Who likes people who are fun and smart.
Who believes in God, always.
Who loves math.
Who loves people with a heart.
Who loves dogs and cats.
Who loves learning math.
Who plans to become a teacher
Who plans to have friends.
Who plans to love the sky.

Nicolette Cunningham, Grade 3
Central Park Elementary School, FL

Light from the Moon

The light from the moon
Is like a cool breeze
Touching my skin.
I was playing with my sister,
Wiggling and giggling,
When we looked out the window
And let the light from the moon
Touch us.

Jeremiah Roland, Grade 3
Lee A Tolbert Community Academy, MO

Blackbird

My blackbird
flies in the sky,
if he falls
he will die.

DuMichael Tutt, Kindergarten
Taylor Road Academy, AL

The Reindeer Are Flying

The reindeer are flying,
The Christmas tree is glowing.
We put reindeer food in the grass,
It's so cold it feels like it's snowing.
My stocking has candy in it,
I wake up when Santa is here.
He turns around…
Then he disappears!

Hailey Fitzgerald, Grade 1
Westlake Christian School, FL

Snow

S now, snow and more snow
N o it didn't snow here.
O h I wish it would snow
W inter is when snow falls.

Jackson Wheeler, Grade 3
Blakeney Elementary School, GA

Fall Colors

Red apples
Yellow leaves
Orange pumpkins
Green grass
Fall colors

Dyala Corrales, Grade 2
Weston Elementary School, NJ

Santa

Santa is very nice.
Santa gives us presents.
Santa lives in the ice.
Santa always rides with his reindeer.
And Santa loves his reindeer.

Jason Lam, Grade 1
Children's Village, PA

Spring

Pitter, patter
Sounds of water running
Pink, plink
Gold, metal
Blue, clue
Colors of umbrellas
Cars go vroom, vroom
Feel dizzy
Running in circles
Around the waterfall
Drops of water
From a leaf fall
Go plip, plop
Into the pond
Some fish scatter
Some things I pass
Are quite exciting
I hear my teacher call, I'm late.

Megan Nishiyama, Grade 3
Coram Elementary School, NY

Bubbles

Bubbles
Bubbles
Bubbles
So sticky
So poppy
Pop
Pop
Pop
They're like a wave of suds
When you poke one
Pop
I love hearing the sound of bubbles
When they all pop
Pop
Pop
Pop
Bye bye
Bubbles

Alex McCullough, Grade 3
Reidville Elementary School, SC

Pug

Cobra is my pug.
He likes to play with me.
I'm his best friend.
We run and play together.
He usually wins the race.

Abbegayle Steighner, Kindergarten
St Mary of the Assumption Catholic School, PA

Going for a Walk

I like going for a walk with my mom and my little sister.
I like to walk and see the dogs down the street.
I like to walk and see the birds fly by.
I like to see the tall buildings and the blue sky.
I like going for a walk.

Cairo Lopez, Grade 1
Mother Seton Inter Parochial School, NJ

A Flower Day

"Buzzzzz" said a bee landing on a flower.
I see a flower budding.
The flower's bright colors shine like a rainbow.
The leaves are great snacks for the ants.
The flowers smell like sweet honey and maple syrup.
The flowers whistle in the wind.
The leaves fly in the sky as the wind passes by.
The flowers feed a hummingbird.
Lunch time for the butterfly
What a great day with the flowers.

WeiXin Du, Grade 2
Worthington Hooker School – K-2 Campus, CT

Balls for Seasons

Wintertime, springtime, summer and fall
all times of year we can have a ball.
In winter's snow and ice, snowballs are great for snowball fights.
In springtime we have lots of fun, with baseball and the grand slam run.
In the summer's heat, beach balls and water balls can't be beat.
In the fall let's not forget that football is the best sport yet.
So grab a ball and don't forget that winter, spring, summer or fall you can
always have fun with your favorite ball.
So the next time you grab a ball remember softball, dodgeball and tennis too
will make your seasons fun and new!

Justin Roth, Grade 3
North Star Elementary School, DE

The Sport of Olympic Luge

My helmet is hard,
I whiz by crowd really fast —
I look like a snake.

Charlotte Angier, Grade 3
Holland Township School, NJ

Autumn

Leaves are falling down
Squirrels are getting acorns
Pumpkins are growing

Will Gilmore, Grade 2
Wellington School, FL

Ocean

Don't you like the ocean?
Seeing the waves crash
Diving
Swimming
Thrashing around
Catching big fish
Little fish
They live all around
Don't you just like sitting
and
Hearing the sound?

Gabriel Onthank, Grade 3
Mission Hill School, MA

Thanksgiving

Thanksgiving
Turkey corn
Eating drinking cooking
Do not eat the skin
Dinner

Cyan Rivera, Grade 3
Marie Curie Institute, NY

My Brother

Sagie is seven.
He plays soccer with me.
He makes lots of goals!

Amit Shpigelman, Grade 1
United Hebrew Institute, PA

Recycling

People help keep the earth clean,
By cleaning pollution wherever it is seen.
People save oxygen by not cutting down trees,
And recycle bottles, cans and old magazines.
We should be good and do what we could.
Recycling trash could help us get cash.

Britny Thomas, Grade 3
Public School 235 Lenox, NY

Soccer

Good soccer player
I steal the ball from players
It's fun to score goals

Andrew Cook, Grade 3
Thelma L Sandmeier Elementary School, NJ

Augustin

Augustin has a busy day.
He sleeps, wets,
wakes-up, drinks milk,
Then he falls asleep again.

Sabrina Nunez, Kindergarten
Mother Seton Inter Parochial School, NJ

Smile Every Day

I have a smile every day.
It makes me bloom in front of the day.
It makes me happy.
It makes people happy too.
And when my mom smiles,
It makes me smile too.

Talia Cordero, Grade 3
St Joseph Catholic Grammar School, NJ

How to Be a Friend

Make them feel good,
Like a swim in the pool,
Or you're snuggled in bed.
Let them feel at home,
When you lay down your head.
And see through their eyes that
They know you're there.

Sidney Kimble, Grade 3
Madison Station Elementary School, MS

Fireworks

Loud, thunder, pretty too.
I love seeing fireworks with you.
I know it's loud and at night.
But I know it looks bright.

Gabriella Turnipseed, Grade 3
Madison Station Elementary School, MS

Dream

Every night we have a dream.
Some dreams are extreme,
Some make us feel bad,
But some make us glad.

Some dreams are in a sad place,
And are impossible to replace.
Sometimes your dream is scary
But sometimes pretty fairy.

Some dreams are fiction
But you can make a prediction.
Some are too short and just one time
But stay with you for a lifetime.

Oh dreams, your wonderful nature
Like a world of unknown venture.
Someone believes it's nothing true
But I'm convinced and trust in you.

Salome Tkebuchava, Grade 3
Memorial-Spaulding Elementary School, MA

How to Describe a Sunset

Look at it.
Say hi to it.
Draw it.
Dance with the sunset.
Say good bye.
Then come back.
Play hide-in-go-seek.
Then the moon comes,
And you cry.
Then it will come again!

Hannah Guimbellot, Grade 3
Madison Station Elementary School, MS

Halloween Night

Halloween night is a scary fright.
It's spooky and filled with scare.
It's more frightening than lightning.
It has more blunder than thunder.

Brody Petree, Grade 3
Cool Spring Elementary School, NC

Rabbit

In the forest grass
The five feet long green rabbit,
Eats crunchy carrots,

Sydney Kendrick, Grade 2
Roseland Park Elementary School, MS

My Cat

Cute, sweet, calm
Playing, hiding, running, sleeping
Scared, fun, nice
Tabitha

Antonia Bellavia, Grade 2
St Mary's School, NJ

Grant

Grant
Weird, tall
Tennis, football, horse riding
Cares about other people
G-man

Sarah Gray Moates, Grade 3
Briarwood Christian School, AL

What My Sister Looks Like…

I love my sister
She is so cool
She has long, red orange hair
And pretty eyes too!
She likes to play dress up,
That's when she's a glow, her eyes
Bright and shining
And her eyes white as snow.

Jessica Lopez, Grade 3
Western Hills Elementary School, AR

Puppy

A brown spotted pup.
She was a pretty puppy.
She does funny tricks.

Carlizia Simmons, Grade 2
Roseland Park Elementary School, MS

Lovely Fall

Wind blows very calm
birds chirping very loudly
trees blow very slow

Jesse Albert, Grade 3
The Parke House Academy, FL

Dear Goldie

Dear Goldie,
I love it when you tackle me
When I get off the bus,
You just love doing that.
I call you over,
You run as fast as you can,
I count,
It only takes you eight seconds,
You are the best dog in the world!

Nicholas Cardona, Grade 3
Cool Spring Elementary School, NC

Austin

A wesome
U nique
S illy
T rue
I nto reading
N ever mean

Austin Rhynes, Grade 3
Pottsville Elementary School, AR

Apples

Grow on tree
Shiny in the sun
Turn to red
Pick them
Eat them

Melanie Castro-Alpizar, Grade 2
Weston Elementary School, NJ

What If

What if my great granddaddy didn't die.
I might go to his house every day after school.

What if I got to live with him before he died, because I only got to see him six times.
I could have woke him up with a hug and kiss. He might get a little scared and yell,
because he usually gets up first, and wakes me up, I so wish he did not die.

What if he didn't die right at this time.
I would not have cried when he died. It just kills me that he died.

Kaitlyn Herrell, Grade 3
Byrns L Darden Elementary School, TN

Animals

I love animals.
Skin: furry, soft, scaly, sticky, slimy, rough, or smooth.
Looks: tall, short, skinny, fat, heavy, or light.
Does: run, walk, trot, leap, swim, climb, fly, hop, or dig.
Feelings: scared, proud, sad, or happy.
Sounds: loud, quiet, roar, groan, chatter, bark, neigh, or squeal.
Life cycle: all animals eat and are prey.
Some animals can be funny and cute —
Others can be mean and scary.
But I still care for them.

Madison Wagoner, Grade 3
Noonan Elementary Academy of Fort Myers, FL

Ode to My Stuffed Bunny

Oh, my marvelous bunny!
You look like you were made from cotton, but I know you were made from love.
You have been with me for seven years.
You are as white as a snow rabbit.
My mom says you came from the toy shop, but I know you came from the jungle.
You are good to fall asleep with
Your fur feels like a cotton ball.
I am going to keep you forever.
When I rub your ears to my face it feels like a feather.
Your eyes are blue like the ocean.
I sewed your name on to your foot, so I would always know your name.
If you went away I would miss tickling your feather like tail to my face.
What would you feel if I went away?
I would feel very sad.
Oh, stuffed bunny I love you so much!

Carly Knibutat, Grade 2
Worthington Hooker School – K-2 Campus, CT

Winter

The snow is freezing.
The snow is wet, white and smooth.
The snow is very thin.

Zack Hull, Grade 3
Tuxedo Park School, NY

Pink Pony

I can run.
I have fun.
I can walk.
But I cannot talk.
I am Pink Pony.

Dayana Gonzalez, Grade 1
Northeast Elementary School, NY

Math

M ath is fun
A lways
T hinking about
H undreds of problems

Jesse Dirkschneider, Grade 3
Bensley Elementary School, VA

Sean

S uper
E xciting
A lone
N eat

Sean Melanson, Grade 2
Long Meadow Elementary School, CT

The King and the Ring

The king needed a wedding ring
He heard a ding
When the door bell ringed
The king opened the door
And heard angels sing!
It was the queen
Who did bring
The king a ring
And she did sing
A ting-a-ling-a-ling!

Maggie Babin, Kindergarten
Northeast Baptist School, LA

One Little Leaf

Swish, swoosh a leaf
Falls from a tree
Up into the sky
Like a jet
Starting its flight
It's a duck migrating
through the unknown places
Far and wide places
Through the trees
It's a journey
With one little leaf
Soaring high in the sky

Austin Tucker, Grade 3
Reidville Elementary School, SC

October

Halloween is cool.
Spooky goblins everywhere.
I love October!

Allison Collins, Grade 2
Wanamassa Elementary School, NJ

Gabriella

G lamorous
A mazing
B rilliant
R adiant
I ntelligent
E njoyable
L ovely
L ikable
A greeable

Gabriella Koskelowski, Grade 2
Long Meadow Elementary School, CT

About Snow

On Sunday I went in the snow.
When I came in I had hot cocoa.
I ran and I had fun.
I like to run.

Ami Birnbaum, Grade 2
Yeshiva Ketana of Long Island, NY

Halloween Night

October is a fun time of year.
Ghost, goblins and lots of fear.

Witches flying about the sky.
Soaring through rooftops oh so high.

Jack-o-lanterns are sometimes frightening.
But watch out for a strike of lightning.

Beware of such a scary sight.
Ghosts and goblins fill the night.

Prowling about for candy and treats.
Freaky monsters fill the streets.

Keana Cozatt, Grade 3
Small World Academy, WV

As It Goes

Falling leaves fall.
Trick-or-treaters call.
We sit down to eat
A little deer meat.
But don't get too stuffed,
Thanksgiving is coming up.
Little animals stuff their burrows to the top.
Winter's almost here.

Gabe Good, Grade 3
Duncan Elementary School, SC

When I'm Alone I…

Laugh at myself,
Sing loud songs,
Pretend I'm in a magical land and I rule it,
Dance to music,
Play on my mom's phone,
Dress up and act like an adult,
Watch TV,
Read books,
Think of candy,
And just play with my hair.

Nicole Bergeron, Grade 3
Madison Station Elementary School, MS

Nicholas/Goof

Nicholas
Cool, fast
Skating, play, jumping
Likes to play hockey
Goof

Nick Falbo, Grade 2
St Stephen's School, NY

Kiana

Best friend
Pretty princess
Plays games
Tells jokes
Wonderful friend

Keisha Torres, Grade 2
Marie Curie Institute, NY

Natural Resources

Trees are the beauty,
Water is our bodies,
Plants are the freshest,
Wood is the hardest.
The natural resources,
are important to help,
our environment.

Zheleca Collins, Grade 3
Public School 235 Lenox, NY

Scarecrows

Scarecrows
Grumpy, unique
Guarding, scaring, watching
Protecting crops each year!
Still

Ava Fernand, Grade 2
Consolidated School, CT

The King

I would like to bring
A roll of string
To my king.

Gracie Stokes, Kindergarten
Northeast Baptist School, LA

Pumpkin

Pumpkin, pumpkin like a ball,
Pumpkin, pumpkin, they grow in the fall.

Pumpkin, pumpkin they are so round,
Pumpkin, pumpkin they are on the ground.

They can be big, they can be small,
They can be short, they can be tall.

Pumpkin, pumpkin they grow on a stem,
Pumpkin, pumpkin how I like them!!!!!

Becca Brockman, Grade 3
Reidville Elementary School, SC

The Problem with Pumpkins

The pumpkin, orange, fat, and round.
The stem is pointy brown.
Quickly did it grow from the ground.
With so many leaves, like a gown.
I cut its face and made a toothy smile.
I turned away very quickly.
Turning back, I saw something quite vile.
The pumpkin's smile was a frown.
Behind its eyes and mouth came an odd goo.
With a rumble, it shot out.
Soaring through the air, the slime flew.
Whatever it touched came to life.
It caused problems with a clamor,
And so, it fell victim to my hammer!

Taryn Wheeler, Grade 3
Coral Springs Elementary School, FL

Christmas Day

C elebrate for Jesus Christ
H anging decorations on the tree
R inging bells
I ce on the bottom of the snow
S nowball fight
T oasty warm fire
M any decorations on the tree
A beautiful holiday
S nowy winter

Brittany Stark, Grade 3
Bradford Township Elementary School, PA

Christmas

Christmas is the day that Jesus Christ was born,
And when I think of Him I think of His crown made of thorns.
Merry, merry Christmas
When all the snow will fall,
That's when you know that it's a merry Christmas for all.

Kacy Cartwright, Grade 2
Foundation Academy, FL

What If?

What if I rode my skateboard on a ramp?
I might sell my skateboard.

What if I jumped off a house and landed on my skateboard?
I could do a flip trick.

What if I made a skateboard shop?
I would like to do a sucker.

What if I was the best skater in the world?

Stacey Tindall, Grade 3
Byrns L Darden Elementary School, TN

The Sea

The sea is where the dolphin dives.
The sea is where the whale swims very proudly.
The ship sinks down into the deep
where the fish swim in the sea.

Anders Pecore, Grade 3
Lincoln Elementary School, PA

Winter Morning

The cool winter morning is nice and quiet, but
the cold breeze whispers to me.
The lawn is covered with frost.
It looks like a long white blanket.
The trees are swaying in the wind.
As I watch through our open window,
A leaf comes dancing in.
The snow glistens as I watch.
Magical snowflakes fall.
It's the most stunning sight, but
all is calm on this winter morning.

Erin Whiting, Grade 3
Lynn Fanning Elementary School, AL

My Dad

He showed me how
to catch a ball.
He showed me how
to swing a bat.
He used to take me
to his baseball games.
Now my dad is in heaven.
I miss him very much.

Marc Vega, Grade 1
James H Bright Elementary School, FL

My Dreams

My dream is to be rich
I dream of having three cars
I dream of having three bikes
I dream of having two dogs
I dream of owning a school
I dream of owning a store
I dream of being famous
That's what I dream about.

Terri Millbrooks, Grade 3
Greenhill Elementary School, MS

Horses

H ave hooves
O utstanding in
R acing
S tallions
E njoy running
S teeds

Alexis Stone, Grade 2
Broadway Elementary School, NC

Sun Rays

Sun rays, sun rays,
Yellow and bright,
You give us warmth,
You give us light.
You work all day,
You rest all night.

Grace Chambers, Grade 2
Briarwood Christian School, AL

The Smell of Rain

The smell of rain
smells misty and foggy
like air except it is cooler
The sky is foggy
The wind is pushing me
Birds are hiding in the nest.
The ground is muddy,
I slip and fall
Trees are wet
All of the house windows are soaked
from the rain
This is a day for indoor play.

Donnie Bell, Grade 3
Lincoln Elementary School, PA

Baylie

Baylie
Nice, tall
Soccer, volleyball, swimming
Always caring about others
Bay

Matthew Norton, Grade 3
Briarwood Christian School, AL

Cheerleading

Cheerleading
Fun, loud
Jumping, stunts, running
Happy, tired, excited, sore
Cheer

Rachel Weathers, Grade 3
Wapping Elementary School, CT

Christmas Is Near

The fire is crackling,
Jesus is here.
The stockings are hung,
Christmas is near.
The children are going to bed,
The lights are gleaming on the tree.
Children dream about their toys,
Santa lands on the roof with glee.

Quinn Hemond, Grade 1
Westlake Christian School, FL

What Is Red?

Paper,
A smooth shake,
A red juicy apple,
Body wash,
Cutting a strawberry and juice coming out.

Lydia Fris, Grade 3
Scott Elementary School, MO

Halloween

Halloween is here tonight
Owls are everywhere through the night
Licking lollipops here and there
Laughing kids everywhere
Oh I want chocolate bars and candy corn!
Won't you wear a costume with big red horns.
Everywhere are black cats
Everyone is wearing red hats
Now I can't wait till Halloween night
When can I give you a fright.

Caitlyn Ghirardi, Grade 3
St Mary's School, NJ

Scary House

Scary house,
Why do you scare me in so many ways?
If I go to you for trick or treating,
I am afraid an old lady
is going to jump out the door and scare me.

Joseph Martin, Grade 3
Cool Spring Elementary School, NC

December

Snow sprinkling softly from the sky
Snowmen stay still and frozen
Santa supplies with surprises for stockings
Jingle bells jangle joyfully
Chomping Christmas cookies
Sleighs slide by
Hot chocolate warms my throat
Winter is wonderful!

Emily Lancia, Grade 3
Cherry Lane Elementary School, NY

Outside

Nice green leaf
Really big leaf
Little red leaf
Little green clover
Big yellow leaf
Nice big cloud
Pretty yellow flower
A little red ant crawled on a sidewalk
With no place to go
And nothing to do.
Julia Josker, Grade 2
John T Waugh Elementary School, NY

The Small Christmas Tree

green beautiful
cool awesome
sweet cute
nice full wide
Ben Viljac, Grade 1
Hilton Head Christian Academy, SC

My Brother

Cute, fun, helpful
Sleeping, playing, drooling, crawling
Sweet, cool, funny
Jude
Seth Otto, Grade 2
St Mary's School, NJ

My Favorite Color

I like red.
A stop sign is red.
Ketchup is red.
An apple is red.
I like red.
Karla Fuentes, Grade 1
Northeast Elementary School, NY

The Olympic Sport of Equestrian

Beautiful horses
Jumping high over the poles
The rider lands it
Miranda Livermore, Grade 3
Holland Township School, NJ

Halloween

Halloween is here!
It is the time of year!
Get your scarecrows ready!
Get your costumes ready!
For Halloween is here!
The scarecrows are ready!
The costumes are ready!
Get your candy
For
HALLOWEEN IS HERE!!!!!!
Hannah Walters, Grade 2
Evangelical Christian School, TN

The Star

Twinkle shiny white
bright space big
celestial body planets
invisible smart
outstanding manners
five points
Reanna Stephens, Grade 2
Hilton Head Christian Academy, SC

Bear

Bear
Hairy, brown
Runs, bites, eats
It is very fast.
Brown bear
Garrett Alldredge, Grade 3
Clinton Christian Academy, MO

I Am From

I am from my soft bedroom
where my rough game makes
the room that I have mine.
I am from my favorite room
where my soft dog is.
I am from my little backyard
where my hard swing is.
Nathan Mendez, Grade 1
Berkeley Lake Elementary School, GA

Nature

I love the garden
We planted one near our class
I planted peppers

Ryan Lang, Grade 2
Virginia A Boone Highland Oaks Elementary School, FL

How to Show No Fear of the Dark

To show no fear of the dark, you must think happy thoughts.
Cuddle up with your stuffed animal.
Make sure your own pillow is comfy.
Get into your comfiest pajamas.

No need to worry, kiddo!
Your mom will tuck you into bed like a teddy bear!
Your dad will read you a story, and you can choose the book too!
Your mom will give you a kiss.
Your dad will give you a hug.

Sleep with your favorite blanket.
Have a night light near your bed.
There will be no monsters under your bed.
If you sleep with your parents, that's okay.
They will be on your side the whole night.

Samantha Tran, Grade 3
Wolcott School, CT

Rusty

Golden, graceful
Prancing, dancing
Slowing down
Nervous, naughty
What a mess!
Slowly creeping
Catch that cat!
Watchful, waiting
'Til we come
Lazy, sickly
To the vet
Hungry hippo
Feed me now!
Golden, graceful
Rusty

Alana Pound, Grade 3
Noonan Elementary Academy of Fort Myers, FL

My Fish

I have a fish
It lives in a dish
Its colors can switch
Sarah Bishop, Kindergarten
Taylor Road Academy, AL

Riegel Ridge Rams

Riegel
Ridge
Rams
rule!
We shout
all the time.
In cheerleading
you need to have
strong movements!
You have to have
teamwork!
Alyssa Schuetz, Grade 3
Holland Township School, NJ

Ice Hockey

Hockey sticks hitting
Pucks are whirling in the air
They fall on ice, GOAL!
Richie Baron, Grade 3
Holland Township School, NJ

Bats/Scary

Bats
little, black
flying, sleeping, eating
Searching for their food.
Scary
Robert Zurzola, Grade 2
Consolidated School, CT

The Moon

The moon is full at night.
The moon is blue
The moon is bright
Charlie Runge, Grade 1
Holland Township School, NJ

Candy

Candy
Round, colorful
Unwrapping, eating, chewing
I like sweet candy.
Bubblegum
Malysa Horton, Grade 3
Chestnut Street Elementary School, PA

My House

My decorated Christmas tree
Wind banging my bells
Chocolate cookies I made for Santa
Wrapped presents Santa gave me
Tasty leftover food
Jacob Carter, Grade 3
Bradford Township Elementary School, PA

Leaves

Leaves
Shapes, colors
Changing, falling, raking
I look at leaves
Plants
Maya Huckabone, Grade 3
Chestnut Street Elementary School, PA

Among the Woods

I've always wondered what roamed the woods.
Could it be a fox?
Could it be a bear?
Could it be raccoons searching for food?
Have you ever roamed the woods?
If so, what did you see?
Kirsten Madick, Grade 3
William Southern Elementary School, MO

Ghosts

Ghosts
Bluish, spooky
Moaning, floating, scaring
They haunt your house
Spirits
Olivia Blackmore, Grade 3
Chestnut Street Elementary School, PA

Candy

Candy
Sugary, yummy
Eating, munching, sucking
I like butterscotch candy.
Lollipops

Nicholas Grube, Grade 3
Chestnut Street Elementary School, PA

The Sun

It shines on us, like a flashlight in the night,
As if a spotlight glows on the ball,
A bright star on the Christmas tree.
Very brightly, it greets in the morning,
It gives the world the warmth it needs,
Hotter than hot cocoa,
Better than freezing cold, ice.
It powers our workforce,
It is the sun!

A.J. Yuan, Grade 3
North Star Elementary School, DE

Rudolph/Reindeer

Rudolph
red-nosed, furry
glowing, eating, flying
dashing through the cold, white snowflakes
reindeer

Joanna Luck, Grade 2
Wells Central School, NY

The Best Christmas Ever!

C hristmas is fun
H olly
R ed and green
I cicles
S anta Claus
T oys
M erry Christmas
A nd Happy New Year
S leighs

Cameron Gasperson, Grade 3
Abbs Valley Boissevain Elementary School, VA

Emily

Emily
cute, funny
piano, drawing, gymnastics
Always kind to others
Elmo

Hunter Wilhelm, Grade 3
Briarwood Christian School, AL

Fall

The air is as breezy as wind.
The trees are as colorful as a rainbow.
The leaves are as yellow as gold.
The birds sound like music.
The cider smells like apples.

Anthony Huertas, Grade 3
Coral Cove Elementary School, FL

Christmas

Look at that Christmas tree
Let's count some ornaments 1, 2, 3…
Such a beautiful design
I wish it was Christmas all the time
God bless the soldiers that are overseas
Merry Christmas to you from me
You're always in my prayers
As I dress up in layers
The weather is very cold
"Stay inside," we tell the old
Christmas warms my heart
I can't wait for the celebration to start!

Izanae Somerville, Grade 3
Marie Durand Elementary School, NJ

For My Mom Because I Love Her*

Every farmer loves a crop.
Every mom loves a shop.
Every floor loves a mop.
And I love you.

Harper Tompkins, Kindergarten
Eden Gardens Magnet School, LA
**Inspired by Jean Marzollo's*
"I Love You: A Rebus Poem"

Love*

Every go loves a stop.
Every bucket loves a mop.
Every frog loves a hop.
And I love you.

Addison Barnard, Kindergarten
Eden Gardens Magnet School, LA
**Inspired by Jean Marzollo's*
"I Love You: A Rebus Poem"

Christmas Day

Snow snow come today
For Christmas day is today

Come outside and play with me
Santa Claus is coming this way.

Kevin Bates, Grade 1
Webster Montessori School, NY

My Bookbag

Bookbag
big, purple
rolling down the hall
carrying all of my stuff.
Bookbag

Amber Jeter, Grade 2
Bensley Elementary School, VA

I Am From

I am from my warm bedroom where
my black skateboard is turned around
and the wheels are going around.
I am from my warm kitchen where
my beautiful pie is cooking.
I am from my grassy park where
my trees are big.

Jose Bielkiewicz, Grade 1
Berkeley Lake Elementary School, GA

Winter

Snow is icy cold,
and snowflakes will fall and crash
Santa's deer are magic

Farha Khalidi, Grade 3
Tuxedo Park School, NY

My Favorite Color

My favorite color is pink.
Pink is a pretty color because it is bright and nice.
My dolls are pink, my clothes are pink and even the bathroom sink.
My favorite color is pink pink pink!

Deborah Merced, Grade 1
Mother Seton Inter Parochial School, NJ

Happiness

Happiness is yellow
It sounds like a cruise ship passing by
It smells like the icing on my birthday cake
It tastes like yummy apples freshly picked from the tree
It looks like a beautiful sunset
It feels like painting with your fingers

Jordyn Taylor Magill, Grade 2
Anne Frank School, PA

Smiles

I smile happy when I go horseback riding.
I smile laughingly when my dog rolls over.
I smile cute when my mom hugs me.
I smile thankfully when I get a new hermit crab.
God smiles when I am nice to Him.

Karina Soudijn, Grade 1
Guardian Angels Catholic School, FL

Books

Books are good to read,
You can read them to your baby sister or brother,
Books can make you relax,
Books make you smart,
You can buy them at the library,
Books tell you about animals,
Books end.

Armanhi Feliciano, Grade 2
Marie Curie Institute, NY

Brave Leaf

I'm red-orange like lava.
I'm soft as cotton.
I'm spinning like a bottle cap.
I'm a brave leaf.

Julien Llaurador, Grade 2
Worthington Hooker School – K-2 Campus, CT

Fall

All the leaves off the trees.
All the leaves make me sneeze.
Look out! There's a lot of bees!
I jump and land on my knees.
Leaves, Leaves, they are everywhere,
Even on my wooden chair.
Oh my goodness…
what to do!
I think there are leaves in my shoes!

Garrett Daniels, Grade 3
Birches Elementary School, NJ

Swimming

stroke, doggie paddle, dive
new and old will survive
jump in, get wet, get dry
it's so fun I think I'll cry
dead man, float, drown
I should win the crown.

Kenzie Oldham, Grade 3
Broadway Elementary School, NC

Dogs Dogs Everywhere

Dogs, Dogs everywhere
On your clothes and your hair.
Dogs, Dogs
Come in all different sizes
Skinny and fat
Tall and short
And that's all fact!

Abby Boren, Grade 3
Evangelical Christian School, TN

Warm Turkey Day

My mom cooks the turkey
on Thanksgiving Day.
It is a feast.
We sit down to eat.
I pray for people who have nothing.
We are lucky to have something.
Most important we have each other.
I love my family.

Amanda Fedele, Grade 3
Our Lady of Hope School, NY

Thanksgiving Day

All from far, come and cheer
Thanksgiving Day is now right here.
Pilgrims and Indians
Will gather to dine
At this great place
Together to shine.
Come one, come all
In this great fall
For a wonderful feast
That's made for us all.
They'll dine on maize
And turkey too,
Let's not forget
The soup and stew.
After the feast they'll sing and dance.
Hope they don't get
Bitten by ants!
At the end of the day
They'll pray and pray
And thank the Lord
For this marvelous day.

Tyler Sills, Grade 2
Evangelical Christian School, TN

The Cute Snowman

funny nice
playful sweet
cute loving
good lovely
cold fluffy
snowy

Brianne Gorddard, Grade 1
Hilton Head Christian Academy, SC

My Favorite Color

I like blue.
My bag is blue.
The sky is blue.
The mat is blue.
I like blue.

Michael Nanan, Grade 1
Northeast Elementary School, NY

Dogs

They howl
And they growl.
They scratch, they drool,
Sometimes they get in a pool.
They bury bones
Sometimes, chew on phones.
I train them to sit and stay
Although it takes all day!
Dogs are wise,
Some with cute, beady eyes.
I love to see, waiting for me…
My little doggie at the tree!

Margaret Badding, Grade 2
Campbell-Savona Elementary School, NY

Great Dad Boulder

Great Dad Boulder you hold yourself so tight
You stop avalanches
You wake me up every morning
You never get mad or angry
You are nice and kind
You are also wise
You are my rock, Great Dad Boulder

Brad Hansell, Grade 3
Sundance School, NJ

Fall

Fall leaves are yellow, purple, and brown.
They fall down to the ground.
The wind outside is cool.
We'll have a bonfire soon.

Lauren Wilms, Grade 2
Eagle's View Academy, FL

Witches/Monsters

Witches
Mean, scary
Flying, sleeping, eating
They have black hats
Monsters

Alyssa Zampogna, Grade 3
Chestnut Street Elementary School, PA

Dogs

Dogs are cool
Dogs are fun

Dogs like to play
Dogs like to run

Some dogs are furry
Some dogs are white

Some dogs are mean
Some dogs are contrite

Dogs like to eat food
Especially treats

Some dogs eat carrots
Some dogs eat meat.

Jessica Boy, Grade 3
St Alexis School, PA

Dogs

Dogs bark! bark! bark!
In the dark! dark! dark!
They run and they play
During the light of day
Dogs come when you call
They love to play ball
Sometimes they get wet
But they're still a favorite pet
When you give them a bath
You can't help but to laugh
Dogs bark! bark! bark!
In the park! park! park!

Jerald Vesel, Grade 3
St Alexis School, PA

My Valentine

It reminds me of friends.
It means you love your
Mom and Dad.
It can make you feel good.

Angelina Tettemer, Grade 1
Holland Township School, NJ

My Brother

My little brother's name is Ryan.
He's really kind and nice.
He says knock knock jokes.
When he was little, he called me Yaya,
But now Yaya slips into the past.
Sometimes he cares for me.
He always leaps across my heart
And always blows through my mind.
He's really loving.
He's sometimes a voice in my head.
Mostly every day he cries when I go to school.
I love my brother Ryan.

Cara Jackson, Grade 3
Oak Ridge Elementary School, PA

Pumpkins

I was eating muffins
when I decided to carve some pumpkins
and make all kinds of faces.
I made mad faces and sad faces.
Some pumpkins were tall
and some were small.
Then I went out to weed
and plant some pumpkin seed.

Audrey Sellers, Grade 3
Nativity Catholic School, FL

Angel in the Sky

Angel in the sky
I will sing with you on high.
Oh,
How pretty colors and different you are.
When I look at you flying in the sky,
How I wish I could be one of you.

Annika Conlee, Grade 2
Evangelical Christian School, TN

Winter Day

Beautiful white trees
Invisible air moving
Delicious hot chocolate my Mom is making
And soft snow.

Christen Wisor, Grade 3
Bradford Township Elementary School, PA

Christmas Time

Christmas is my favorite time of year.
It brings us lots of cheer.
My favorite things are decorating our tree
and when Santa and Hermie come visit me.
Hermie is our elf you see.
He brings us lots of joy.
He only awakes and plays at night while we are sleeping tight.
But he hides again when it is light.
When Santa comes on Christmas Eve,
Hermie has to leave.
He always leaves us a little treat.
Our elf Hermie can't be beat!

Bailey Black, Grade 3
Pike Liberal Arts School, AL

Halloween

I see lots of candy in my big pillow case.
I smell the candy in my bucket.
I hear kids knocking on the door.
I feel a little pirate tapping on my leg with his sword.
I touch something slimy and yucky.

HALLOWEEN

Gregory Culbreath, Grade 3
Wellington School, FL

The Sky

Bees are flying high
Up above the big white clouds
In the pretty sky

Hannah Ferber, Grade 2
Virginia A Boone Highland Oaks Elementary School, FL

Sick Day

Today I have the flu
I can't believe it's true
When I wake up in the middle of the night
I sneeze all over my room
When I went to the doctor
He says I will be feeling like a rose
Blooming and like and angel flying up for peace
So the angel could see Jesus and giving world peace.

David Ramirez, Grade 3
Walnut Street School, NY

The Sun

The sun gives us light.
It is circled like a cookie.
Bright fiery hot star.

Brandon Sones, Grade 2
Roseland Park Elementary School, MS

Who Is It?

He was a puppet
He wanted to be a star
His nose grew

Pinocchio

Jacques Legrand, Grade 1
Northeast Elementary School, NY

Flowers

Water lily, sunflower, violet, rose
You can smell flowers with your nose

Some seeds you can eat
Some you cannot

Some plants you can plant
Some stay in a pot

Mackenzie O'Hara, Grade 3
Webster Montessori School, NY

A Season

As spring comes
everything blooms
just for me and you.
Soft and sweet like
a hummingbird tweet
as the summer comes.
As the wind blows
the pumpkins grow
as fall comes.
Soft as snow
like a silver glow
as the winter comes.

Julia Swords, Grade 2
Briarwood Christian School, AL

Bubbles

My brother ate some bubbles
And let me tell you why
Mom told him to brush his teeth
And that did not go right
He bursted Mommy's bubbles
That night he got a bubble bath
And ate even more bubbles
When he went down for a nap
He looked a little weird
When he got up — POP!
And he was gone!

Taylor Schiavone, Grade 3
Marie Durand Elementary School, NJ

Christmas, Christmas!

Christmas, Christmas
It is almost here!
A Christmas tree
and holiday cheer!

Snow falls everywhere
so go out and play.
There will be snowmen, snowballs,
and even a sleigh.

When it's Christmas Eve,
Santa stops at your house.
Nobody's awake —
not even a mouse!

On Christmas morning
when Santa is done,
we unwrap our presents —
which makes Christmas so fun!

Michael Szczechowski, Grade 3
North Star Elementary School, DE

Mark

M ice — I like 'em
A pples —I eat 'em
R ocks — I throw 'em
K angaroos — I like 'em

Mark Mitchell, Kindergarten
Eden Gardens Magnet School, LA

Beautiful Flower

Oh, flower,
How have you grown to be so beautiful?
Flower, oh flower,
Will you grow oh so beautiful even more?
I hope so.
And you do too, I think.
You will grow too beautiful.
I know it.

Olivia Slotman, Grade 3
John T Waugh Elementary School, NY

Turkey

Turkey
Brown, big
Gobbling, running, eating
Turkeys can run fast
Bird

Cameron Biel, Grade 3
Chestnut Street Elementary School, PA

Grace

Friendly
Funny
Loves to cook
Loves to play
Wishes to get a mouse for a pet.
Dreams of being a doctor.
Wants to be healthy.
Who wonders how many stars are in the sky.
Who fears really bad hurricanes.
Who is afraid there maybe no more water.
Who likes fresh strawberries with sugar.
Who believes in world peace.
Who loves fruit.
Who loves bumble bees.
Who loves orange juice.
Who loves playing outside.
Who plans to have a good life.
Who plans to not smoke.
Whose final destination is the country.

Grace Plass, Grade 3
Central Park Elementary School, FL

My Favorite Place
Michigan
football team
aunts, cousins, uncles
geese, frogs, tadpoles at the lake
good vacation
Joseph Meade, Grade 1
Sundance School, NJ

Rainbows
Rainbows are beautiful.
Rainbows are pretty,
Rainbows are not plentiful.
The ones you see are pretty.
Katie Valadez, Grade 3
Mendenhall Elementary School, FL

Autumn
Autumn spills in with
squirrels gathering nuts
and pumpkins growing from vines
on a cold sunset night
with children jumping in the leaves
as mom bakes pumpkin pies
smelling up the house
Lexi Buchan, Grade 3
Wellington School, FL

Fall
Fall leaves fall down
to the ground.
They have different colors
Like red, orange, purple, and blue.
And all the animals
Gather up their food.
Shane Adams, Grade 2
Eagle's View Academy, FL

Rain
R ain falls from the sky
A nd makes me wet.
I ce cold water
N ice cold water
Yucorian Black, Grade 1
Annie Belle Clark Primary School, GA

Thanksgiving
Thanksgiving
Fun, exciting
Feasting, playing, learning
The pilgrims feasted today.
Holiday
Matthew Drury, Grade 3
Landmark Christian School, GA

Winter/Season
winter
icy, freezing
throwing, snowboarding, ice skating
I throw snowballs at my brother.
season
Ryan Bolebruch, Grade 2
Wells Central School, NY

Winter
Christmas
Santa's coming
Snow is falling
down the chimney and
...away!
C. Blair Marine, Grade 3
New Canaan Country School, CT

Time for Fall
The leaves change colors
The birds fly south from the cold
It is time for fall!
Dillon Clark, Grade 3
Ross Elementary School, PA

Purim
I am going to get a new costume
And it's going to be a Purim costume.
It is a bride costume.
It covers your head and is white.
Purim makes me happy.
I love Purim.
Yael Bruce, Kindergarten
United Hebrew Institute, PA

Football

I love football,
It is very fun.
Sometimes it rains,
But I usually play in the sun!

Marley Felder, Grade 2
Virginia A Boone Highland Oaks Elementary School, FL

I Am

I am Jackson who plays video games.
I wonder if I will be a car designer.
I hear cheering when I open my store for cars.
I feel great when I get new video games.
I want more Yogos.
I am a person who loves my family.

I pretend to be a Yogo.
I feel strength when I eat healthy foods.
I touch a car when I play with them.
I worry that I will die.
I cry because I am sick.
I am a person who's playful.

I understand that I hear God in my heart.
I say, "I am strong."
I dream to live 1000 years.
I try to do math.
I hope I succeed in math.
I am a person who cares about myself.

Jackson DeGirolamo, Grade 3
McKinley Elementary School, PA

All About Fall

In the fall, I smell hot, mashed up pumpkins in a pie on a windowsill.
In the fall, I feel a soft, warm, electric blanket on me when I'm cold.
In the fall, I taste brown, hot, chocolaty cocoa with melted marshmallows in it after I was outside playing.
In the fall, I hear crunchy leaves on the ground crunching when I walk up and down the sidewalk.
In the fall, I see dormant flowers out back in my garden.
In the fall, I don't see snowmen outside standing in the snow, unless it was this year!

Vivianne Bricker, Grade 3
Watsontown Elementary School, PA

Believe in Myself
Believe in myself
Determined to win my game
Strong, powerful and hopeful
Amalia Crevani, Grade 3
Holland Township School, NJ

Star!
I saw from afar
A bright little star
That lay in the night
Of beauty bright
A sight of light
That gave me delight
That led the way
As He lay
On the hay!
Warren Matthews, Grade 3
Fort Dale Academy, AL

My Dog
My dog
is Elmo
He is taller than
my elbow.
David Werking, Kindergarten
Taylor Road Academy, AL

Christy
Best mother
Pretty face
Plays doctor
Plays tag
Cuddly mom.
Kiana Prusky, Grade 2
Marie Curie Institute, NY

Cloud
The giant puffy white cloud
In the sunset
Floated like a butterfly
Gliding in a meadow.
Allison Quintin, Grade 3
Wellington School, FL

I Am From
I am from my quiet bedroom
where my soft dog is staring at me.
I am from my warm game room
where I watch TV on Saturday morning.
I am from my big yard
where my big pool is waiting for me to dive in.
Jaylen Gonzalez, Grade 1
Berkeley Lake Elementary School, GA

Spring
Spring comes and goes by
Say good-bye until next year
Have fun while it's here.
Matthew Clementoni, Grade 3
Catherine A Dwyer Elementary School, NJ

A Walk in the Woods
I went with my dad to the woods for a walk.
We stopped by the water to talk.
We saw birds flying by.
Up they went to the sky.

On the hill we saw a deer.
It ran away when we got near.
The woods are a good place to play.
But when it gets dark, it is the end of the day.
Bernard Lindinger, Grade 2
McKinley Elementary School, PA

My Grammy's House
When I go to my Grammy's house,
I will play with her cats and kittens.
She has a dog too.
His name is Thomas.
He loves me and I love him too.
He is a nice dog.
There are lots of cats there.
One of the cat's names is Tiger.
I love Tiger too and he loves me.
I love to go to my Grammy's house.
I love my Grammy and she loves me too.
I have a great time there.
Bailey Blake, Grade 2
Contentnea Elementary School, NC

My Dog

I wrestled with my dog after I went swimming.
I was slippery and wet so he was winning.
We played tug-of-war with the towel.
We had so much fun we began to howl.
We played lions too.
Mom said we belong in a zoo.
When she said put him back in his pen,
I was sad and I almost cried.
I love my dog and it's always hard to say bye.

Alex Charles Ormond, Grade 2
Contentnea Elementary School, NC

Monster in My Closet

There is a monster in my closet
I am pretty sure
I saw him bounce across my floor
He has three eyes, a long tail and pointy horns
Really I know what I saw
I am not making it up all
Mom come and check
Dad come see
He keeps grabbing my covers from under me
I pulled my covers over my head
Closed my eyes and scared to death
Hurry, hurry Mom he's here
I feel him nibbling on my ear
He is going to eat me
I am sure of that
Well, Looky here
It is my silly cat

Joseph Holmes, Grade 2
Carr Elementary School, NC

Lovely Fall

Plentiful leaves fall and change color
Wonderful pumpkin and cinnamon apple pie
And yummy applesauce in my stomach
Crunching leaves and branches
Fluffy owls hooting, light blowing wind
I love fall!

Milan Parker, Grade 2
Wellington School, FL

The Olympic Snowboarder

He is fast and dangerous.
He flips and jumps through the
cold air.

Logan Devitt, Grade 3
Holland Township School, NJ

Night Street

At night the city sleeps.
The city is dark but the moon is bright.
I see a car shining in the moonlight.
Now I must go home.
Good night.

Chris Beaulieu, Grade 2
Tamaques Elementary School, NJ

Pumpkin

The pumpkin is fat.
It is orange.
Make a face on it.
Seeds are in the pumpkin.
Make it pumpkin pie.

Ryan Moosbrugger, Grade 2
Hilton Head Christian Academy, SC

Basketball

ball, hoop, team
winning makes you gleam
play, shoot, score
game's not a bore
dribble, bounce, throw
to the hoop we go

Lyndy Boggs, Grade 3
Broadway Elementary School, NC

Sports

I love sports.
Baseball, skiing, swimming
Sports are so much fun!
I just love this thing
called winning!

Shimon Katz, Grade 2
Yeshiva Ketana of Long Island, NY

Polar Bear

Polar bear, polar bear I see you
Swimming in the ocean blue

I wonder why your fur is white
I wonder where you sleep at night

I wonder if you like the zoo
With all the people looking at you

I wonder what you'd say to me
If I were able to set you free

No more bars, no zoo keeper
I'll take you where the water's deeper

You'll swim and play, eat fish all day
I wish we could do it this way

Megan Ellery, Grade 3
St Alexis School, PA

Winter

Children have coats on
In winter it's cold outside
At home it is warm

Binyomin Edell, Grade 3
Yeshiva Ketana of Long Island, NY

Megan

M eaningful
E xcellent
G rateful
A mazing
N ice

Megan Gould, Grade 2
Long Meadow Elementary School, CT

Thanksgiving

Thanksgiving
Family, home
Eating, drinking, thanking
Thanksgiving is a feast.
Holiday

Paloma Malavé-Reyes, Grade 3
Marie Curie Institute, NY

The Environment

Roses are red violets are blue you should help the environment too.
The Environment, The Environment
It means so much to me and it should to you.
It means a lot to my family and I
If you would help the environment by recycling, and stop littering.
Remember to help the environment!

Anayiah Brathwaite, Grade 3
Public School 235 Lenox, NY

My Pumpkin

My Pumpkin falls down on the porch
And crashes on the floor.
Then my baby brother plays in the pumpkin smoosh.

Ashley DeBenedictus, Kindergarten
Marlboro Elementary School, NY

My Teachers

At the beginning in kindergarten,
I had Mrs. Masemore.
She filled my head with brain power just before I left school,
To go to the seashore.

When I had my head filled with the basics,
I strolled over to the room of Mrs. Russell.
Since she was my first grade teacher,
To the door I did hustle.

In second,
I had Mrs. Howe.
In the end,
She made me as smart as a barn owl.

Now in third, right now,
I have Mrs. Ronyack.
Soon my brain
Will be as sharp as a tack.

I wrote about my teachers,
Because they fill my brain with knowledge.
And I'm sure they'll do this,
Until college.

Kiran Pandey, Grade 3
Hanover Elementary School, PA

Umbrellas at the Beach

The beach is a place
To bring your umbrella
The sun beams on you
And the umbrella
You play in the water
And in the sand
Then you eat your lunch

Cameron Barbosa, Grade 3
Coram Elementary School, NY

Winter

In winter it snows.
In winter the ground is white.
In winter ice comes.
In winter snowmen are born.
But when winter ends,
It all goes away.

Anne Harrington, Grade 3
John Ward Elementary School, MA

July 4th

Eeeeeeeeee pow! July Fourth is here!
The crowds cheering wooo-hooo!
Finding the fireworks isn't hard.
Instead of moping I can keep hoping.
Eeeeeeeeee pow! Eeeeeeeeee pow!
This was a great Fourth of July.
Now I have to go home and wash up.

Noah Graham, Grade 3
Briarwood Christian School, AL

Snowflakes

S now is fun to play in.
N o one doesn't like it.
O ne of my friends plays with me a lot.
W ith snow you can do a lot.
F our kids play with me.
L ick the snowflakes
A nd have fun.
K ick and play with the snow.
E at some of the snow.
S now is very fun to play with.

Emily DiFerdinando, Grade 3
Evergreen Elementary School, PA

What's That Noise?

Ding dong, what's that noise?
Through the house,
Check all the toys.
Oh, it's just the Liberty Bell.
Boy, that sound is not swell!

Zachary Dinch, Grade 2
Trinity West Elementary School, PA

Things

Things are all
Around you
Things to do
And things to eat
There are so many things
So little time to see it

Claire Graves, Grade 3
North Ridge Elementary School, NC

To Have Fun

My kind father
comes from the Dominican Republic
six days before Thanksgiving
to Williams Island
to have fun with me

Matías Julían Mariné Cerra, Grade 3
Miami Country Day School, FL

Leap Frog

Leap frog, leap frog
Jump over here,
Leap frog, leap frog
Jump over there.
Leap frog, leap frog
Like clouds floating in through the air.
Leap frog, leap frog
In the sparkling blue sky
Ten million minnows fly in the sky.
Leap frog, leap frog
Then the sun left to go and
Off flowers of lilly closed up on the go.

Helene Schaffhauser, Grade 3
Oak Ridge Elementary School, PA

Movie Theater

Tall, high movie screen
Lots of unique, different noises
The popping, salty popcorn
The soft, furry seats
Sweet, yummy Junior Mints

Zane Morgan, Grade 3
Bradford Township Elementary School, PA

Winter

I know winter is lurking near,
by the gusts of wind swooshing by me
and making me shiver

I hear winter lurking near,
by listening to the animals outside,
gathering food to feast on
when winter finally comes

I feel winter lurking near,
by the swooshing wind
and the silent blankets of snow and ice

I taste winter lurking near,
when I stick my tongue out
and a snowflake lands on it,
but quickly melts away

I smell winter lurking near,
when I smell the cold, crisp air,
and inhale the aroma of warm hot chocolate
coming from the kitchen

Alison Sivitz, Grade 3
Lincoln Elementary School, PA

My House

The clean table
People talking loudly
My mom's hay cookies
Dogs that are furry and soft
Sparkling cold water

Lauren Stover, Grade 3
Bradford Township Elementary School, PA

Horse-ku

Horse is very cute.
I like horses. They are neat.
I just like the horse.
Yulisa Royston, Grade 2
Paine Primary School, AL

Hockey

men falling down hard
pushing the puck for a goal
sliding and gliding
Jordan Dely, Grade 3
Holland Township School, NJ

Elijah

Likes dancing
Sharing everything
Kind person
Cat person
Wanting something
Johnathan Wilson, Grade 2
Anne Frank School, PA

Football

It looks like a eye.
You can throw it.
You can kick it.
You can play football with it.
It looks like lips on my mouth
You can kick it off too.
Logan Ruthe, Grade 1
Holland Township School, NJ

Isabella

I sabella likes Halloween.
S occer.
A pples are my favorite.
B allerina.
E ats ice cream.
L ikes horses.
L oves turtles.
A girl.
Isabella Ziolkowski, Grade 1
St Stephen's School, NY

Dogs Are Running in the Lake

Dogs are running in the lake.
It's filling up the blank and keeping Blake
from making his cake.
Bradford Pattillo, Grade 3
Briarwood Christian School, AL

Football and Basketball

Football is my favorite sport.
I also like to play on the basketball court.
I like to shoot, catch, and run.
I like both of them because they are so fun.
Ta'Quan Roberson, Grade 2
Forest Street Elementary School, NJ

Summer

I like summer because it's fun,
It's cool, with no homework to do.
I love summer — it's nice and fun.
I love summer — it's cool and good.
And you play and run —
And there's the carnival.
Mathew Botros, Grade 3
St Joseph Catholic Grammar School, NJ

Salamanders

The salamander, a wildlife creature,
Was oddly made by Mother Nature.

It is the cousin of the lizard,
And they both can survive a blizzard.

Their habitats are different places,
And sometimes they have different faces.

You can find them under rocks or logs,
They may be sitting with a bullfrog.

They all come in different shades,
Some see them and they become afraid.

Finding them is really cool,
Wish I could bring one to school.
Sydney Palmer, Grade 3
St Alexis School, PA

Baseball and Me

My favorite sport is baseball.
I like to watch it and play it, too.
There is pitching and catching
And sliding and hitting.
To get in the game, you cannot be sitting.
First base, second, base, third base, and home,
Make sure you touch them all,
Or otherwise your team might fall.
A glove, a ball, a bat, and a helmet,
With this equipment, you are all set.
The Miramar Canes is my team,
And our colors are orange and green.
The Marlins, the Tigers and the Red Sox are cool,
I wish I could bring the players to school.
Miguel Cabrera, Miguel Olivo, David Ortiz, and Tankersly,
These are some of the players that I aspire to be.
So hopefully some day you will see,
in the Major Leagues will be me.

Kyle Acosta, Grade 3
Coral Cove Elementary School, FL

Nature

There are beautiful trees and flowers, bushes too.
In the world of sunshine and beauty there are wonderful things happening.
And when we go outside for recess, if we do,
We might be able to see them.
I am so glad that God gave us so many good things to see.

Ayodele Oluyemi, Grade 1
Collingwood Park SDA School, NJ

Winter

Winter is fun, winter is cold, and winter is chilly
And makes me shiver through my bones.
Winter is white, winter is nice
Everything is covered, with a blanket of snow.
Winter is entertaining, winter is play
I get to ride down the hill, with my snowboard and sleigh.
Winter is peace, winter is calm
Trees are covered with ice and are shining in the sun.
Winter is love, winter is peace
Everything looks magic and unreal.

Isabelle Coupet, Grade 3
Collingwood Park SDA School, NJ

Who Has Seen a Baseball?

Who has seen a baseball?
Not me, not you
But when the hitter hits a home run
The baseball is passing through.

Who has a seen a baseball?
Not you, not I
But when the pitcher throws a fast ball,
The baseball is passing by.

Nathan Hefner, Grade 1
Sundance School, NJ

Dogs

Dogs
Eat a lot
Furry animals
Growl and bark
But I LOVE dogs!

Jarrett Johnson, Grade 3
A L Burruss Elementary School, GA

Winter Snow

Winter snow tickles my nose
and freezes my toes.
My cold ears are red,
so I warm them in my bed.
So I don't have to go out in the storm,
I go to sleep without a peep.

Anna Williard, Grade 2
Briarwood Christian School, AL

My Favorite Day

My favorite day
I saw my little brother
for the first time.
It was really fun.
He was really tiny,
He was very, very cute.
He is two years old now,
I like to play with him.

Kaitlin Harkey, Grade 1
Cool Spring Elementary School, NC

Michael

M agnificent
I nteresting
C harming
H andsome
A wesome
E xtraordinary
L oving

Michael Reilly, Grade 2
Long Meadow Elementary School, CT

Thanksgiving

Thanksgiving Day
We went away
For a long ride
On the south side
We ate alone
In the Jamaica's Comfort Zone
The food was so delicious
The turkey was vicious
My aunt had to bake
A nice pineapple cake
I ate until I was full
I was stuffed like a bull
We had a fantastic time
Then we went home to unwind
This was the end of my day
When I went away!

ShiAnn Santiago, Grade 3
Marie Durand Elementary School, NJ

Dear Skeletons

Dear skeletons,
You scare me.
Please, don't eat me.
Please, don't kill me.

Hunter Wilhelm, Grade 1
Cool Spring Elementary School, NC

Sun

The sun is a star
the sun is so very bright
the sun to big too.

Keitrel, Grade 2
Joan Walker Elementary School, FL

Fall Leaves

Fall leaves
Fall leaves
Oh how I love
Fall leaves
With my sister
Playing in the leaves
We first rake the leaves up
Then we, then we
Jump in the leaves
Fall leaves
Fall leaves
Oh how I love
Fall leaves

Taylor Leigh Wendell, Grade 2
Thomas Jefferson Elementary School, VA

Halloween

Halloween is very scary.
That makes me think of being a pretty fairy.
Halloween has scariness.
It gives me a weakness.
There is so much to do on Halloween night.
It also has a witches' broom flight.
Happy Halloween! Be safe!

Zoya Sadowski, Grade 3
McKinley Elementary School, PA

Mother Love

Hugs and kisses and all of your wishes,
Mother love.
Kisses and hugs and ladybugs,
Mother love.
Bandage finders and all-the-timers,
Mother love.
Funny jokers and belly pokers,
Mother love.
Awesome gamers and "what-a-shamers,"
Mother love.
Silly sallies and dilly dallies,
Mother love.

Sophie Williams, Grade 3
Loomis Elementary School, PA

Penguins
Penguins pip.
Penguins slide.
Penguins flop, flop, flop!
Juliet Alvarez, Grade 1
Northeast Elementary School, NY

November/Thanksgiving
November
Cool, windy
Stuffing big turkeys
Colorful leaves are falling
Thanksgiving
Kayla Flemming, Grade 3
Northeast Elementary School, NY

My Teacher
You teach great things.
Your love is good.
You have a sweet spirit.
You give us mercy,
and you help me remember things.
Now I have a memory!
I love you.
Katie Grippe, Grade 2
Somerset Christian School, KY

Penguins
Penguins dive.
Penguins slide.
Penguins pip, pip, pip!
Aliyah Codner, Grade 1
Northeast Elementary School, NY

My Favorite Bed
I love my bed,
It is so red.
When I sleep,
I'm counting sheep.
I love the sound,
When no one's around.
The pillows are so soft,
When I go upstairs to my loft.
Victoria Krastev, Grade 3
Ellicott Road Elementary School, NY

Frog-ku
Slimy, yucky, gross,
Eats insects and flies, yum! Yum!
Jumps, ribbitt, hop hop!
Sam Hayes, Grade 2
Paine Primary School, AL

Autumn
Squirrels bury nuts
Striped fast squirrels collect nuts
They come at daytime
Jackson Powell, Grade 2
Wellington School, FL

Daddy
A strong horse
A horse reminds me of my home
Rocks on the ground
Horses running
Taylor Hancock, Grade 1
Stone Academy, SC

Poodles
I like big poodles.
Golden poodles are special.
Dogs run very fast.
Dovid Werzberger, Grade 3
Yeshiva Ketana of Long Island, NY

Pumpkins
People plant pumpkins
Pumpkins have seeds inside them
People carve pumpkins
Giovanni Locham, Grade 2
Weston Elementary School, NJ

My Favorite Sport
My favorite sport is baseball.
It is so much fun!
I love it so much!
Especially when I run!
Chaim Goodman, Grade 2
Yeshiva Ketana of Long Island, NY

The Star Above the Holy One

The holy star of Bethlehem,
stood high above a holy stable
in the holy town of Bethlehem
a holy son was born.
In this manger many came to see.
For in this manger there lay the holy one.
For Lord Jesus be His name.
He is the son of God.
He was born to Mary and Joseph on this holy day.
But crucified for a nice, kind, loving soul.
My heart tells me that this work does not please the holy eye.
Those 40 days were long and hard.
But He rose again.
He came.
We hoped He would stay, but He couldn't.
But we love Him.

Nicole Souza, Grade 3
Wolcott School, CT

My Wolf

I wish I had a wolf.
I would play with him in the woods.
We could play in the snow and build a fort.
He would be my best friend.

Braedan Collins, Kindergarten
St Mary of the Assumption Catholic School, PA

Ice Cream

At night when it is time for bed,
I kick and scream,
and when my parents let me stay up late
I eat ice cream.

When I finish my ice cream
They say, "Go to bed!"
But I don't want to
I want to eat more ice cream.

So then they say, "You can eat more ice cream tomorrow."
"Ok," I say and I go to bed
But dreams of ice cream fill my head.

Kara Travers, Grade 3
McKinley Elementary School, PA

Fall

In the fall
I love it all
Red, yellow, and orange leaves
Fall, fall, fall to the ground
Lauryn Mattox, Grade 2
Eagle's View Academy, FL

5 W's

I
love to look at planets
in the night
in my house
'cause they are interesting
Kiana McQuade, Grade 1
Sundance School, NJ

Fire Football

Looks like an oval eye.
My dad and I playing
catch.
Lips.
At a football game.
A monkey head.
It is brown and white and
has lines.
Michael VanDine, Grade 1
Holland Township School, NJ

Clint

C lean
L istener
I nspiring
N ephew
T ogether
Clint Hovis, Grade 2
Park Elementary School, AR

December Is Awesome

December is here,
I can feel the wind in my hair,
It is my birthday.
Rio Hito, Grade 3
Tuxedo Park School, NY

The Guy Lost in the Woods

There was a guy lost in the woods
He heard a noise that made him jump,
But it was his cabin mate!
Adam Hassan, Grade 3
St Joseph Catholic Grammar School, NJ

Trees

There are many kinds of trees in the world
I like them very much
Oak trees are my favorite
Their leaves are so bright
Giulia Bronzi, Grade 3
Miami Country Day School, FL

Dogs

I like dogs.
I like dogs because they like to play ball.

I like dogs because they like to chase cats.
I like dogs because they are fluffy and nice.
I like dogs because they are cool.
William Holahan, Grade 3
McKinley Elementary School, PA

Dogs

Dogs are furry and cuddly.
Dogs can be very good friends.

Dogs are very playful too.
Four paws of softness and fun.

Dogs come in different sizes.
Dogs are different colors.

Dogs like to roll on the grass.
Dogs jump up on people.

Dogs like to chew many things.
Dogs chew ropes, bones, balls, and treats.

Dogs like to take walks with you.
That's why they are man's best friend.
Matthew Beck, Grade 3
St Alexis School, PA

The Legend of the Gingerbread Girl

sweet brown
warm frosty
nice colorful
lovely good
fast hard
cool awesome
smart bright

Samantha Norton, Grade 1
Hilton Head Christian Academy, SC

Princess

Beautiful, adorable,
Lovable, soft,
Fluffy cat.

Come lay on my bed.
I'll pet you and love you.
I'll scratch your head
If you want me to.

Your purr box is loud!
OUCH!
You bit my nose!
Off my bed and outside for you.

I'll feed your breakfast.
Now earn your keep and
Go catch a mouse!

Mackenzie McCotter, Grade 3
Thomas Jefferson Elementary School, VA

Fruit

Fruit is healthy.
Fruit is good.
I'd eat it all day,
If my mom said I could.
Apples, oranges, lots of berries,
Bananas, grapes, and bright, red cherries,
I love them all, this is true,
Do you love fruit like I do?

Cole Starr, Grade 2
Briarwood Christian School, AL

Rudolph/Reindeer
Rudolph
shiny, red-nosed
flying, playing, eating
he leads Santa's sleigh Christmas Eve
reindeer
Sheyenne Beach, Grade 2
Wells Central School, NY

Fire Safety
Fire
Alarms
Sirens
Fire trucks
Water
Fire out
Melany Solis, Grade 2
Weston Elementary School, NJ

Happy Halloween!
Halloween is great.
I see black cats everywhere.
Happy Halloween!
MacKenzie Hawes, Grade 2
Wanamassa Elementary School, NJ

Animals
cat
fat, fluffy
eating, meowing, purring
milk, kittens, bones, puppies
barking, swimming, running
dirty, fast
dog
Savannah Wade, Grade 2
Bensley Elementary School, VA

Dolphins
Dolphins in water.
I like to watch them swim some.
My room has dolphins.
Makahla Brown, Grade 3
Clinton Christian Academy, MO

Basketball
My defense goes on the court,
They set up like a fort.
My favorite player is Shaquille O'Neal,
Because he's the real deal.
When I get hot,
I don't miss a shot.
My favorite game is Horse,
I always win of course.
In basketball we play with five,
We run fast and the crowd stays alive.
Every shot counts for two,
If you're lucky, I'll play with you.
Charlie Neuweiler, Grade 3
Our Lady of Hope School, NY

Reese's Cup
Round and chocolate.
With peanut butter inside.
It's my favorite.
Nicholas Schaaf, Grade 2
St Peter the Apostle School, GA

Rainbow
What is more beautiful
Than looking at the colorful rainbow,
After the boring rain?

Nothing…

After a boring rainy day
When that shining rainbow appears

It refreshes my mind
It fills my heart
It just makes my day.
Merlinda Kovacevic, Grade 3
Public School 48, NY

Clouds
Clouds are in the sky
They look like cotton candy
Clouds make rain fall down
Chenny Kim, Grade 3
John Ward Elementary School, MA

Sydney

S pecial
Y oung
D ancer
N ice
E nergetic
Y outhful

Sydney Warsing, Grade 3
Virginia A Boone Highland Oaks Elementary School, FL

Chocolate

Warm, gooey, delicious chocolate
Melting in your mouth
Through the wrapper you can feel the cold hard candy
You can feel the texture of the Hershey bar
You wish it could last forever
But it's already gone.

Darby McCaslin, Grade 3
Lincoln Elementary School, PA

Jessica

J oy
E nthusiastic
S inger
S weet
I ntelligent
C entered
A wesome

Jessica Zeitlin, Grade 3
Virginia A Boone Highland Oaks Elementary School, FL

School

People like to learn and play,
when they go to school every single day.

Come home from school and get a good rest,
wake up again time to do your best!

If you have a bad day don't make it worse,
go grab a friend and make burst.

And if you make A's and B's you will be the best!

Mia Smith, Grade 3
Pike Liberal Arts School, AL

Flowers

When the bright sun rises
In the morning,
I go outside and see
If the beautiful flowers
Need some water.
When I fill the
Red bucket up with
Cold water and bring it
To the dazzling garden and
Water the colorful plants.
Day by
Day by
Day I wait to
See the colorful, dazzling
Flowers
Sprout.
Every day when the sunset
goes down, I go into
My big, soft, cozy bed.
then see the flowers
Winking and smiling at me!

Bianca Carbone, Grade 3
Oak Ridge Elementary School, PA

The Ocean

Fishermen catch shrimp.
Ocean islands are little.
Walk across sand bars.

Rin Richardson, Grade 2
St Peter the Apostle School, GA

Fishes

Kitty, Kitty, Kitty
She is as cute as a puppy
Kitty is small
like a chick
She is also orange like the fruit
how sweet!
She is like a dolphin
jumping in the aquarium
Kitty, Kitty, Kitty
I love you!

Kelly Yu, Grade 3
Public School 148 Ruby Allen, NY

Days of the Week

Days of the week, oh!
Seven in all.
School days, five in all.
Monday begins the school week
With lots of work and fun.
Followed by Tuesday, then
Wednesday and on to Friday.
Five learning days!
So much work,
So much fun.

Saturday a break from
Regular work.
Day to relax,
Day to visit friends,
Visit zoos and museums
And theaters too.
Hang out
And have a ball.

Sunday a day for worship
And praising God.

Kaile Reid, Grade 3
John Hus Moravian School, NY

Bats

Bats fly high
Up in the sky.

At night they play
So they sleep all day.

They will stay out of sight
When they are out at night.

Bats use sonar
To go near and far.

Bats always cause alarm
But they never mean any harm.

Josh Graham, Grade 3
Pike Liberal Arts School, AL

Rocks

Rocks, rocks everywhere,
Red, blue, black and green.
I see them up
I see them down.
I even see them in the ground.
Some are big
Some are little.
Some are even smaller than a penny.
Some you can crack with crystals inside.
"Oh, how I wish I could be one, too!"

Ben Sciacchetano, Grade 2
Evangelical Christian School, TN

The Uninvited Guests

It's hot there is no water,
but still they march.
They march up and down
like little soldiers.
Marching, up twisted metal pipes,
up drains, into the bathroom,
searching for water.
One by one
marching out of the big bowl
in the center of drawers.
Slowly but silently
marching around the bathroom floor.
I count them when they come out of the drain.
They crawl up the side of the bathtub
under rugs on cabinets.
Who are these uninvited guests?
Ants!

Sarah Finleyson, Grade 3
Reidville Elementary School, SC

Candy

Candy
Sweet, juicy
Munching, sucking, chewing
Very good to eat!
Chocolate

Lauren Gentile, Grade 3
Chestnut Street Elementary School, PA

Autumn
Leaves, pumpkins, scarecrows
Squirrels, crow, flower, yellow
The trees are dying
Ryan Bell, Grade 2
Wellington School, FL

Nicholas/Scrat
Nicholas
Fast, tall
Playing, running, laying
I like playing hockey
Scrat
Nicholas Lenz, Grade 2
St Stephen's School, NY

Frost/Snow
Frost
Cold, slippery
Coating, touching, glittering
Shiny on the grass.
Snow
Kellie Murtha, Grade 2
Consolidated School, CT

My Favorite Place
New York
The skyline, the high buildings
Museums
I really like it
Brian Odiase, Grade 1
Sundance School, NJ

Toys
I see toys everywhere,
You can bring toys anywhere,
Dolls to play with,
Teddy bears to snuggle,
Blocks to build with,
Cars to race with,
Now I put my toys away.
Vanessa Bellamy, Grade 2
Marie Curie Institute, NY

Siblings
Usually there is only one,
And most of the time they're lots of fun.

Sometimes they're my closest friend,
But niceness always has to end.

I sometimes wish I had another,
That's how I feel about my brother.
Spencer Carter, Grade 3
Madison Station Elementary School, MS

Halloween
Halloween is fun.
I like trick-or-treating,
I love costumes!
Costumes like devils and witches.
They're the costumes I like.
I also like getting candy!
Ariel Williams, Grade 3
St Joseph Catholic Grammar School, NJ

My House
It is bright in here.
It is smokey here.
Open up the windows in our house.
Brown bottom and red top of my house.
Hope Ann Cowder, Grade 3
Bradford Township Elementary School, PA

Fall Leaves
What is yellow and brown and falls all around?
Fall leaves of course!
So graceful as they fall,
You never see them bounce like a ball.
When fall leaves are here,
Turkey time is near,
The air is nice,
A little like ice.
Soon the leaves will be gone,
The wind will become strong,
Winter will be near, but never fear,
Fall leaves will return again next year!
Sara Mulkey, Grade 3
A L Burruss Elementary School, GA

The Twilight Zone

Dusk is when you can see dew spangled webs.
Dusk is when the sky changes colors like a chameleon.
Dusk flushes millions of mosquitoes.
Dusk is a community of nocturnal animals.
Dusk gives the signal for night to be born.
Dusk is when shooting stars look like explosions.
Dusk polishes the baseball diamond.
The figures of the night look like gargoyles.
Well, dawn is coming, I should go to bed.
I will see you next twilight!

Aidan Hughes, Grade 3
Jeffrey Elementary School, CT

Autumn

A pples are good to eat in the fall.
U p and down, leaves in the wind.
T hanksgiving is a good time with my family.
U p in the tree, a squirrel is getting nuts.
M aking jack-o'-lanterns is good for fall.
N uts are for squirrels, not for people.

Javier Jimenez, Grade 3
Central Park Elementary School, FL

Black

Black is the color of darkness.
The night.
A bat creeping in your attic.
Black is the man that you imagine in your dreams,
Or the panther ready to strike!
Black is the color of evil not to shame.
Black is as dark as the water in the ocean at night.

Caleb Rhodes, Grade 3
John Ward Elementary School, MA

Autumn

A pples are really tasty at harvest time.
U seful pumpkins to carve.
T urkey is good to eat for Thanksgiving time.
U p down all around, leaves flying everywhere.
M outh watering food.
N ice ripe pumpkins for pumpkin pie.

Rachel Thompson, Grade 3
Central Park Elementary School, FL

My Pet

Dog
White
Barks at the door
Jumps up
Super loud when phone rings
Lives inside
Love my dog
When I give her a treat
She will sit
Doggy

Aiden McLaughlin, Kindergarten
Broadway Elementary School, NC

All About My Mom

My mom is cute.
I love her.
When I am with her
I feel like a beautiful
white flower.
I love my mom, mom, mom
It's all about my mom,
She is very sweet
like a lollipop. But...
when she dresses all
brown she looks like a
yummy chocolate chip
cookie. Yum, yum, yum,
When my mom sleeps
she looks like a beautiful
angel when I touch her
she is like a soft cloud

Camila Analuisa, Grade 3
Public School 148 Ruby Allen, NY

Fall

Fall flies in with
colorful leaves on the green grass
with pumpkins growing bigger
on a cool windy morning
with my mom making pumpkin pies

Channing Chambers, Grade 3
Wellington School, FL

Light

Light
Is sight
Makes things bright
Makes you feel brave
Light!

Toni Ann Jackson, Grade 3
A L Burruss Elementary School, GA

Autumn

A ll the leaves fall from the tree.
U nder the leaves is the ground.
T hanksgiving is coming.
U ntil the leaves fall I can't wait.
M y brothers like fall.
N uts are eaten by squirrels.

Jacob Kaplan, Grade 2
United Hebrew Institute, PA

Christmas Eve

We open one present
On Christmas Eve.
We feed the reindeer
Before they leave.
It's hard to sleep.
We get lots of toys.
The snow falls on us.
Stockings are for girls and boys.

Tucker Gleason, Grade 1
Westlake Christian School, FL

Who Has Seen Life?

Who has seen life?
Not I, not you.
But, when life is touching your cheek,
It's nice to speak.
The life is passing through.

Who has seen life?
Not I, not you.
But, when life is happening,
The power is coming through.
The life is passing by.

Steven Rhein, Grade 2
Sundance School, NJ

Red

There once was a boy named Red,
Who had a friend named Ned.
Red had a fear,
That he would die here.
But now he is really dead!

Robert Jessie, Grade 3
John H Winslow Elementary School, NJ

Jesus Was Born on Christmas Night

Jesus was born on Christmas night.
The three kings saw a bright light.
The three kings saw a star.
They traveled very far.

Jesus was born in a manger.
Jesus was not in danger.
Jesus was born in a barn.
Jesus, Mary, and Joseph were not in any harm.

Hayley Morgan, Grade 3
St Edward the Confessor School, LA

Karate

Karate.
Karate is fun.
Sometimes we run.
We use weapons,
but only for protection.
We always do our best,
even when we are put to the ultimate test!
Karate.

Jonathan Pinghera, Grade 3
North Star Elementary School, DE

Chanukah at My House

My dreidels were on a table.
I played with the little one.
My sister, Rachel, brought two packs of oil
To my house.
There was eight days and nights.
Chanukah makes me happy.

Jonathan Rutta, Kindergarten
United Hebrew Institute, PA

Cats

Cats
Dogs aren't better,
Eat fish,
Fur is soft,
Cats are my favorite!
Kamila Teruel, Grade 3
A L Burruss Elementary School, GA

Wonder Cow

I make milk.
It feels like silk.
I like to hit rocks.
Even though they feel like blocks.
I am Wonder Cow.
David Flores, Grade 1
Northeast Elementary School, NY

Brown Horse

I am tall
You will never fall
I jump
But never bump
I am Brown Horse.
Dashne Flores, Grade 1
Northeast Elementary School, NY

The Santa Bell

green nice
beautiful cute
Christmas cool
good loud
noisy hand
small
Jacey Robinson, Grade 1
Hilton Head Christian Academy, SC

BMXing
Fun, Tricky
Big air, Wipe out, Sweating
Awesome, Cool, Fantastic, Scary
Biking
Justice Wells, Grade 3
Wapping Elementary School, CT

My Pet

Dog
Brown and white
Runs
Rolls over
Wags tail
I feed him
I show him tricks
Doggy fun
Lacey Ingram, Kindergarten
Broadway Elementary School, NC

Jumping on Beds

I like jumping on beds
bouncing up and down —
popping up like a rabbit —
up to the ceiling
then falling down again.
Just be careful when you're jumping
or you might bump your head!!!
Rachel Deligdish, Grade 2
Bnos Malka Academy, NY

Sounds

I can see the bee it said
buzzzzzzzzzzzzzzzzzzzzzz

I can see the lion it said
roar

I can see the boy walking
boom boom boom

I can see the hand clapping
clap clap clap clap

I can see the phone ringing
ring ring ring ring

I can see the horse say
naah naah naah naah
Andres Alberto, Grade 2
Public School 148 Ruby Allen, NY

My Bunny

The habits of my bunny are very funny
He has big round eyes and a huge furry tummy

He lives underground
And he never makes a sound

My bunny can hop
To the very top

My bunny hops through the yard
But trying to catch him is hard

When my bunny is in the garden he looks for treats
And nibbles on all he likes to eat

He likes to have some fun
When he is done he lies in the sun

Gabrielle Martin, Grade 3
St Alexis School, PA

School

In school, you learn a lot.
At recess, you play in the parking lot.
In gym, you exercise and play games,
And in other subjects, you exercise your brain.
When you eat lunch, you eat a bunch of food.
In spelling, you learn new words.
And in art, you learn new words too.

Andrew Wenzler, Grade 3
Our Lady of Hope School, NY

Mrs. Cohen

M arvelous
R ealistic
S tar

C aring
O utstanding
H ysterical
E xciting
N ice

Alexis Fried, Grade 3
Virginia A Boone Highland Oaks Elementary School, FL

Baseball
It's a circle.
You throw it.
You catch it.
You hit it.
It reminds me of games.
Baseball is fun.
Tennis is fun.
Jason LaVigna, Grade 1
Holland Township School, NJ

Baseball
I love to play baseball.
I love it the best.
I love to hit home runs.
I want to beat the rest.
Stephen Vasile, Grade 3
Our Lady of Hope School, NY

The Sport of Boxing
My gloves are moving
My shirt is all sweaty now
I am punching him
Jake Petro, Grade 3
Holland Township School, NJ

Winter
Clouds are like a bunny.
Snow is white with ice —
Polar bunnies are like snow.
Erik Shaw, Grade 3
Tuxedo Park School, NY

Popcorn
Once a
POP!
Once a
POP!
What can it be?
It could be a balloon or tire!
But what can it be?
Yi Xi Pan, Grade 3
Public School 131, NY

Turkey
Turkey
Fat, colorful
Stuffing, cooking, eating
Turkeys are very good
Bird
Madyson Whippo, Grade 3
Chestnut Street Elementary School, PA

The Flag
The flag blows red, white and blue
Outside on a pole
High in the sky.
Sebastian Pena, Kindergarten
Mother Seton Inter Parochial School, NJ

The Frog
Croak croack croack splish splash splatter
the frogs are making quite a chatter.
They are making so much noise
it sounds like a group of boys.
Emma Faulkner, Grade 3
Briarwood Christian School, AL

Fun in the Snow
In the white snow I play.
I do it all day!
In the snow my hand got cold.
I didn't want my mother to scold!
My gloves they did hide,
So I went inside!
Sarah McLain, Grade 1
St Vincent De Paul Elementary School, MO

The Sunset and Me
I gaze at the sunset
Go down the hill
I watch the slow moment
Of the sunset
The light and beauty gets tinier and tinier
Until it goes away
Goodbye sunset
I will see you again.
Miranda Griffin, Grade 3
Oak Ridge Elementary School, PA

Sports

I like to play sports.
There are all different sorts.
Hockey is my favorite game.
My favorite player is in the Hall of Fame.
The game is so hot!
I like it a lot.

Jessica Opiela, Grade 3
Ellicott Road Elementary School, NY

Cool Pumpkins

Big
Thin
Orange
Cool
Make faces out of them
See them everywhere, especially at Halloween
Round
Fat
Nice-looking
Use them for pies
PUMPKINS!

Anna Marie Herin, Grade 2
Evangelical Christian School, TN

Will

W orthy
I nspiring
L oyal
L adies choice and quick on his feet

Will Scobey, Grade 2
Park Elementary School, AR

Veteran

V ery kind
E asy to get hurt
T hink of plans to win the war
E ager to visit their family
R escues America
A dmit they will not stop working
N ervous to start going to war

Carlee Walker, Grade 3
Bradford Township Elementary School, PA

Halloween

Roses are red.
Violets are blue.
The sky is as blue
As a pencil gripper.
A cloud is as white
As an angel in the sky.
The night time sky
Is as dark as Halloween night.
When the ghosts fly around
On the scariest night of all…
Boo! BOO!
Did you hear that?!

Sierra Amo, Grade 2
Annsville Elementary School, NY

Bears

Tall, furry, hairy
Growls for food and at people
The fur is so soft

Juancruz Lorenzino, Grade 3
Miami Country Day School, FL

Color the World

Beautiful blue,
the color of the silent sky.

Unique yellow,
the color of the shining sun.

Grand green,
the color of the growing grass.

Perfect purple,
the color of glorious grapes.

Precious pink,
the color of pure pink lemonade.

Radiant red,
the color of fantastic flowers.

Madison Paige, Grade 3
Reidville Elementary School, SC

My Hermit Crab

Tiny, rough, tough
Sleeping, climbing, eating, running
Stubborn, fun, happy
Tex

Jevawn Wright, Grade 2
St Mary's School, NJ

The Dark

Afraid in the dark,
Because I'm so small,
Can't sleep tonight — at all!
Darkness all around,
A light in the night,
Would be such a wonderful sight!

Donte Hines, Grade 3
A L Burruss Elementary School, GA

At the Old Ball Game

Peanuts and cracker jacks,
Hot dogs and snacks.
I can't wait to go,
To the old ball game!

Baseballs and bats,
Soft gloves and hats.
Bases and cleats,
Equipment!

Shortstop or pitcher,
First base or catcher.
Where will I be?
Positions!

Short sleeve or long sleeve,
Belts and tight pants.
Don't forget stirrups,
Uniforms!

The umpires and coaches,
The dirt and the sweat.
I never want to hear,
"Three strikes and you're out!"

Benjamin Painter, Grade 2
Home School, KY

Gators

The Gators are awesome,
They're very, very cool;
When you think of a win,
Think orange and blue.

Max Kurkin, Grade 3
Virginia A Boone Highland Oaks Elementary School, FL

Boom, Boom, Crack!

The firework display was awesome.
The first one went off with an enormous "Boom!"
The sky was dead black after the show.
It was scary standing right below.

Will Carlisle, Grade 3
Briarwood Christian School, AL

November

My favorite month of the year is November.
It has my birthday, a day I will always remember.
There is Thanksgiving with turkey, stuffing, and pumpkin pie.
Sometimes when I eat too much I just want to cry!

Alexandra Muro, Grade 3
Our Lady of Hope School, NY

The Bible

The Bible is full of things God wants us to know,
And you can read it through rain or snow.
It says things that are helpful, like this,
"It is more blessed to give than to receive,"
And "You should trust and believe."
God is powerful and strong,
And you can trust Him even if your life is challenging and long.
He chose some special men to write the Bible, and thus,
now we can read it, all of us.

Mary Kathryn Hutcheson, Grade 3
Victory Christian School, GA

Playgrounds

Playgrounds are fun,
You could swing on the swing set.
There's dirt on the ground,
You don't have to go home yet!

Brian Acebo, Grade 2
Virginia A Boone Highland Oaks Elementary School, FL

She's a Schooly Girl

Her name is Gloribel Stephanie Momin
She seems so smart
I love the way her backpack goes
up and down every step she takes.
She wants to be a lawyer
She always knows the answer to a test
She's good at spelling
She helps me with my
homework when I need it
That's why I love her
and she loves me!

Ishika Momin, Grade 3
Public School 148 Ruby Allen, NY

Scary Pumpkin

Scary pumpkin!
We picked you,
From the pumpkin patch,
With not even a scratch.
Then, I saw a ghost,
That scared a host.
But not my pumpkin,
My pumpkin scared the ghost!

Luke Jennings, Grade 3
Coral Springs Elementary School, FL

Summer

Summer is fun
I play in the sun
All day I wish
It was summer
Every day.

Audrey Noel, Grade 3
Miami Country Day School, FL

The Cars

Cars are cool.
Cars are hot.
They go fast.
They use gas.
Cars have colors.
And cars go vroom!

Jordan Walker, Grade 1
Forest Street Elementary School, NJ

An Older Dog

Our dog Annie is old and gray
But still she brightens up our day.

Our dog Annie can sit and stay
And Annie really *loves* to play.

When we run around and skip
Our old dog Annie will bark and yip.

One time Annie tried to chomp on bees
Down by the playground and the trees.

Dogs like Annie still have lots to give
By your side as long as they live.

We love Annie for she is our friend
Our love for Annie will never end

Julia Maruca, Grade 3
St Alexis School, PA

Andrew

A happy person
N ever down
D oes lots of things
R eads a lot
E lephant is favorite animal
W ent to Colorado

Andrew Kristofferson, Grade 3
Clinton Christian Academy, MO

I Am From

I am from my pretty bedroom
where my books are in my bed
waiting for me to come and read them.
I am from my nice kitchen where
my warm cookies are in the oven
cooking and cooking.
I am from my hilly backyard
where I like swinging on my swing
going back and forth.

Amiree Cage, Grade 1
Berkeley Lake Elementary School, GA

Leaves

Leaves
Colorful, flat
Flying, laying, tumbling
I like keeping leaves.
Plant

Charles Ball, Grade 3
Chestnut Street Elementary School, PA

Turkey/Meat

Turkey
Stuffed, brown
Hunting, killing, eating
We hunt the turkey
Meat

McKenna Ennis, Grade 3
Chestnut Street Elementary School, PA

RV's

RV's are so big
And they drive so fast.
But if you drive with your awning out…
You might get arrested!

Jacob Huller, Grade 3
Evergreen Elementary School, PA

Chanukah

Running, running!
We have to get the place ready for Chanukah!
We have to make the latkes!
Do you want to play the dreidel game?
Spin the dreidel! I win!
I get all of the gelt!

Adina Bell, Kindergarten
United Hebrew Institute, PA

Lynnie

When I am sad she makes me happy.
When I am holding her she makes me joyful.
When I hold her she seems to listen to me.
Lynnie is the best guinea pig in the world.

Michaela Rieser, Grade 2
St Anselm School, PA

Alex

A lex likes cats.
L ikes books.
E ats steak.
X -Men is my favorite show.

Alex Nemeth, Grade 1
St Stephen's School, NY

Ethan

E ater
T all
H appy
A wesome
N ovember baby

Ethan McKinney, Grade 2
Park Elementary School, AR

Beth

My mom
Green eyes
Rides bikes
Likes swimming
Very pretty

Wesley Williams, Grade 2
Marie Curie Institute, NY

Black Cats/Kitten

Black cats
Furry, black
Balancing, moving, hunting
Come out in October.
Kitten

Trey Iacovelli, Grade 2
Consolidated School, CT

Thanksgiving

Thanksgiving
Food drinks
Thanking giving thinking
We eat a lot
Feast

Ryan Rivera, Grade 3
Marie Curie Institute, NY

On the Computer

I was
on the
computer when
the computer turned
OFF!

I turned it
back on but
it turned back
OFF!

I thought the
computer was
BROKEN but
there was
only a

BUG

Ashley Kreider, Grade 3
Hunter GT Magnet Elementary School, NC

Maizie

We have a pet named Maizie.
Not the normal pet, now is she?
She isn't a dog, or even a cat,
A pig, or bird, or anything like that.
She once had spots that are now all gone.
She now has grown and lives on her own.
She runs really fast and jumps really high.
We miss her so much we all could just cry!
Can you guess what she is?
To me it's so clear,
Our pet Maizie is a doe deer!

Christopher Farrar, Grade 3
Pike Liberal Arts School, AL

There Was a Man

There was an old man with a beard.
He said, "It's just as I feared.
2 owls, a hen,
4 larks, and a wren
have all built their nest in my beard."

Andriy Mulyar, Grade 3
Springfield Park Elementary School, VA

Rainbows

Rainbows are beautiful.
Rainbows are so beautiful and bright,
They make you want to blink and think.
Rainbows have many different colors.
You wear the colors of the rainbow every day.
When it rains you may be seeing, a rainbow on the road.
That's why rainbows are so beautiful!

Emily Payamps, Grade 3
St Joseph Catholic Grammar School, NJ

My Dog Sunshine

When I wake up in the morning,
My sunshine does not mind to rise,
She quickly plays and kisses me,
I sure don't make myself hard to find.

When I leave to school she runs and says goodbye,
Goodbye my sunshine, I'll have you on my mind.
In the afternoon when I arrive,
My playful Sunshine is waiting, I know that she is all mine.

At home she runs and plays with me,
She plays fetch and also hide and seek,
I can't resist her kisses,
My heart misses when each other we don't see.

She is one fine dog and loving,
Obeying all the time,
I love her because,
She is always by my side.

Daisy Gongar, Grade 3
Coral Cove Elementary School, FL

Fall

In the fall, I taste warm tasty apple cider at a Bucknell University football game.
In the fall, I smell really delicious pumpkin pie in my house
at the Thanksgiving table.
In the fall, I feel windy, rainy weather when I am outside.
In the fall, I hear noisy crashing cars at a Nascar race in the Poconos.
In the fall, I see crashing helmets in a football game at Bucknell.
In the fall, I don't see baseball players hitting a ball.

Garrett Ruch, Grade 3
Watsontown Elementary School, PA

Keep Christ in Christmas

When Jesus came
Nothing was the same
But when Jesus died,
Everyone cried.

In December
We remember
That Mary's Son
Made us all one.

Rebekah Stoll, Grade 3
St Edward the Confessor School, LA

Something Fun to Do in Fall

Something fun to do in fall
Is play in leaves or with a ball.
I ride my bike all day long.
Then sometimes I want to
Sing a silly song.

Alexis Ford, Grade 2
Melwood Elementary School, MD

Art

Art is everywhere.

Art is like colors
in the sky
making a picture.

All of these lovely colors in the sky!
Look like dozens and dozens
of rainbow colors.

Art is everywhere you look!
Art is in books, beaches and
lots of other
wonderful
things too.

Art is lots and lots
of rainbows.

Kevin Kerliu, Grade 3
Public School 48, NY

I Dream in Pink

Shades of pink line up the sky
shades of pink light up my life
shades of pink lift up
my spirits with delight.

Butterflies shape the clouds
with shades of pink
all about making my dreams
in pink come around.

Pink gowns, pink diamond shoes
Pink crowns and pink ribbons, too.

These are my dreams
that I hope one day will come true.

Naomi R. Baca, Grade 3
Coral Cove Elementary School, FL

Kinley

K ind
I ndependent
N utty
L ittle
E mperor
Y elling

Whitney Key, Grade 3
Pottsville Elementary School, AR

Splish Splash

Fun, fun, fun
it is all wet
Splish, splish, splish
Splosh, splosh, splosh
water sparkling blue
Scary ride green and black
Lots of floaties to float on
food and rides
Hot, hot, hot
Lots of people wait in line
Splish splash is
huge, huge, huge
songs to sing and dancing too.

Marcela Madrid, Grade 3
Public School 148 Ruby Allen, NY

My Fish

Sunny when I caught
fish at Hoffman parks
and big mouth bass.
Water is blue and wiggly.
I fish with pink worms and squid lures.
Fish are tough.
Happy when I fish.

Ethan Dean, Grade 1
Holland Township School, NJ

Me and You

Me and you have the same shoes
We stick together just like glue.
Whenever I am sad I look at you.
You are cheerful and nice.
Me and you have lots of spice.
I'm sure we'd be best friends if we met!

Hadassah Betapudi, Grade 3
Evangelical Christian School, TN

Winter

Winter is a season
Where it's freezing cold
Winter is a season
Where you can watch the snow fall
Winter is season
Where you can make snowman out of snow
Winter is a season
Where you can do snowball fight
Winter is a season
Where you can drink hot cocoa
Winter is a season
Where you get cold and cough
Winter is a season
Where you wear warm clothes
Winter is the best season
Of all I love winter,
Winter and all!!!!

Kavya Kosana, Grade 2
Dutch Neck Elementary School, NJ

Santa/St. Nick

Santa
plump, red, active
giving, working, singing
bringing gifts to all boys and girls
St. Nick

Joe Wilson, Grade 2
Wells Central School, NY

Christmas Day

Christmas is a day
To get together and play.
We go to parties
And have lots of fun
And celebrate God's love for us!
Christmas is a wonderful day!

Carson Moriarty, Grade 2
Evangelical Christian School, TN

Snowflakes

Here come the snowflakes
They fall all over the place
Snowflakes are the best!

Jacob Tuck, Grade 2
Coral Cove Elementary School, FL

What Is Blue?

Blue is the color of the sky,
Also blue tastes like blueberries,
Blue smells like a blue marker,
Blue also feels like a hard book,
Blue also sounds like a bird chirping.

Jalun Branch, Grade 3
Scott Elementary School, MO

Green

My favorite color
Green grass
Money
Green paper
Fish
Green
My favorite color.

Tyler Ridener, Grade 2
Southside Elementary School, KY

My Pet

Dog
Dachshund
Barks at mean people
Flips
Runs
Chases his tail
Loves me
Does not like cats
Wiener Dog

Charles Nelson, Kindergarten
Broadway Elementary School, NC

Night Time

It was a dark night.
The moon was shining bright.
It was time for bed
Because my mom said.
Now I am asleep
With my brother who is a creep.

Cade Calhoun, Grade 3
Pike Liberal Arts School, AL

Chase

We play pool
I always win
We love to swim
The water is cold
We play on the computer
I like the games
We have fun sleepovers
In the morning we play football

Joshua Abeckjerr, Grade 3
Miami Country Day School, FL

The Fair

I like the Fair
It has fun roller coasters
It has roller coaster swings
You have to be safe when you ride
So you won't slide

Kourtney Battle, Kindergarten
J E S Memorial SDA School, FL

Family

F athers will always show love.
A unt Ashley loves my family.
M y mom is beautiful.
I love all of the members in my family.
L ove is all around our house.
Y ou should make sure you family is loved.

Cinamyn Seward, Grade 3
Bensley Elementary School, VA

Veteran's Day

V eteran's Day is celebrated for the people who fought for our freedom.
E ven teachers can be a veteran.
T hey always bring a back up weapon just in case one runs out of ammo.
E ven if they are at work they need to go right away.
R ed is the color of blood.
A rch-rivals,
N o one should be on the arch-rival's team.
S ome veterans use swords in fights.

D anger means your are in trouble
A person like me should celebrate for Veteran's Day
Y ou could grow up to be a veteran.

Seth Acosta, Grade 3
Susquehanna Community Elementary School, PA

Trees

All trees have bark
Bark is hard
When the wind blows, the leaves shake
Squirrels like trees
There are different trees.
Trees have stems
Trees grow on the ground
Trees don't have leaves when it is winter
On trees leaves are yellow, red, orange, and green.
You can't break big trees.
Trees live in the woods sometimes and in the forests.
Trees are outside in nature.
Trees are pretty.
Trees grow with water.
I like trees.

Zack Littrell, Grade 1
Alvaton Elementary School, KY

Red Apples

It is a heart shape.
It is good for you!
It is a food.

Red and green —
I love apples
because they are
healthy!

Nicholas Hults, Grade 1
Holland Township School, NJ

Favorite Sport

My favorite sport
Is baseball
I'm not too short
To catch the ball
I throw a pitch
I hit a run
I get the itch
Until we've won.

Salvatore Ferro, Grade 3
Our Lady of Hope School, NY

The Heart

It is red.
It is round.
It is pretty.
It has curves.
It feels like love.
It is inside of us.
You see it in stores.

Rachel Kraycirik, Grade 1
Holland Township School, NJ

Leaves/Beautiful

Leaves
Red, crunchy
Falling, blowing, jumping
Colorful trees are bare.
Beautiful

Andy Maiorano, Grade 2
Consolidated School, CT

Two Good Kids

They ran up the stairs
Quietly, quietly
Who doth the little fro
Ever ran so quietly?
They went to their room
Quietly, quietly
Who could have
Ever been so quiet?
They took out their books
Smiling a lot
They did their work
About how horses could trot!
It was hard for them
To go to bed
So secretly, they stayed up
And did their work instead!

Lucy Krogh Whitwam, Grade 1
Childrens House Montessori School, MS

My Sister

My sister is very pretty
but also very greedy.

When my sister has candy
she only shares with Mandy.

My sister likes to go to the mall
with her boyfriend who is tall.

My sister goes to school
and she thinks she's all cool.

Even though my sister is greedy
I will always love her 'cause she is pretty.

Kasy Almonte, Grade 3
Mother Seton Inter Parochial School, NJ

My Mom and Me

My mom and me love to play with each other.
We have fun.
We like to go home with each other too.
We have fun all day long.

Callie Chen, Grade 1
Children's Village, PA

Penguins

Penguins hop.
Penguins slide.
Penguins dive, dive, dive!

Ahmad Perez, Grade 1
Northeast Elementary School, NY

Sun

Round, fiery, gleaming
Moving, shining, keeping dry
Magical bright star

Connor Davis, Grade 2
Roseland Park Elementary School, MS

Red

I am a rose.
I am lips.
I am blood.
I am red.

Ericka Alvarez, Grade 1
Northeast Elementary School, NY

Happy

If happy were a color
It would be yellow
As yellow as a Hi-lighter.

Bailey Zalepeski, Grade 2
Annsville Elementary School, NY

Penguins

Penguins swim.
Penguins waddle.
Penguins dive, dive, dive!

Amrita Deonanan, Grade 1
Northeast Elementary School, NY

Yellow

I am a star.
I am the sun.
I am a crayon.
I am yellow.

Cristian Mejia, Grade 1
Northeast Elementary School, NY

The Shamrock

green Ireland
plain clover
emblem leaf
icon flower
Saint Patrick's Day
luck mostly 3 leaves
spiritual march
solitaire game
seamrog

Lauren Reed, Grade 2
Hilton Head Christian Academy, SC

Frosty

Frosty is a snowman
Who always says "Happy birthday."
Frosty likes his friends.
Frosty has a carrot nose
And a pebble mouth.
I will always remember Frosty
As well as he can be!
When Frosty melts
I will be sad.

Alyssa Dunne, Grade 3
Evergreen Elementary School, PA

Bullfrogs

B ig
U sually fat
L aughing
L arge
F rog
R ibbit
O vergrown
G entle
S mart

Evan Lambert, Grade 3
McKinley Elementary School, PA

Trees

Need lots of water
Both big and small trees give air
Make a lot of homes

David Bensabat, Grade 3
Miami Country Day School, FL

Eagle

The eagle is a tornado.
It spins to the ground to capture its prey.
Grabbing its prey and carrying it up and up until it's gone.

Matt Kaczor, Grade 3
KC Heffernan Elementary School, NY

Super Horse

I am fast.
I do not like to be last.
I can run.
It is lots of fun.
I am Super Horse.

Rossemary Perez, Grade 1
Northeast Elementary School, NY

Baby Isabella

Baby is fun
She hits and runs all day long in the sun
It is so much fun to see her run
She pulls my hair all day
She cannot stop
She wants to play

Alexia Barroso, Grade 3
Miami Country Day School, FL

Fall

Fall looks like leaves
Fall looks like trees
Fall looks like scarecrows
Fall looks like dead grass
Fall looks like haunted houses
Fall looks like birds flying south
Fall feels like cool wind
Fall feels like chilly air
Fall feels like the wind
Fall feels good!

Tori Dyer, Grade 1
Alvaton Elementary School, KY

Gabriella

G abriella loves her sisters!
A beautiful girl...
B est sister...
R ed-haired Gabby...
I love my family!
E njoys school...
L ovely hair...
L oves her pets...
A smart girl!

Gabriella Lugo, Grade 1
Chelsea Heights Elementary School, NJ

Hockey

I like to skate fast.
So I can get past,
And shoot for a goal.
I must aim for the hole.

I raise my arms in the air.
My friends all stare.
We all jump up and scream.
Then go home for ice cream!

Evan Menard, Grade 2
McKinley Elementary School, PA

Rain

R ain is fun
A pples grow in the rain
I ce is cold
N ests are wet

Brisa Gomez, Grade 1
Annie Belle Clark Primary School, GA

Index

Author Autograph Page

Author Autograph Page

Author Autograph Page

Author Autograph Page

Author Autograph Page

Author Autograph Page

Author Autograph Page

Author Autograph Page

Author Autograph Page

Author Autograph Page